Constraint-Based Syntax and Semantics

CSLI Lecture Notes Number 223

Constraint-Based Syntax and Semantics
Papers in Honor of Danièle Godard

Edited by
Anne Abeillé &
Olivier Bonami

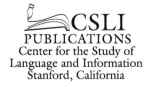

CSLI
PUBLICATIONS
Center for the Study of
Language and Information
Stanford, California

Copyright © 2020
CSLI Publications
Center for the Study of Language and Information
Leland Stanford Junior University
Printed in the United States
24 23 22 21 20   1 2 3 4 5

Names: Abeillé, Anne, editor. | Bonami, Olivier, editor. | Godard, Daniele,
   honoree.

Title: Constraint-based syntax and semantics: papers in honor of Danièle Godard /
   edited by Anne Abeillé and Olivier Bonami.

Description: Stanford, Calif. : CSLI Publications, 2018. | Series: CSLI lecture notes
   ; 223 — Papers presented at the 4th European HPSG symposium. | Includes
   bibliographical references.

Identifiers: LCCN 2018027633 (print) | LCCN 2018050316 (ebook) |
   ISBN 9781684000470 (Electronic) | ISBN 1684000475 (Electronic) |
   ISBN 9781684000463 (pbk. : alk. paper) | ISBN 1684000467 (pbk. : alk. paper

Subjects: LCSH: Grammar, Comparative and general–Syntax–Congresses. |
   Language and languages–Semantics–Congresses. | Constraints (Linguistics)
   Classification: LCC P26.G635 (ebook) | LCC P26.G635 C66 2018 (print) |
   DDC 415–dc23

LC record available at https://lccn.loc.gov/2018027633

CIP

∞ The acid-free paper used in this book meets the minimum requirements of the
American National Standard for Information Sciences—Permanence of Paper for
Printed Library Materials, ANSI Z39.48-1984.

CSLI Publications is located on the campus of Stanford University.

Visit our web site at
http://cslipublications.stanford.edu/
for comments on this and other titles, as well as for changes
and corrections by the author and publisher.

Contents

Contributors

ANNE ABEILLÉ: Laboratoire de Linguistique Formelle, CNRS – UMR 7110, Université de Paris, Batiment Olympe de Gouges, 8 rue Albert Einstein, 75013 Paris, France
abeille@linguist.univ-paris-diderot.fr

AHMAD ALOTAIBI: 3626 - Al-Imam University, Unit No. 47, Riyadh 7493-13318, Saudi Arabia
asdotaibi@imamu.edu.sa

GABRIELA BÎLBÎIE: Faculty of Foreign Languages and Literatures, University of Bucharest, Strada Pitar Edgar Quinet 5-7, Bucureşti 010017, Romania
gabriela.bilbiie@lls.unibuc.ro

OLIVIER BONAMI: Laboratoire de Linguistique Formelle, CNRS – UMR 7110, Université de Paris, Case 7031 – 5, rue Thomas Mann, 75205 Paris cedex 13, France
olivier.bonami@u-paris.fr

ROBERT D. BORSLEY: Department of Language and Linguistics, University of Essex & School of Languages, Literatures and Linguistics, Bangor University, College Road, Bangor, Gwynedd LL57 2DG, UK
rborsley@essex.ac.uk

ROBIN COOPER: Department of Philosophy, Linguistics and Theory of Science, University of Gothenburg, Box 200, S-405 30 Gothenburg, Sweden
robin.cooper@ling.gu.se

FRANCIS CORBLIN: Sorbonne-Université & Institut Jean Nicod (CNRS), UFRLangue française, 108 Bd Malesherbes, 75850 Paris Cedex 17, France
francis.corblin@paris-sorbonne.fr

DENIS CREISSELS: Université Lyon2, France;
513 route de la Combette, 38410 Saint Martin d'Uriage, France
denis.creissels@univ-lyon2.fr

MATHILDE DARGNAT: Analyse et Traitement Informatique de la Langue Française, Nancy, UMR 7118, CNRS & Université de Lorraine; ISC: Institut des Sciences Cognitives, Bron, UMR 5304, CNRS & Lyon 1, France
mathilde.dargnat@univ-lorraine.fr

ELISABET ENGDAHL: Department of Swedish, University of Gothenburg, Box 200, S-450 30 Gothenburg, Sweden
Elisabet.Engdahl@svenska.gu.se

JONATHAN GINZBURG: LLF, CNRS – UMR 7110, Université Paris Diderot-Paris 7, Case 7031 – 5, rue Thomas Mann, 75205 Paris cedex 13, France
yonatan.ginzburg@u-paris.fr

JULIAN HOUGH: Cognitive Science Group, School of Electronic Engineering and Computer Science, Queen Mary University of London, Mile End Road, London E1 4NS, UK
j.hough@qmul.ac.uk

JACQUES JAYEZ: ENS de Lyon and Institut des Sciences Cognitives – Marc Jeannerod, CNRS – UMR 5304, Université Lyon 1, 67 Bd Pinel, 69675 BRON CEDEX, France
jacques.jayes@ens-lyon.fr
jjays@isc.cnrs.fr

JEAN-PIERRE KOENIG: Department of Linguistics, 609 Baldy Hall, University at Buffalo, North Campus, Buffalo, NY 14260-6420, USA
jpkoenig@buffalo.edu

JOAN MALING: Linguistics Program, Volen National Center for Complex Systems, Brandeis University, 415 South Street, Waltham, MA 02453, USA0
maling@brandeis.edu

KARIN MICHELSON: Department of Linguistics, 609 Baldy Hall, University at Buffalo, North Campus, Buffalo, NY 14260-6420, USA
kmich@buffalo.edu

DAVID SCHLANGEN: Department Linguistics, University of Potsdam, Haus 14, Karl-Liebknecht-Straße 24-25, 14476 Potsdam, Germany
david.schlangen@uni-potsdam.de

JESSE TSENG: Cognition, Langues, Langage, Ergonomie (UMR 5263), CNRS & University of Toulouse Jean Jaurès, 5 allées Antonio Machado, 31058 Toulouse Cedex 9, France
Jesse.Tseng@univ-tlse2.fr

ANNIE ZAENEN: Center for the Study of Language and Information, Stanford University, Panama Street, Stanford, CA 94304, USA
azaenen@stanford.edu

1

Introduction

ANNE ABEILLÉ AND OLIVIER BONAMI

As its title implies, this book collects work carried out within the family of frameworks that the late Ivan A. Sag called *constraint-based grammars*. In his usage, a framework for grammatical analysis is constraint-based if it takes the form of a set of constraints on surface expressions that need to be satisfied simultaneously (Sag, Wasow & Bender 2003, Appendix B).[1] Constraint-based grammars in this sense emerged in the late 1970s, mostly in the form of models of grammars combining formal syntax and formal semantics, enriching tree representations with feature structures combined by unification.

Within this framework, taking lexicon and semantics and their interface to syntax more seriously than transformational grammar, Lexical Functional Grammar (LFG; Bresnan w& Kaplan 1982) and Generalized Phrase Structure Grammar (GPSG; Gazdar et al. 1985) allowed new analyses for English and other languages. Using a restricted formal apparatus, they were pursuing the double ambition of psycholinguistic

---

[1] The notion of a constraint-based grammar is arguably related to but distinct from notions of *unification-based grammars* (Shieber 1986), *model-theoretic grammars* (Pullum & Scholz 2001), and *non-transformational grammar* (Borsley & Borjars 2011), which all pick out different subsets of grammatical frameworks contrasting with mainstream generative grammar.

realism and straightforward computational applicability through direct implementation of the grammars written by linguists.

Danièle Godard has been an important contributor to the development of this family of approaches, and in particular phrase structure grammar, in France and Europe. Initially trained as a sociolinguist at the University of Pennsylvania (Godard 1977),[2] she kept an interest in syntactic variation throughout her career (Godard 1989b, Abeillé, Godard & Miller 1997, Abeillé & Godard 2007). She wrote her dissertation on French relative clauses (Godard 1986b, 1992b), using then current Government and Binding Theory with a critical point a view. She notably challenged the Complex NP constraint (Godard 1980, 1992a), the subject island and the *wh*-island constraint. She has been influential in many respects, and was a key actor in the development of Head-driven Phrase Structure Grammar (HSPG; Pollard & Sag 1987, 1994). Like GPSG and LFG, HPSG is surface-based (strings are built by syntax without movement rules), lexicalist (words are built by morphology and not by syntax) and declarative (HPSG grammars can be used for parsing and generation). But HPSG goes further in exploring the importance of viewing grammars as sets of constraints, to be satisfied by well-formed sequences of a language, rather than as generative devices. It also offers a unique framework for describing all linguistic levels inside a single representation, the *sign*.

Within this framework, Danièle has published major papers on syntax, semantics and interfaces. Her work with Anne Abeillé provided new analyses of most of the major aspects of French syntax (tense auxiliaries in Abeillé & Godard 1994, 1996, 2002; negation in Abeillé & Godard 1997; quantifier floating in Abeillé & Godard 1999a; adjective ordering in Abeillé & Godard 1999b; adverb ordering in Abeillé & Godard 2003b; interrogatives in Abeillé & Godard 2011, etc.), aiming to overcome the shortcomings of transformational analyses. Her work with Anne Abeillé, Philip Miller and Ivan Sag dealt with causatives and clitic climbing (Abeillé, Godard, Miller & Sag 1997, Abeillé, Godard & Sag 1998). She also worked with Ivan Sag on extracting complements of noun (Sag & Godard 1993 Godard & Sag 1996), and with Olivier Bonami and Jean-Marie Marandin on French subject inversion (Bonami, Godard & Marandin 1999, Bonami & Godard 2001). In parallel, she conducted work on ontology and lexical semantics with Jacques Jayez (e.g. Godard & Jayez 1993a, b; Jayez & Godard 1999), and on the syntax–semantics interface with Olivier Bonami (e.g. Bonami & Godard 2007a, b; 2008a, b).

In later work she focused on integrating descriptions of syntax and discourse, notably in studies of French object fronting (Abeillé, Godard & Sabio 2008a, b), reinforced Italian negation (Godard & Marandin 2006, 2007) and French declarative questions (Abeillé, Crabbé, Godard & Marandin 2012, Abeillé, Godard & Marandin 2014).

Animated by an exceptionally open and collaborative spirit, Danièle was an active member of the CNRS Laboratoire de linguistique formelle (LLF), where she introduced unification-based grammars and formal semantics, with Francis Corblin, Jean-Marie Marandin and Anne Abeillé. She was responsible for an NSF grant (1995–1998) on French syntax with Ivan Sag (Stanford), and for the Alliance project *Grammatical Interfaces* (2004–2006) with Doug Arnold (University of Essex). She was an active member of the French–Dutch PICS 1998–2001 *Formal Semantics and French Data*, and of the GDR *Semantics and Modelisation* (2002–2005). She has founded (with Francis Corblin) the French online encyclopaedia of formal semantics Sémanticlopédie (writing the entries on Secondary Predicates, Compositionality and Logophoricity), and coauthored the *Handbook of French Semantics* (Bonami, Godard & Kampers-Manhe 2004, Godard 2004). With Annie Delaveau and Anne Abeillé, she has undertaken a major French grammar project, covering the syntax of contemporary French, spoken and written, with more than 50 collaborators, to be published in 2021 (Abeillé, Delaveau & Godard 2007, Abeillé & Godard 2012, Abeillé & Godard forthcoming).

A specialist in French and the Romance languages (Godard 2003, 2010), she has also had wider linguistic interests, as shown by her work on Tswana with Denis Creissels (Creissels & Godard 2005), and by the research group she created with Sophie Vassilaki, within the *Empirical Foundations of Linguistics* excellence cluster, on the subjunctive in French and Balkan languages (Godard & de Mulder 2011, Godard 2012, Godard, Hemforth & Marandin 2017).

This volume gathers nine contributions by Danièle's co-authors, students, and friends. Most have chosen topics related to Danièle's work: the copula (Abeillé & Godard 2000b), quantification (Abeillé & Godard 1999a), relative clauses (Godard 1992b), the passive (Abeillé & Godard 2002), non-at-issue meaning (Bonami & Godard 2008a), tense auxiliaries (Abeillé & Godard 1994, 1996), subjunctive mood (Godard & de Mulder 2011, Godard 2012) and questions (Abeillé & Godard 2011, Abeillé, Godard & Marandin 2014). Three deal primarily with syntax, three with semantics, and three with the 'integration of linguistic dimensions' (Bonami & Godard 2007a). We outline them in turn.

The first of the syntax papers, by AHMAD ALOTAIBI and ROBERT D. BORSLEY, presents a detailed HPSG analysis of the copula in Modern Standard Arabic. The main challenge here is to account for the absence of overt realization of positive present forms. The authors argue that capturing the similarities and differences between sentences with and without an overt copula requires the postulation of a phonologically empty positive present form.

DENIS CREISSELS discusses an intriguing relativization strategy found in the languages of Senegal: when the relative clause attributes an individual-level property (as opposed to a stage-level property) to a referent, there is the possibility of inserting an intermediate clause translatable as 'which you know that'. Creissels shows that the intermediate clause, while being historically motivated, is not literally interpretable, and hence argues that the relevant languages have innovated a distinct relative clause type. It is noteworthy that this happened in parallel in an area in which the languages are only distantly related and have otherwise strikingly different relativization strategies.

Jesse Tseng discusses the agreement of past participles with objects in French. While French prescriptive grammars consistently posit that participles agree with preceding objects in periphrastic tenses, this generalization is disputed by HPSG analyses due to Abeillé & Godard (1994, 1996, 2002) and Miller & Sag (1997), who propose instead that agreement is found with *noncanonical* objects, i.e. clitic, relativized, or *wh*-extracted objects. Tseng reviews the evidence, highlighting the subtle role of sociolinguistic variation: agreement is known to be optional and rare in informal spoken French, where other factors, such as the clause-finality of the participle, seem to play a conditioning role.

In the first of the semantics contributions, Francis Corblin revisits the distinction between pure indexicals, like the pronoun *I*, and demonstratives, like the noun phrase *this person*. Although the distinction has been argued to be spurious by many, Corblin argues that it can be maintained, provided one makes a sharp distinction between the anchor of an indexical and its referent: the anchor is some entity that helps locate the referent by standing in some salient relation with it, without that relation being identity in most situations. The paper shows that expressions such as *here* and *now* can then truly be considered pure indexicals, and discusses the conditions under which a demonstration may accompany a pure indexical without changing its place in the classification.

The paper by Mathilde Dargnat and Jacques Jayez is a critical evaluation of the pragmatic theory of presupposition projection based on the *Questions under Discussion* (QUD). In this theory, presuppositions project if and only if they do not address the QUD and can escape the scope of belief predicates. The authors deploy a wealth of evidence to show that the biconditional is too strong: while not addressing the QUD entails projection, content that addresses the QUD can still project under some lexical or contextual circumstances. In particular, embedding predicates making no contribution to the QUD favor projection, as do triggers making no contribution to the main content.

Jean-Pierre Koenig and Karin Michelson provide an overall analysis of the quantification system of the Iroquoian language Oneida. They show that quantification over individuals in Oneida is almost exclusively expressed by combining the main verb with an internally-headed relative clause whose predicate is a 'counting verb', possibly combined with number names denoting numbers. As a result, Oneida does not seem to make use of generalized quantifiers – relations between sets – in its semantics. A striking consequence is that Oneida has no direct semantic way of expressing proportional quantification (*most*) or negative universals (*no*).

In the opening chapter of the 'integration of linguistic dimensions' strand, Gabriela Bîlbîie attempts to account for the diversity of uses of the subjunctive in interrogatives in Romanian. Having shown that the occurrence of the subjunctive in matrix clauses has to be taken at face value and cannot be reduced to ellipsis of a matrix modal predicate, she distinguishes five distinct patterns of use on the basis of their illocutionary contribution. What the patterns have in common is conveying a weak commitment of the speaker together with a weak call on the addressee, which is never required to provide an answer. Interestingly though, these illocutionary situations do not give rise to the use of a single mood in other Romance languages.

The paper by ELISABET ENGDAHL, ANNIE ZAENEN and JOAN MALING explores the properties of 'pivots' in Swedish presentational sentences and contrasts them with those of canonical subjects. Differences between the two emerge from the interaction of syntactic, lexical semantic, and information-structural constraints on the realization of arguments, coupled with the observation that pivots are systematically part of focus, while subjects tend to be topics. Interestingly, the authors show that the assignment of grammatical functions is not entirely determined by lexical properties of the predicate, but also depends on information structure.

JONATHAN GINZBURG, ROBIN COOPER, JULIAN HOUGH and DAVID SCHLANGEN propose a general strategy to recast HPSG as an incremental grammatical framework. They first justify briefly the claim that grammars should classify utterances as they occur in conversation, and then provide explicit representations of partial utterances and linguistic reactions from all discourse participants to such partial utterances. They then outline a view of dialogue processing where content is integrated in dialogue in a word-by-word fashion, building on the framework of KoS. Interestingly, KoS uses as a component part of its representation of individual increments in dialogue an utterance type that has the same structure as an HPSG *sign*. This justifies the claim that HPSG can be made compatible with an incremental view of grammar.

2

Danièle Godard's Bibliography

Abeillé, Anne, Olivier Bonami, Danièle Godard & Michèle Noailly. 2017. Adjectives and adverbs in the *Grande Grammaire du français*. In Martin Hummel & Salvador Valera (eds.), *Adjective–Adverb Interfaces in Romance*, 113–139. Amsterdam: John Benjamins.

Abeillé, Anne, Olivier Bonami, Danièle Godard & JesseTseng. 2003. The Syntax of French *à* and *de*: An HPSG Analysis. *Proceedings of the ACL-SIGSEM Workshop on the Linguistic Dimensions of Prepositions and their Use in Computational Linguistics Formalisms and Applications*, 133–144. Toulouse.

Abeillé, Anne, Olivier Bonami, Danièle Godard & JesseTseng. 2004. The Syntax of French *de*-N′ Phrases. In Stefan Müller (ed.), *Proceedings of the 11th International Conference on Head-driven Phrase Structure Grammar*, 6–26. Stanford, CA: CSLI Publications.

Abeillé, Anne, Olivier Bonami, Danièle Godard & JesseTseng. 2006. Les syntagmes nominaux français de la forme *de*-N′. *Travaux de linguistique* 50:79–95.

Abeillé, Anne, Olivier Bonami, Danièle Godard & JesseTseng. 2006b. The syntax of French *à* and *de*: An HPSG Analysis. In Patrick Saint-Dizier (ed.), *Dimensions of the Syntax and Semantics of Prepositions*, 147–162. Dordrecht: Springer.

Abeillé, Anne, Benoît Crabbé, Danièle Godard & Jean-Marie Marandin. 2012. French Questioning Declaratives: A Corpus Study. In Sarah Brown-Schmidt, Jonathan Ginzburg & Staffan Larsson (eds.), *Proceedings of SemDial 2012 (SeineDial): The 16th Workshop on the Semantics and Pragmatics of Dialogue*, 70–79. Paris.

Constraint-Based Syntax and Semantics: Papers in Honor of Danièle Godard.
Anne Abeillé and Olivier Bonami (eds.).
Copyright © 2020, CSLI Publications.

Abeillé, Anne, Annie Delaveau & Danièle Godard. 2007. *La Grande Grammaire du français:* principes de construction. *Revue roumaine de linguistique* 52(4):403–419.

Abeillé, Anne & Danièle Godard. 1994. The Complementation of Tense Auxiliaries in French. In Raul Aranovich, William Byrne, Susanne Preuss & Martha Senturia (eds.), *Proceedings of the Thirteenth West Coast Conference on Formal Linguistics* (WCCFL 13), 157–173. Stanford, CA: CSLI Publications.

Abeillé, Anne & Danièle Godard. 1996. La complémentation des auxiliaires en français. *Langages* 122:32–61.

Abeillé, Anne & Danièle Godard. 1997. The Syntax of French Negative Adverbs. In Danielle Forget, Paul Hirschbühler, France Martineau & María-Luisa Rivero (eds.), *Negation and Polarity: Syntax and Semantics*, 1–27. Amsterdam: John Benjamins.

Abeillé, Anne & Danièle Godard. 1999a. A Lexical Approach to Quantifier Floating in French. In Gert Webelhuth, Jean-Pierre Koenig & Andreas Kathol (eds.), *Lexical and Constructional Aspects of Linguistic Explanation*, 81–96. Stanford, CA: CSLI Publications.

Abeillé, Anne & Danièle Godard. 1999b. La position de l'adjectif épithète en français: le poids des mots. *Recherches linguistiques de Vincennes* 28:9–32.

Abeillé, Anne & Danièle Godard. 2000a. French Word Order and Lexical Weight. In Robert D. Borsley (ed.), *The Nature and Function of Syntactic Categories*, 325–360. New York: Academic Press.

Abeillé, Anne & Danièle Godard. 2000b. Varieties of *esse* in Romance Languages. In Dan Flickinger & Andreas Kathol (eds.), *Berkeley Formal Grammar Conference*, 2–22. Stanford, CA: CSLI Publications.

Abeillé, Anne & Danièle Godard. 2001a. A class of lite adverbs in French. In Joaquim Camps & Caroline Wiltshire (eds.), *Romance Syntax, Semantics and L2 Acquisition*, 9–25. Amsterdam: John Benjamins.

Abeillé, Anne & Danièle Godard. 2001b. Deux types de prédicats complexes dans les langues romanes. *Linx. Revue des linguistes de l'université Paris X Nanterre* 45:167–175.

Abeillé, Anne & Danièle Godard. 2002. The Syntactic Structure of French Auxiliaries. *Language* 78:404–452.

Abeillé, Anne & Danièle Godard. 2003a. Les prédicats complexes dans les langues romanes. In Danièle Godard (ed.), *Les langues romanes. Problèmes de la phrase simple*. Paris: CNRS Éditions.

Abeillé, Anne & Danièle Godard. 2003b. The Syntactic Flexibility of Adverbs: French Degree Adverbs. In Stefan Müller (ed.), *Proceedings of the 10th International Conference on Head-driven Phrase Structure Grammar*, 26–46. Stanford, CA: CSLI Publications.

Abeillé, Anne & Danièle Godard. 2003c. The Syntax of French Adverbs without Functional Projections. In Martine Coene, Gretel de Cuyper & Yves D'hulst (eds.), *Current Studies in Comparative Romance Linguistics*, 1–39. Amsterdam: John Benjamins.

Abeillé, Anne & Danièle Godard. 2004a. De la légèreté en syntaxe. *Bulletin de la Société de Linguistique de Paris* XCIX:69–106.

Abeillé, Anne & Danièle Godard. 2004b. Les adjectifs invariables comme compléments légers en français. In Jacques François (ed.), *L'adjectif en français et à travers les langues*, 209–224. Caen: Presses Universitaires de Caen.

Abeillé, Anne & Danièle Godard. 2006. La légèreté en français comme déficience de mobilité. *Lingvisticæ investigationes* 29(1):11–24.

Abeillé, Anne & Danièle Godard. 2007. Les relatives sans pronom relatif. In Michaël Abecassis (ed.), *Le francais parlé. Normes et variations*, 37–60. Paris: L'Harmattan.

Abeillé, Anne & Danièle Godard. 2010a. The Grande Grammaire du français project. In Nicoletta Calzolari, Khalid Choukri, Bente Maegaard, Joseph Mariani, Jan Odijk, Stelios Piperidis, Mike Rosner & Daniel Tapias (eds.), *Proceedings of the International Conference on Language Resources and Evaluation, LREC 2010*, 687–692. European Language Resources Association (ELRA).

Abeillé, Anne & Danièle Godard. 2010b. Complex Predicates in the Romance Languages. In Danièle Godard (ed.), *Fundamental Issues in the Romance Languages*, 107–170. Stanford, CA: CSLI Publications.

Abeillé, Anne & Danièle Godard. 2011. Les interrogatives compléments en français. *Cahiers de lexicologie* 98:161–176.

Abeillé, Anne & Danièle Godard. 2012. *La Grande Grammaire du français* et la variété des données. *Langue française* (4):47–68.

Abeillé, Anne & Danièle Godard (eds.). Forthcoming. *La Grande Grammaire du français*. Arles: Actes Sud/Imprimerie nationale éditions.

Abeillé, Anne, Danièle Godard & Jean-Marie Marandin. 2014. French Questioning Declaratives in Question. In Philip Hofmeister & Elisabeth Norcliffe (eds.), *The Core and the Periphery: Data-driven Perspectives on Syntax Inspired by Ivan A. Sag* (Lecture Notes), 129–161. Stanford, CA: CSLI Publications.

Abeillé, Anne, Danièle Godard & Philip [H.] Miller. 1997. Les causatives en français: un cas de compétition syntaxique. *Langue française* 115:62–74.

Abeillé, Anne, Danièle Godard, Philip [H.] Miller & Ivan A. Sag. 1997. French Bounded Dependencies. In Sergio Balari & Luca Dini (eds.), *Romance in HPSG*, 1–54. Stanford, CA: CSLI Publications.

Abeillé, Anne, Danièle Godard & Frédéric Sabio. 2008a. Two Types of NP Preposing in French. Stefan Müller (ed.), *Proceedings of the 15th International Conference on Head-driven Phrase Structure Grammar*, 306–324. Stanford, CA: CSLI Publications.

Abeillé, Anne, Danièle Godard & Frédéric Sabio. 2008b. Deux constructions à SN antéposé en français. In Jacques Durand, Benoît Habert & Bernard Laks (eds.), *Actes du premier Congrès Mondial de Linguistique Française*, 2361–2376. Paris: Institut de Linguistique Française.

Abeillé, Anne, Danièle Godard & Ivan A. Sag. 1998. Two Kinds of Composition in French Complex Predicates. In Erhard Hinrichs, Andreas Kathol & Tsuneko Nakazawa (eds.), *Complex Predicates*, 1–41. New York: Academic Press.

Bonami, Olivier & Danièle Godard. 2001. Inversion du sujet, constituance et ordre des mots. In Jean-Marie Marandin (ed.), *Cahier Jean-Claude Milner*, 117–174. Paris: Verdier.

Bonami, Olivier & Danièle Godard. 2005a. Evaluative Adverbs and Underspecified Semantic Representations. In Frank Richter & Manfred Sailer (eds.), *Proceedings of the ESSLLI'05 Workshop on Empirical Challenges and Analytical Alternatives to Strict Compositionality*, 59–78. Edinburgh.

Bonami, Olivier & Danièle Godard. 2005b. Les adverbes évaluatifs dans une approche multidimensionnelle du sens. In Injoo Choi-Jonin, Myriam Bras, Anne Dagnac & Magali Rouquier (eds.), *Questions de classification en linguistique: méthodes et descriptions*, 19–37. Bern: Peter Lang.

Bonami, Olivier & Danièle Godard. 2007a. Integrating Linguistic Dimensions: The Scope of Adverbs. In Stefan Müller (ed.), *Proceedings of the 14th International Conference on Head-driven Phrase Structure Grammar*, 25–45. Stanford, CA: CSLI Publications.

Bonami, Olivier & Danièle Godard. 2007b. Parentheticals in Underspecified Semantics: The Case of Evaluative Adverbs. *Research on Language and Computation* 5:391–413.

Bonami, Olivier & Danièle Godard. 2007c. Quelle syntaxe, incidemment, pour les adverbes incidents? *Bulletin de la Société de Linguistique de Paris* CII:255–284.

Bonami, Olivier & Danièle Godard. 2007d. Adverbes initiaux et Types de phrase en français. In Alexandra Cunita, Coman Lupu & Lilianne Tasmowski (eds.), *Studii de Lingviistică şi Filologie Romanică*, 50–57. Bucarest: Editura Universităţii din Bucureşti.

Bonami, Olivier & Danièle Godard. 2008a. Lexical Semantics and Pragmatics of Evaluative Adverbs. In Louise McNally & Chris Kennedy (eds.), *Adverbs and Adjectives: Syntax, Semantics, and Discourse*, 274–304. Oxford: Oxford University Press.

Bonami, Olivier & Danièle Godard. 2008b. On the Syntax of Direct Quotation in French. In Stefan Müller (ed.), *Proceedings of the 15th International Conference on Head-driven Phrase Structure Grammar*, 358–377. Stanford, CA: CSLI Publications.

Bonami, Olivier & Danièle Godard. 2008c. Syntaxe des incises de citation. In Jacques Durand, Benoît Habert & Bernard Laks (eds.), *Actes du premier Congrès Mondial de Linguistique Française*, 2395–2408. Paris: Institut de Linguistique Française.

Bonami, Olivier, Danièle Godard & Brigitte Kampers-Manhe. 2004. Adverb Classification. In Francis Corblin & Henriëtte de Swart (eds.), *Handbook of French Semantics*, 143–184. Stanford, CA: CSLI Publications.

Bonami, Olivier, Danièle Godard & Jean-Marie Marandin. 1998. French Subject Inversion in Extraction Contexts. In Gosse Bouma, Geert-Jan M. Kruijff & Richard T. Oehrle (eds.), *Proceedings of the Joint Conference on Formal Grammar, Head-driven Phrase Structure Grammar and Categorial Grammar*, 101–112. Saarbruecken.

Bonami, Olivier, Danièle Godard & Jean-Marie Marandin. 1999. Constituency and Word Order in French Subject Inversion. In Gosse Bouma, Erhard Hinrichs, Geert-Jan M. Kruijff & Richard T. Oehrle (eds.), *Constraints and Resources in Natural Language Semantics*, 21–40. Stanford, CA: CSLI Publications.

Creissels, Denis & Danièle Godard. 2005. The Tswana Infinitive as a Mixed Category. In Stefan Müller (ed.), *Proceedings of the 12th International Conference on Head-driven Phrase Structure Grammar,* 70–90. Stanford, CA: CSLI Publications.

Godard, Danièle. 1977. Same Setting, Different Norms: Phone Call Beginnings in France and the United States. *Language in Society* 6(2):209–219.

Godard, Danièle. 1980. Les relatives parenthétiques du Français, la contrainte du syntagme nominal complexe (CNPC) et les. *Linx* 2(1):35–88.

Godard, Danièle. 1986a. Les déterminants possessifs et les compléments de nom. *Langue française* (72):102–122.

Godard, Danièle. 1986b. *Propositions relatives, relations anaphoriques et predication. Études sur* dont. Ph.D. dissertation, Université Paris 7.

Godard, Danièle. 1988. Sujet et compléments génitifs dans le groupe nominal. In Jean-Claude Milner (ed.), *Recherches nouvelles sur le langage*, 7–50. Paris: Laboratoire de linguistique formelle.

Godard, Danièle. 1989a. Empty Categories as Subjects of Tensed Ss in English or French? *Linguistic Inquiry* 20:497–506.

Godard, Danièle. 1989b. Français standard et non-standard: les relatives. *Linx* 20(1):51–88.

Godard, Danièle. 1991. Le test en grammaire générative. L'exemple de la structure de la phrase. *Histoire, Epistémologie, Langage* 13:27–56.

Godard, Danièle. 1992a. Extraction out of NP in French. *Natural Language & Linguistic Theory* 10:233–277.

Godard, Danièle. 1992b. *La syntaxe des relatives en français*. Paris: Editions du CNRS. [Originally published in 1988.]

Godard, Danièle. 1992c. Le programme labovien et la variation syntaxique. *Langages* 108:51–65.

Godard, Danièle. 1996. Les phrases compléments de Nom sont-elles des arguments. In Nelly Flaux, Michel Glatigny & Didier Samain (eds.), *Les noms abstraits. Histoire et théories*, 301–311. Villeneuve d'Ascq: Presses universitaires du Septentrion.

Godard, Danièle. 2003. *Les langues romanes: problèmes de la phrase simple*. Paris: Éditions du CNRS.

Godard, Danièle. 2004. French Negative Dependency. In Francis Corblin & Henriëtte de Swart (eds.), *Handbook of French Semantics*, 351–389. Stanford, CA: CSLI Publications.

Godard, Danièle. 2005. Problèmes syntaxiques de la coordination et propositions récentes dans les grammaires syntagmatiques. *Langages* (4):3–24.

Godard, Danièle. 2010. *Fundamental Issues in the Romance Languages*. Stanford, CA: CSLI Publications.

Godard, Danièle. 2012. Indicative and Subjunctive Mood in Complement Clauses: From Formal Semantics to Grammar Writing. In Christopher Piñón (ed.), *Empirical Issues in Syntax and Semantics 9*, 129–148. Paris: Centre National de la Recherche Scientifique.

Godard, Danièle & Walter de Mulder. 2011. Infinitif et subjonctif dans les complétives en français. *Cahiers de Lexicologie* 98: 145–160.

Godard, Danièle, Barbara Hemforth & Jean-Marie Marandin. 2017. Le subjonctif en contexte négatif en français: une approche expérimentale. *Omagiu profesorului Emil Ionescu la 60 de ani*, 27–39. Bucarest: University of Bucarest,

Godard, Danièle & Jacques Jayez. 1993a. Towards a Proper Treatment of Coercion Phenomena. In Steven Krauwer, Michael Moortgat & Louis des Tombe (eds.), *Sixth Conference of the European Chapter of the Association for Computational Linguistics*, 168–177. Utrecht.

Godard, Danièle & Jacques Jayez. 1993b. Le traitement lexical de la coercion. *Cahiers de linguistique française* 14:123–149.

Godard, Danièle & Jacques Jayez. 1996. Types nominaux et anaphores: le cas des objets et des événements. In Walter De Mulder, Liliane Tasmowski-De Ryck & Carl Vetters (eds.), *Anaphores temporelles et (in)cohérence*, 41–58. Amsterdam: Rodopi.

Godard, Danièle & Jacques Jayez. 1999. Quels sont les faits? In Marc Plénat, Michel Aurnague, Anne Condamines, Jean-Pierre Maurel, Christian Molinier & Claude Muller (eds.), *L'emprise du sens: structures linguistiques et interprétation. Mélanges de syntaxe et de sémantique offerts à Andrée Borillo par un groupe d'amis, de collègues et de disciples*, 117–136. Amsterdam: Rodopi.

Godard, Danièle & Jean-Marie Marandin. 2006. Reinforcing Negation: The Case of Italian. In Stefan Müller (ed.), *Proceedings of the 13th International Conference on Head-driven Phrase Structure Grammar*, 174–194. Stanford, CA: CSLI Publications.

Godard, Danièle & Jean-Marie Marandin. 2007. Aspects pragmatiques de la négation renforcée en italien. In Franck Floricic (ed.), *La négation dans les langues romanes*, 136–160. Amsterdam: John Benjamins.

Godard, Danièle & Walter de Mulder. 2011. Infinitif et subjonctif dans les complétives en français. *Cahiers de Lexicologie* 98:145–160.

Godard, Danièle & Ivan A. Sag. 1996. Quels compléments de nom peut-on extraire en français? *Langue française* 109:60–79.

Jayez, Jacques & Danièle Godard. 1999. True to Fact. In Paul Dekker (ed.), *Proceedings of the 12th Amsterdam Colloquium*, 151–156. Amsterdam: ILLC/Department of Philosophy, University of Amsterdam.

Sag, Ivan A. & Danièle Godard. 1993. Extraction of *de*-phrases from the French NP. In Mercè Gonzàlez (ed.), *Proceedings of the North East Linguistic Society* (NELS 24), 519–540. Amherst, MA: GLSA, University of Massachusetts Amherst.

3

The Copula in Modern Standard Arabic

AHMAD ALOTAIBI AND ROBERT D. BORSLEY

1 Introduction

Like its counterparts in many languages, the Modern Standard Arabic (MSA) copula allows a variety of complements and has both predicational and equative uses. Predicational uses may involve PP, AP, and NP complements, and also verbal complements. Equative uses have a distinctive syntax with an optional pronoun between the two arguments. There are also syntactic differences between predicational examples with a non-verbal complement and predicational examples with a verbal complement. Further complications arise with the present tense of the copula. This is only used in a restricted set of contexts. Where a present tense form of the copula might be expected, MSA normally has a verbless clause, traditionally known as a nominal sentence. The present tense also has a special negative form – *laysa* – which appears in most but not all of the contexts in which the past tense forms appear. In this paper, we will develop an analysis of the data within Head-driven Phrase Structure Grammar (HPSG). We will argue that an appropriate type hierarchy and associated constraints, and a phonologically null present tense form of the copula can handle the full set of facts, accommodating the similarities and differences among predicational examples with a non-verbal complement and a verbal complement and equative examples, and the

Constraint-Based Syntax and Semantics: Papers in Honor of Danièle Godard.
Anne Abeillé and Olivier Bonami (eds.).
Copyright © 2020, CSLI Publications.

similarities and differences between examples with a visible copula and examples with no visible copula.

The paper is organized as follows. In Section 2, we compare and contrast predicational and equative uses of the copula. We argue that the facts support an approach in which there is a lexical type *copula* with two subtypes: *predicational-copula* and *equative-copula*. In Section 3, we argue that it is necessary to recognize two subtypes of the former for examples with a non-verbal and a verbal complement. In Section 4, we focus on the present tense of the copula. We argue that the verbless clauses involve a phonologically null form of the copula, and we propose that *laysa* is subject to a special constraint. In Section 5, we develop a detailed HPSG analysis of the MSA copula incorporating that positions that we have argued for in the preceding sections. Finally, in Section 6, we summarize the paper.

2   Predicational and Equative Uses

The Modern Standard Arabic (MSA) copula has a variety of uses like the copula in many languages. This raises the question whether there is one lexeme or more than one. Like its counterparts in many languages, the MSA copula appears with a variety of complements. It allows PP, AP, and NP complements:

(1) kaana   T-Tifl-u   fii   l-ħadiiqat-i
     be.PAST.3SG.M   the-child.SG.M-NOM   in   the-garden-GEN
     'The child was in the garden.'

(2) kaana   xalid-u-n   xaaʔif-a-n   min
     be.PAST.3SG.M   Khalid-NOM-NN   afraid.SG.M-ACC- NN   from
     l-ʕanaakib-i
     the-spiders-GEN
     'Khalid was afraid of spiders.'

(3) kaana   zayd-u-n   muʔallif-a   riwaayaat-i-n
     be.PAST.3SG.M   Zaid-NOM-NN   author.SG.M-ACC   novels-GEN-NN
     'Zaid was an author of novels.'

It also combines with both present and past tense verbs:[1]

---

[1] What we are calling present and past forms are sometimes called imperfective and perfective. The present tense forms should perhaps be viewed as tenseless since they do not always have a present tense meaning.

(4) kaana   zayd-u-n   yaktubu   t-taqriir-a
be.PAST.3SG.M Zaid-NOM-NN write.PRES.3SG.M the-report-ACC
'Zaid was writing the report.'

(5) kaana   zayd-u-n   kataba   t-taqriir-a
be.PAST.3SG.M Zaid-NOM-NN write.PAST.3SG.M the-report-ACC
'Zaid had written the report.'

With a present tense verb, it gives a progressive interpretation and with a past tense verb a perfect interpretation.

It is clear from work like Sag et al. (1985) on English that a variety of complements does not necessarily mean that there is more than one copula lexeme. However, this is not the only complication that an analysis needs to deal with. Like the copula in many languages, the MSA copula has both predicative uses, as in (1)–(5) above, and equative uses, as in the following:

(6) kaana   hišaam-u-n   muħammad-a-n
be.PAST.3SG.M   Hisham-NOM-NN   Muhammad-ACC-NN
'Hisham was Muhammad.'

This might suggest that there are two copula lexemes. However, in some analyses a single copula lexeme appears in both types of sentence. For example, Williams (1983) and Partee (1986) propose that the copula is always predicative but that there is a mechanism turning a referential expression like *Muhammad* in (6) into a predicative expression. On this approach, if *Muhammad* is normally m, it will be $[\lambda y[y=m]]$ in (6). In contrast, Van Eynde (2009), building on Montague (1974), argues that many apparent predicative uses of the copula are really equative uses.

It is clear that the existence of predicative and equative uses of the copula does not necessarily mean that there are two copula lexemes. However, in MSA, equative uses of the copula have a distinctive syntax. They allow an optional pronoun between the two noun phrases. Thus, as well as (6), we have (7):

(7) kaana   hišaam-u-n   huwa   muħammad-a-n
be.PAST.3SG.M Hisham-NOM-NN   he   Muhammad-ACC-NN
'Hisham was Muhammad.'

The pronoun is always third person but agrees in number and gender with the subject, as the following illustrate:

(8) kuntu   ?anaa   huwa   mu?allif-a   r-riwaayat-i
be.PAST.1SG   I   he   author-ACC   the-novel-GEN
'I was the author of the novel.'

(9) kaanat   l-fataat-u   hiya/*huwa   l-munassiqat-a
be.PAST.3SG.F   the-girl-NOM   she   he   the-coordinator-ACC
'The girl was the coordinator.'

(10) kaana   ha?ulaa?i   hum/*huwa   ?afDal-a   fariiq-i-n
be.PAST.3SG.M   those   they   he   best-ACC   team-GEN-NN
'Those were the best team.'

Predicative uses of the copula do not allow a pronoun. Thus, the following are not possible as alternatives to (1)–(4):

(11) *kaana   T-Tifl-u   huwa   fii
     be.PAST.3SG.M   the-child.SG.M-NOM   he   in
l-ħadiiqat-i
the-garden-GEN
'The child was in the garden.'

(12) *kaana   xalid-u-n   huwa
     be.PAST.3SG.M   Khalid-NOM-NN   he
xaa?if-a-n   min   l-ʕanaakib-i
afraid.SG.M-ACC-NN   from   the-spiders-GEN
'Khalid was afraid of spiders.'

(13) *kaana   zayd-u-n   huwa   mu?allif-a
     be. PAST.3SG.M   Zaid-NOM-NN   he   author.SG.M-ACC
riwaayaat-i-n
novels-GEN-NN
'Zaid was an author of novels.'

(14) *kaana   zayd-u-n   huwa   yaktubu
     be.PAST.3SG.M   Zaid-NOM-NN   he   write.PRES.3SG.M
t-taqriir-a
the-report-ACC
'Zaid was writing the report.'

This contrast suggests that MSA has not a single copula which is associated with two distinct meanings but two distinct copulas with different semantic and syntactic properties. However, the same set of forms are used in predicative uses and equative uses. We will capture this by assuming a single lexical type with two subtypes, as follows:

(15)
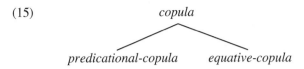

copula

predicational-copula   equative-copula

We will discuss the constraints on these types in Section 5.

3   Verbal and Non-verbal Predicational Uses

There is a further syntactic difference that we need to consider between predicational examples with a non-verbal complement and predicational examples with a verbal complement.

We noted in the last section that the copula allows PP, AP, and NP complements. As we would expect, P, A, and N and their complements in examples like (1)–(3) can be fronted.

(16) fii   l-ħadiiqat-i   kaana   T-Tifl-u
     in   the-garden-GEN   be.PAST.3SG.M the-child.SG.M-NOM
     'The child was in the garden.'

(17) xaaʔif-a-n   min   l-ʕanaakib-i   kaana
     afraid.SG.M-ACC-NN from   the-spiders-GEN be.PAST.3SG.M
     xalid-u-n
     Khalid-NOM-NN
     'Khalid was afraid of spiders.'

(18) muʔallif-a   riwaayaat-i-n   kaana   zayd-u-n
     author.SG.M-ACC novels-GEN-NN be.PAST.3SG.M Zaid-NOM-NN
     'Zaid was an author of novels.'

One might assume that the copula also allows a VP complement and that this is what we have in examples like (4) and (5) above. However, V and its complement NP cannot be fronted. The following are ungrammatical:

(19) *yaktubu   t-taqriir-a   kaana   zayd-u-n
     write.PRES.3SG.M the-report-ACC be.PAST.3SG.M Zaid-NOM-NN
     'Zaid was writing the report.'

(20) *kataba   t-taqriir-a   kaana   zayd-u-n
     write.PAST.3SG.M the-report-ACC be.PAST.3SG.M Zaid-NOM-NN
     'Zaid had written the report.'

This suggests that the predicational copula with a verbal complement is rather like the French auxiliaries *avoir* 'have' and *être* 'be' as analysed by Abeillé & Godard (2002) and appears in an argument composition structure with a verb and the complements of the verb as its complements. Thus, whereas (1) has the schematic structure in (21), (4) has that in (22).

(21)

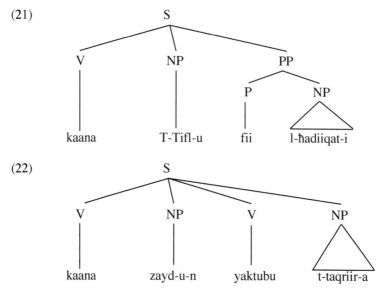

(22)

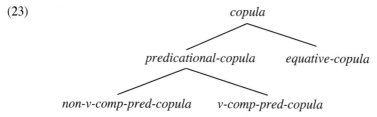

To implement this position, we will need two subtypes of the type *predicational-copula*, giving the following type hierarchy:

(23)

copula

predicational-copula   *equative-copula*

non-v-comp-pred-copula   *v-comp-pred-copula*

We will provide appropriate constraints in Section 5.

4   Present Tense Sentences

All the examples in the preceding sections contain a past tense form of the copula. This is because complications arise in the present tense. In particular, present tense is unacceptable in many contexts. It also has a special negative form – *laysa*. In this section, we explore these facts.

The following are counterparts of (1)–(3) and (6)/(7) with a present tense form of the copula, and all are unacceptable:

(24) *yakuunu   T-Tifl-u   fii   l-ħadiiqat-i
      be.PRES   the-child.SG.M-NOM in   the-garden-GEN
      'The child is in the garden.'

(25) *yakuunu   xalid-u-n   xaaʔif-a-n   min
      be.PRES   Khalid-NOM-NN   afraid.SG.M-ACC-NN from
      l-ʕanaakib-i
      the-spiders-GEN
      'Khalid is afraid of spiders.'

(26) *yakuunu   zayd-u-n   muʔallif-a   riwaayaat-i-n
      be.PRES   Zaid-NOM-NN author.SG.M-ACC novels-GEN-NN
      'Zaid is an author of novels'

(27) *yakuunu hišaam-u-n   (huwa)   muħammad-a-n
      be.PRES Hisham-NOM-NN   he   Muhammad-ACC-NN
      'Hisham is Muhammad.'

Present tense forms of the copula are only acceptable in a restricted set of contexts, e.g. after *qad* 'may', as in the following:

(28) qad yakuunu T-Tifl-u   fii   l-ħadiiqat-i
      may be.PRES the-child.SG.M-NOM in   the-garden-GEN
      'The child may be in the garden.'

(29) qad yakuunu   xalid-u-n   xaaʔif-a-n
      may be.PRES   Khalid-NOM-NN afraid.SG.M-ACC-NN
      min   l-ʕanaakib-i
      from the-spiders-GEN
      'Khalid may be afraid of spiders.'

(30) qad   yakuunu zayd-u-n   muʔallif-a
      may   be.PRES Zaid-NOM-NN author.SG.M-ACC
      riywaayaat-i-n
      novels-GEN-NN
      'Zaid may be an author of novels.'

(31) qad   yakuunu hišaam-u-n   (huwa)
      may   be.PRES Hisham-NOM-NN he
      muħammad-a-n
      Muhammad-ACC-NN
      'Hisham may be Muhammad'

In most situations where a present tense form of the copula might be expected, MSA has a verbless sentence, traditionally known as a nominal sentence. Thus, instead of (24)–(27), we have the following:

(32) T-Tifl-u   fii   l-ħadiiqat-i
      the-child.SG.M-NOM in   the-garden-GEN
      'The child is in the garden.'

(33) xalid-u-n   xaaʔif-u-n   min   l-ʕanaakib-i
      Khalid-NOM-NN   afraid.SG.M-NOM-NN from   the-spiders-GEN
      'Khalid is afraid of spiders.'

(34) zayd-u-n   muʔallif-u   riwaayaat-i-n
      Zaid-NOM-NN   author.SG.M-NOM   novels-GEN-NN
      'Zaid is an author of novels.'

(35) hišaam-u-n   (huwa)   muħammad-u-n
      Hisham-NOM-NN   he   Muhammad-NOM-NN
      'Hisham is Muhammad.'

Note that whereas the adjectival and nominal complements in (29) and (30) are accusative, the adjectival and nominal predicates in (33) and (34) are nominative. Apart from this, these sentences look like copula sentences without an overt form of the copula.

There is a further important similarity between ordinary copula sentences and verbless sentences: both allow an existential interpretation with the expletive *hunaaka* 'there'. The following illustrate:

(36) kaana   hunaaka   Taalib-u-n   fii
      be.PAST.3SG.M there   student.SG.M-NOM-NN   in
      l-ħadiiqat-i
      the-garden-GEN
      'There was a student in the garden.'

(37) hunaaka   Taalib-u-n   fii   l-ħadiiqat-i
      there   student.SG.M-NOM-NN   in   the-garden-GEN
      'There is a student in the garden.'

MSA verbless sentences have been discussed within a Chomskyan approach, e.g. by Fassi Fehri (1993) and Aoun, Benmamoun & Choueiri (2010), and similar verbless sentences in other languages have been discussed within HPSG. For example, Bender (2001) discusses African American Vernacular English (AAVE), in which the sentence in (38) means 'You are in trouble' and is much like (1) above:

(38) You in trouble.

Essentially two types of analysis have been proposed for such sentences. Some, e.g. Fassi Fehri (1993) and Bender (2001), assume that they contain a phonologically empty form of the copula. Others, e.g. Aoun et al. (2010), reject this assumption. The problem with the latter type of analysis is that it makes the similarities between verbless sentences and sentences with an overt form of the copula an accident. In contrast, on the first type of analysis, they are unsurprising. We will assume, therefore, that MSA verbless sentences involve a phonologically empty form of the copula with properties similar but not identical to overt forms.

There is some independent motivation for such an analysis from *wh*-interrogatives.[2] Consider the following:

(39) a. mimma   kaana   xalid-u-n
         from.what   be.PAST.3SG.M   Khalid-NOM-NN
         xaaʔif-a-n?
         afraid.SG.M-ACC-NN
         'Of what was Khalid afraid?'

    b. *mimma   xalid-u-n   kaana
         from.what   Khalid-NOM-NN   be.PAST.3SG.M
         xaaʔif-a-n?
         afraid.SG.M-ACC-NN
         'Of what was Khalid afraid?'

MSA generally allows a subject to either precede or follow the associated verb. However, (39b) suggests that it does not allow the sequence *wh*-phrase – subject before the verb. Consider now the following:

(40) mimma   xalid-u-n   xaaʔif-u-n?
      from.what   Khalid-NOM-NN   afraid.SG.M-NOM-NN
      'Of what is Khalid afraid?'

Here the sequence *wh*-phrase – subject is perfectly acceptable. This is unsurprising if such sentences contain a phonologically empty form of the copula. We can assume that this is located between the *wh*-phrase and the subject and hence that (40) is like the grammatical (39a) and unlike the ungrammatical (39b).

We assume that the phonologically empty form of the copula differs from overt forms in taking an adjectival or nominal complement which is nominative. We also assume one further difference. One might suppose that the verb in the following is the complement of a phonologically empty form of the copula:

(41) r-rajul-u   yaktubu   t-taqriir-a
      the man NOM   write.PRES.3SG.M   the report ACC
      'The man writes the report.'

---

[2] This argument comes from Alotaibi (2015: Chapter 3).

However, there is evidence that such examples must have an analysis in which the overt verb is the only verb. We noted earlier that the copula can be preceded by *qad* 'may'. The same is true of ordinary verbs, as (42) illustrates:

(42) r-rajul-u   qad yaktubu   t-taqriir-a
      the-man-NOM   may write.PRES.3SG.M   the-report-ACC
      'The man may write the report.'

But a verb that is the complement of an overt form of the copula cannot be preceded by *qad*:

(43) *r-rajul-u   kaana   qad   yaktubu
       the-man-NOM   be.PAST.3SG.M   may   write.PRES.3SG.M
       t-taqriir-a
       the-report-ACC

This suggests that examples like (41) must have an analysis in which the verb is not the complement of the phonologically empty form of the copula. To avoid two analyses for such examples, we will assume that the phonologically empty form of the copula never takes a verbal complement.

Thus, we assume that there are two differences between the phonologically empty form of the copula and overt forms: (i) it takes a nominative and not an accusative complement, and (ii) it does not allow a verbal complement. In other respects, however, it is like the overt forms. In particular, it allows the same phrasal complements and it allows an existential construction with *hunaaka*. We will account for the similarities and differences in the next section.

We turn now to special negative present tense form of the copula – *laysa*. Present tense negation normally involves the particle *laa* and a present tense verb, and past tense negation normally involves the particle *lam* and a jussive present tense verb.[3] In the past tense, the copula has the expected form. Thus, (44) is a negative counterpart of (1).

(44) lam   yakun   T-Tifl-u   fii
      NEG.PAST   be.PRES.JSV.3SG.M   the-child.SG.M-NOM   in
      l-ħadiiqat-i
      the-garden-GEN
      'The child was not in the garden.'

However, in the present tense, MSA has not (45) but (46).

---

[3] All the other present tense verbs presented here are indicative.

(45) *laa   yakuunu   T-Tifl-u   fii
      NEG.PRES   be.PRES.3SG.M the-child.SG.M.NOM in
      l-ħadiiqat-i
      the-garden-GEN
      'The child is not in the garden.'

(46) laysa   T-Tifl-u   fii   l-ħadiiqat-i
      be.NEG.PRES.3SG.M the-child.SG.M-NOM in   the-garden-GEN
      'The child is not in the garden.'

Thus, negation has an irregular realization in the present tense of the copula. The precise nature of the irregularity depends on whether sequences like *lam yakun* are two words or one with a prefix. In the latter case, it is a fairly standard case of suppletion, rather like the appearance of *went* instead of **goed* in English. In the former case, it is rather like the situation with French comparatives, where most adjectives have periphrastic comparatives but a handful have synthetic comparative forms. (See Bonami 2015 for discussion.) We will not try to decide which is the right position.[4]

Laysa takes the full range of predicative phrasal complements. It has a PP complement in (46). It can also have an AP and an NP complement, as in the following:

(47) laysa   xalid-u-n   xaaʔif-a-n   min
      be.NEG.PRES.3SG.M Khalid-NOM-NN   afraid.SG.M-ACC-NN from
      l-ʕanaakib-i
      the-spiders-GEN
      'Khalid is not afraid of spiders.'

(48) laysa   zayd-u-n   muʔallif-a
      be.NEG.PRES.3SG.M Zaid-NOM-NN   author.SG.M-ACC
      riwaayaat-i-n
      novels-GEN-NN
      'Zaid is not an author of novels.'

It also appears in equative sentences:

(49) laysa   hišaam-u-n   (huwa)
      be.NEG.PRES.3SG.M Hisham-NOM-NN   he
      muħammad-a-n
      Muhammad-ACC-NN
      'Hisham is not Muhammad.'

In contrast to what we assume to be the case with the phonologically empty present tense form of the copula, it also allows a verbal complement:

---

[4] This issue is discussed inconclusively in Krer (2013).

(50) laysa   zayd-u-n   yaktubu
      be.NEG.PRES.3SG.M   Zaid-NOM-NN   write.PRES.3SG.M
      t-taqriir-a
      the-report-ACC
      'Zaid is not writing the report.'

However, the verbal complement may not be past tense:

(51) *laysa   zayd-u-n   kataba
      be.NEG.PRES.3SG.M   Zaid-NOM-NN   write.PAST.3SG.M
      t-taqriir-a
      the-report-ACC
      'Zaid has not written the report.'

Thus, this form is less restricted than the phonologically empty present tense form, but it is still subject to an important constraint.

5 An HPSG Analysis

We will now outline an HPSG analysis incorporating the conclusions reached in the preceding sections. We will first discuss the constraints that are necessary for the various phrasal types we are assuming, and then consider the additional constraints necessary to account for the present tense of the copula.

5.1 Basic Constraints

We are assuming the hierarchy of types in (23), repeated here as (52).

(52)

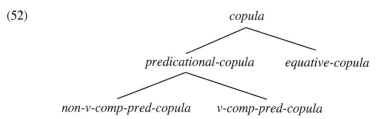

We assume that *copula* is a subtype of *verb-lexeme* and that this is subject to something like the following constraint:[5]

---

[5] A separate constraint will ensure that the value of SUBJ is either a singleton list or the empty list.

$$(53) \; \textit{verb-lexeme} \quad \rightarrow \quad \begin{bmatrix} \text{HEAD } \textit{verb} \\ \text{SUBJ}[1] \\ \text{COMPS}[2] \\ \text{ARG-ST}[1] \oplus [2] \end{bmatrix}$$

This means that there is no need to say anything about the values of HEAD, SUBJ and COMPS for *copula* and its subtypes.

We noted in Section 2 that the same set of forms is used in predicative uses and equative uses of the copula. To capture this fact we simply need to assume that the constraints that are responsible for the various forms refer to the type *copula*.

Following fairly standard assumptions, we assume that the *predicational-copula* is a semantically empty raising verb. We can capture this with the following constraint:

$$(54) \; \textit{predicational-copula} \; \rightarrow \quad \begin{bmatrix} \text{CONT}[2] \\ \text{ARG-ST} \; < [1], \begin{bmatrix} \text{SUBJ} < [1] > \\ \text{CONT}[2] \end{bmatrix} > \oplus \text{L} \end{bmatrix}$$

This ensures that *predicational-copula* forms share a SUBJ value and a CONT value with their first complement. In the case of *non-v-comp-pred-copula*, this will be the only complement.

We turn now to the constraints on the maximal subtypes. For *non-v-comp-pred-copula*, we propose the following constraint:

$$(55) \; \textit{non-v-comp-pred-copula} \; \rightarrow \quad \begin{bmatrix} \text{ARG-ST} \; < [], \begin{bmatrix} \text{HEAD} \neg \textit{verb} \\ \text{LEX} - \end{bmatrix} > \end{bmatrix}$$

This ensures that this form of the copula takes a single complement which is non-verbal and [LEX −], hence a phrase. For *v-comp-pred-copula*, we need the following constraint:

$$(56) \; \textit{v-comp-pred-copula} \; \rightarrow$$
$$\begin{bmatrix} \text{ARG-ST} < [], \begin{bmatrix} \text{HEAD } \textit{verb} \\ \text{LEX} + \\ \text{COMPS}[1] \end{bmatrix} > \oplus [1] \end{bmatrix}$$

This ensures that the first complement of this form of the copula is verbal and [LEX +], hence a verb, and that the other complements are whatever the verb requires. In other words, it ensures an argument composition structure.

Finally, for *equative-copula*, we propose the following (where 'NP' is an abbreviation for a number of features):

(57) *equative-copula* →

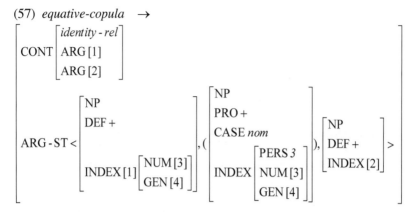

This ensures that this form of the copula has an identity interpretation and that the optional pronoun is third person but agrees in number and gender with the subject.

We can now provide analyses for some past tense examples. The copula in (1) will have the properties in (58), and the example will have the structure in (59) (which is simplified in various ways).

(58)

$$
\begin{bmatrix}
\text{CAT} \begin{bmatrix} \text{HEAD} \begin{bmatrix} verb \\ \text{TENSE } past \end{bmatrix} \\ \\ \text{SUBJ} < [1] > \\ \text{COMPS} < [2] > \end{bmatrix} \\
\text{CONT} [3] \\ \\
\text{ARG-ST} < [1] \begin{bmatrix} \text{NP} \\ \text{PERS } 3 \\ \text{NUM } sing \\ \text{GEN } masc \end{bmatrix}, [2] \begin{bmatrix} \text{PP} \\ \text{SUBJ} < [1] > \\ \text{CONT} [3] \end{bmatrix} >
\end{bmatrix}
$$

(59)

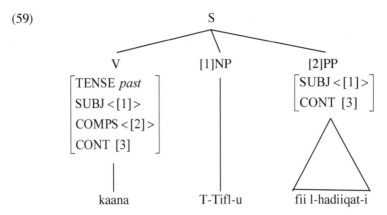

$$
\begin{array}{ccc}
& S & \\
V & [1]NP & [2]PP \\
\left[\begin{array}{l} \text{TENSE } past \\ \text{SUBJ} <[1]> \\ \text{COMPS} <[2]> \\ \text{CONT} [3] \end{array}\right] & & \left[\begin{array}{l} \text{SUBJ} <[1]> \\ \text{CONT} [3] \end{array}\right] \\
\text{kaana} & \text{T-Tifl-u} & \text{fii l-hadiiqat-i}
\end{array}
$$

The copula in (4) will have the properties in (60), and the example will have the structure in (61).

(60)

$$
\left[\begin{array}{l}
\text{CAT} \left[\begin{array}{l} \text{HEAD} \left[\begin{array}{l} verb \\ \text{TENSE } past \end{array}\right] \\ \\ \text{SUBJ} <[1]> \\ \text{COMPS} <[2],[3]> \end{array}\right] \\
\\
\text{CONT} [4] \\
\\
\text{ARG-ST} <[1] \left[\begin{array}{l} NP \\ \text{PERS } 3 \\ \text{NUM } sing \\ \text{GEN } masc \end{array}\right], [2] \left[\begin{array}{l} V \\ \text{TENSE } pres \\ \text{SUBJ} <[1]> \\ \text{COMPS} <[3]> \\ \text{CONT} [4] \end{array}\right], [3]NP >
\end{array}\right]
$$

(61)

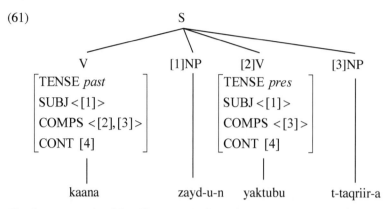

Finally, we can consider (7) – an equative with a pronoun. Here, we simplify by ignoring CONT. The copula will have the syntactic properties in (62) and the example will have the structure in (63).

(62)

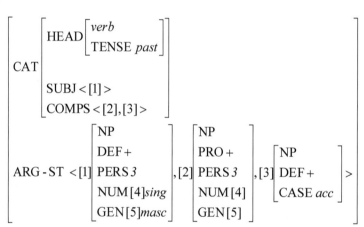

(63)

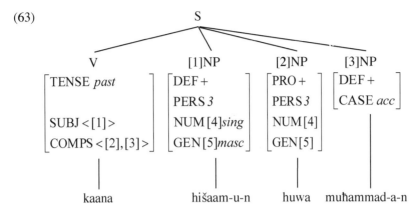

5.2 Present Tense of the Copula

We now consider the special properties of the present tense of the copula. On the one hand, we have a phonologically empty positive form, which takes a nominative and not an accusative complement, and does not allow a verbal complement. On the other hand, we have the special negative form *laysa*, which allows a verbal complement but not a past tense one.

We will assume that the phonologically empty form of the copula is [NULL +] and that this is required by the following constraint:

(64) $\begin{bmatrix} copula \\ \text{HEAD} \begin{bmatrix} \text{POL } pos \\ \text{TENSE } pres \end{bmatrix} \end{bmatrix} \rightarrow$ [NULL +]

We assume, following e.g. Bonami, Borsley and Tallerman (2016), that constraints can be overridden by more specific constraints and that (64) is overridden by more specific constraints in the contexts in which overt present tense forms such as *yakunnu* appear. We also assume that nominal and adjectival complements of a verb are generally accusative as a result of the following constraint:

(65) $\begin{bmatrix} \text{HEAD } verb \\ \text{COMPS} < ... \begin{bmatrix} \text{HEAD } noun \vee adj \\ \text{CASE}[1] \end{bmatrix}, ... > \end{bmatrix} \rightarrow [1] = acc$

In the case of the phonologically empty form of the copula this constraint will be overridden by the constraint in (66):

(66) $\begin{bmatrix} \text{HEAD}[\text{NULL}+] \\ \text{COMPS} < ... \begin{bmatrix} \text{HEAD } noun \vee adj \\ \text{CASE}[1] \end{bmatrix}, ... > \end{bmatrix} \rightarrow [1] = nom$

The constraint in (65) will also be overridden by the constraint on the type *equative-copula*, in (57) above, which requires the optional pronoun to be [CASE *nom*]. Finally, we need to ensure that the phonologically empty form of the copula never takes a verbal complement. We can do this with the constraint in (67):

(67) $\begin{bmatrix} \text{HEAD}[\text{NULL}+] \\ \text{COMPS} < [\text{HEAD}[1]], ... > \end{bmatrix} \rightarrow [1] = \neg verb$

We can now provide some analyses for some positive present tense examples. The copula in (32) will have the properties in (68) and the example will have structure in (69).

(68)

$$\begin{bmatrix} \text{CAT} \begin{bmatrix} \text{HEAD} \begin{bmatrix} verb \\ \text{TENSE } pres \\ \text{POL } pos \\ \text{NULL}+ \end{bmatrix} \\ \\ \text{SUBJ} < [1] > \\ \text{COMPS} < [2] > \end{bmatrix} \\ \\ \text{CONT}[3] \\ \\ \text{ARG-ST} < [1] \begin{bmatrix} \text{NP} \\ \text{PERS } 3 \\ \text{NUM } sing \\ \text{GEN } masc \end{bmatrix}, [2] \begin{bmatrix} \text{PP} \\ \text{SUBJ} < [1] > \\ \text{CONT}[3] \end{bmatrix} > \end{bmatrix}$$

(69)

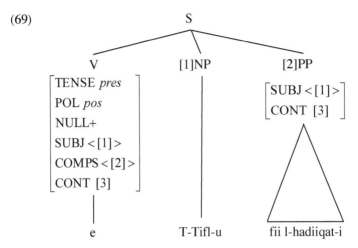

```
                              S
          ┌───────────────┬──────────────┐
          V            [1]NP          [2]PP
  ┌                    ┐              ┌           ┐
  │ TENSE pres         │              │ SUBJ <[1]> │
  │ POL pos            │              │ CONT [3]   │
  │ NULL+              │              └           ┘
  │ SUBJ <[1]>         │
  │ COMPS <[2]>        │
  │ CONT [3]           │
  └                    ┘
          │              │              △
          e           T-Tifl-u      fii l-hadiiqat-i
```

The equative copula in (35) will have the properties in (70) and the example
will have structure in (71).

(70)

$$
\begin{bmatrix}
\text{CAT}
\begin{bmatrix}
\text{HEAD}
\begin{bmatrix}
verb \\
\text{TENSE } pres \\
\text{POL } pos \\
\text{NULL}+
\end{bmatrix} \\[2mm]
\text{SUBJ} <[1]> \\
\text{COMPS} <[2],[3]>
\end{bmatrix} \\[4mm]
\text{ARG-ST} <[1]
\begin{bmatrix}
\text{NP} \\
\text{DEF}+ \\
\text{PERS } 3 \\
\text{NUM}[4]sing \\
\text{GEN}[5]masc
\end{bmatrix},
[2]
\begin{bmatrix}
\text{NP} \\
\text{PRO}+ \\
\text{PERS } 3 \\
\text{NUM}[4] \\
\text{GEN}[5]
\end{bmatrix},
[3]
\begin{bmatrix}
\text{NP} \\
\text{DEF}+ \\
\text{CASE } nom
\end{bmatrix} >
\end{bmatrix}
$$

(71)

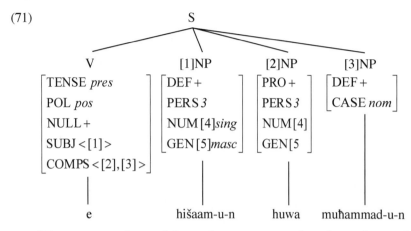

We turn now to the special negative present tense form *laysa*. As noted above, we will not consider how to deal with the fact that the copula has this special form. We will just deal with its selectional properties. Essentially, we need to say that when a negative present tense form of the copula has a verbal complement, the complement has present tense. The following constraint does this:

(72)
$$
\begin{bmatrix}
copula \\
\text{HEAD}\begin{bmatrix} \text{POL } neg \\ \text{TENSE } pres \end{bmatrix} \\
\\
\text{COMPS} < \begin{bmatrix} \text{HEAD } verb \\ \text{TENSE}[1] \end{bmatrix}, ... >
\end{bmatrix}
\rightarrow \quad [1] = pres
$$

6 Conclusions

We have been concerned in this paper with the properties of the copula in MSA. They are quite complex and challenging although probably no more so than those of the copula in many other languages. We have developed an analysis involving two main ideas:

- The similarities and differences among the various uses of the MSA copula can be captured with an appropriate type hierarchy and associated constraints.

- The similarities and differences between verbless sentences and sentences with an overt copula can be captured by assuming that the former contain a phonologically empty form of the copula with similar but not identical properties to overt forms.

The first idea is just standard HPSG. The second is more controversial. There has been some skepticism within HPSG about the value of phonologically empty elements (see especially Sag 1997). However, as noted above, Bender (2001) argues for a phonologically empty copula in AAVE. Whatever may be the case in other languages, it seems to us that there is a strong case for a phonologically empty form of the copula in MSA.[6] Without it, the similarities between verbless sentences and sentences with an overt copula are essentially an accident.

Acknowledgements

An earlier version of this paper was presented at the Constraint-based Syntax and Semantics Meeting in Honour of Danièle Godard, Paris, 27 March 2017. We are grateful to members of the audience for a number of helpful comments. We alone are responsible for what appears here.

---

[6] We would not want to claim that verbless clauses always involve an empty copula. Arnold and Borsley (2014) present arguments that there is no empty copula in the versions of (i) and (ii) with no overt copula.

(i) This is hard to teach, no matter how good the students (are).

(ii) The better the students (are), the more fun the class (is).

4

Relativization and the Grammaticalization of the Stage-Level vs. Individual-Level Distinction in the Languages of Senegal

Denis Creissels

1 Introduction

An areal feature of the languages spoken in Senegal is that, regardless of their genetic affiliation (Atlantic or Mande), they have grammaticalized a distinction between relative clauses expressing a stage-level property of their head, and relative clauses expressing individual-level properties. As illustrated in (1), in the languages in question, relative clauses expressing individual-level
properties of their head can be introduced by a complex expression whose literal meaning, originally 'which you know that', has undergone a process of semantic bleaching (and is not immediately perceived by speakers any-more).

Constraint-Based Syntax and Semantics: Papers in Honor of Danièle Godard.
Anne Abeillé and Olivier Bonami (eds.).
Copyright © 2020, CSLI Publications.

(1) *Fóoñi (Jóola, Atlantic)* – pers. doc.

 ka-jiil-a-k   **k-an** **u-manj-umi**
 CLk-stump-D-CLk CLk-REL 2SG-know-SBD
 k-oo-k-u   **tiitooraay** **di**
 CLk-LCOP-CLk-DX in_the_middle LOC
 ba-ŋaan-a-b
 CLb-clearing-D-CLb
 'a stump which is in the middle of the clearing'
 lit. /a stump / which / you know (that) / it is / in the
 middle / in / the clearing/

To the best of my knowledge, the possibility of a grammaticalized distinction between stage- and individual-level properties in the 'noun + relative clause' construction has not been discussed so far in the general literature on relativization. As regards the languages of Senegal, it was mentioned for the first time in Creissels et al. (2015), a paper devoted to impersonality in the languages of Senegal.

This paper is organized as follows. Section 2 consists of a succinct presentation of the relativization strategies found in the languages of Senegal. In Section 3, I provide illustrations of relative clauses expressing individual properties of their head in various Senegalese languages. In Section 4, I analyze the semantic evolution underlying the use of 'which you know that' to introduce relative clauses referring to an individual-level property of their head. In Section 5, I discuss the apparent mismatch between syntax and semantics that characterizes this construction in its present-day use. Section 6 summarizes the conclusions.

2 Relativization Strategies in the Languages of Senegal

Senegal is a multilingual country. *Ethnologue* lists 38 living languages. Of these, 31 are indigenous, and seven non-indigenous.[1] Apart from the Portuguese-based creole traditionally spoken in the town of Ziguinchor and some of the surrounding villages, the indigenous languages of Senegal belong either to the Western branch of the Mande family, or to the Atlantic family as delimited by Pozdniakov & Segerer (forthcoming).[2] Typologically, At-

---

[1] https://www.ethnologue.com/country/SN/languages (accessed 3 September 2017).

[2] Pozdniakov & Segerer's Atlantic is more restricted than Atlantic as delimited in the classical works of Greenberg and Sapir, since it excludes Mel languages (considered now as a distinct branch of the Niger-Congo macro-family) and some languages, previously classified as Atlantic, whose Niger-Congo affiliation is probable, but whose inclusion in one of the well-established branches of Niger-Congo is problematic.

lantic and Mande languages sharply contrast in many respects, including their relativization strategies. For an overview of the structural particularities of Atlantic and West Mande languages, the interested reader is referred to Lüpke (forthcoming), a volume on Atlantic languages which includes sketches of several Atlantic languages, but also of Mandinka (West Mande).

2.1 Relativization Strategies in West Mande Languages

Mandinka, mainly spoken in Middle Casamance, is one of the important regional languages of Senegal.[3] Closely related Manding varieties (Niokolo Maninka, Dantila Maninka, etc.) are spoken in Eastern Senegal. The other two representatives of West Mande in Senegal, Soninke and Dialonke, are only distantly related to Mandinka, but their relativization strategies are basically the same. On the classification of Mande languages, see Vydrin (2009).

The most common relativization strategy in Mandinka, illustrated in (2) below, is a correlative strategy in which the relative clause is not embedded in the matrix clause. It may precede or follow it, but the order 'relative clause – matrix clause' is much more frequent than the order 'matrix clause – relative clause'. Within the relative clause, the relativizer *mîŋ* (dialectal variants: *mêŋ*, *mûŋ*) occupies the position of the relativized NP, either alone of combined with the noun acting as the semantic head of the relative clause.[4]

---

[3] Mandinka is also spoken in Gambia and Guinea Bissau. In Gambia, it is spoken as a first language by about 40% of the population, and is widely used as a lingua franca. In Guinea Bissau, the dominant language is the Portuguese-based Guinea Bissau Creole, but Mandinka is one of the important regional languages.

[4] Comparative data show that the relativizer *mîŋ* originates from a demonstrative.

(2) *Mandinka (West Mande)* – pers. doc.

a. **Mùsôo yè kèwôo lá kódóo tǎa.**
woman.D CPL man.D GEN money.D take
'The woman took the man's money.'

b. **mùsôo mîŋ yè kèwôo lá kódóo tǎa**
woman.D REL CPL man.D GEN money.D take
'the woman who took the man's money'

c. **mîŋ yè kèwôo lá kódóo tǎa**
REL CPL man.D GEN money.D take
'the one who took the man's money'

d. **mùsôo yè kèwôo mîŋ ná kódóo tǎa**
woman.D CPL man.D REL GEN money.D take
'the man whose money was taken by the woman'

e. **mùsôo yè mîŋ ná kódóo tǎa**
woman.D CPL REL GEN money.D take
'the one whose money was taken by the woman'

f. **mùsôo yè kódòo míŋ tǎa**
woman.D CPL money.D REL take
'the money that the woman took'

g. **mùsôo yè míŋ tǎa**
woman.D CPL REL take
'the one that the woman took', 'what the woman took'

As illustrated in (3), the relativized NP is resumed in the matrix clause by a pronoun.

(3) *Mandinka (West Mande)* – pers. doc.

a. **[Mùsôo yè kèwôo_i mîŋ ná kódóo tǎa],**
woman.D CPL man.D REL GEN money.D take
ŋ́ níŋ wǒo_i běn-tà.
1SG with DEM meet-CPL
'I met the man whose money was taken by the woman.'
lit. something like 'The woman took which man's money, I met that one.'

b. **[Mùsôo_i mîŋ yè kèwôo lá kódóo tǎa],**
woman.D REL CPL man.D GEN money.D take
ŋ́ níŋ wǒo_i běn-tà.
1SG with DEM meet-CPL
'I met the woman who took the man's money.'
lit. something like 'Which woman took the man's money, I met that one.'

Two other relativization strategies are found in Mandinka. In the first one, the relative clause precedes the matrix clause and is resumed by a pronoun, like in canonical relativization, but the head noun is found on the left edge of the relative clause, immediately followed by the relativizer and resumed by a pronoun occupying the position of the relativized NP – (4b), to be compared with the canonical construction in (4a). Both have the same meaning.

(4) *Mandinka (West Mande)* – pers. doc.

    a. [Í   bè   súwòo$_i$ mîŋ dâa   tó],
       2SG LCOP house.D REL door.D LOC
       wó$_i$ lè   mú   ŋ́   yàâ   tí.
       DEM FOC EQCOP 1SG home.D POSTP
       'The house at whose door you are is my home.'

    b. [Súwòo$_i$ mîŋ í   bé   à$_i$ dâa   tó],
       house.D REL 2SG LCOP 3SG door.D LOC
       wó$_i$ lè   mú   ŋ́   yàâ   tí.
       DEM FOC EQCOP 1SG home.D POSTP

In the second type of non-canonical relatives, the internal structure of the relative clause is identical to that of canonical relatives, but it occurs as a constituent of the matrix clause. However, this is only possible if the relative clause occupies a peripheral position which may be either the subject position at the beginning of the clause, as in (5), or an oblique position at the end of the clause.

(5) *Mandinka (West Mande)* – pers. doc.

    [Sàâ   mîŋ mú   súŋkútóo kèemáa tì]
    snake.D REL EQCOP girl.D   husband POSTP
    múrù-tá   nǎŋ.
    return-CPL CTRP
    'The snake who was the girl's husband came back.'

For a more detailed description of relativization in Mandinka, the reader is referred to Creissels & Sambou (2013).

2.2 Relativization Strategies in Atlantic Languages

The vast majority of the languages of Senegal belong to one of the two branches of the Atlantic family as delimited by Pozdniakov & Segerer (forthcoming): Northern Atlantic and Bak. The Northern Atlantic branch includes Wolof, by far the most important language of Senegal (spoken natively by at least 40% of the population, also spoken as a lingua franca throughout the country, and widely used in all areas of public life except formal education), and important regional languages such as Seereer and Pulaar. The Bak branch includes Jóola (aka Diola), an important regional language.

Atlantic languages have post-nominal relatives. There is variation as regards the use of verb forms distinct from those found in plain assertive clauses, the presence of pronouns resuming the head noun within the relative clause, and the presence of linkers at the junction between the head noun and the relative clause. The special verb forms found in relative clauses are typically also used in *wh*-questions, and in focalization. The linkers found at the junction between the head noun and the relative clause express gender-number agreement with the head noun, like determiners and other noun modifiers, but they provide no indication about the function of the relativized NP within the relative clause. They are often labeled 'relative pronouns' in the available descriptions, since they occupy a position superficially similar to that occupied by relative pronouns in many European languages. They are pronominal in the sense that, in the absence of a lexical head, they act as the head of the relative clause, but they do not have the properties that could justify analyzing them as real relative pronouns extracted from the relative clause.

For example, in Ganja (Balant, Bak, Atlantic), relative clauses are immediately postposed to their head. As illustrated in (6), the gap strategy is not limited to the relativization of subjects and objects. A resumptive element is used only in the relativization of genitives. The verb is marked for backgrounding in the completive aspect, but in the incompletive aspect, the forms used in relative clauses are not different from those found in plain assertive clauses.[5]

---

[5] For a more detailed description of relativization in Ganja, see Creissels & Biaye (2016).

(6) *Ganja (Balant, Atlantic)* – Creissels & Biaye (2016)
  a. **à-láantὲ   mà wús-nì   f-ñjʊ́gʊ́b**
     CLha-man D   buy-BGR CLf-chair
     'the man who bought a chair'

  b. **f-ñjʊ́gʊ́b mà   à-láantὲ   mà   wús-nì**
     CLf-chair D   CLha-man D   buy-BGR
     'the chair that the man bought'

  c. **hɔ̀tɔ́   mà   n-tɔ́ɔ-nì   Dàagâr**
     (CLu)car D   1SG-go-BGR Dakar
     'the car with which I went to Dakar'
     lit. 'the car (that) I went to Dakar'

  d. **b-tá   mà   bì-bíʊθá-nì   hás**
     CLb-tree D   CLbi-see-BGR (CLu)monkey
     'the tree on which they saw a monkey'
     lit. 'the tree (that) they saw a monkey'

  e. **à-láantὲ   mà à-nîn   ní   mà**
     CLha-man D   CLa-woman POSS.CLha D
     dée-nì
     give_birth-BGR
     'the man whose wife has given birth'
     lit. 'the man (that) his wife has given birth'

In the languages of Sub-Saharan Africa in general, and in Atlantic languages in particular, it is common that the verb forms found in relative clauses are distinct from those found in the corresponding independent clauses. However, most descriptions do not discuss the precise nature of the verb forms in question: do such 'relative verb forms' constitute a *dependent mood*, i.e. a set of verb forms that, although distinct from those found in independent clauses, are structurally similar to them (in the same way as 'subjunctives' in European languages)? or do they show the kind of deviation from the standard of the independent clause predicate that characterizes the forms traditionally designated as *participles*? In other words, in reference to the distinction between *deranking* and *balancing* introduced by Stassen (1985: 76–83), are relative clauses headed by special verb forms *balanced* or *deranked* dependent clauses?

In most cases, there does not seem to be evidence that the relative clauses of Atlantic languages involving special verb forms should be analyzed as deranked (i.e. participial). A relativization strategy involving verb forms analyzable as participles is however found in Jóola Fóoñi (Atlantic), a language using distinct relativization strategies for subject and non-subject relativization.

Both types of relative verb forms found in Jóola Fóoñi are morphologically distinct from the verb forms used in the corresponding independent
clauses, and at the same time do not show evidence of deranking as regards
the TAM and polarity distinctions they express, or their behavior with
respect to grammatical relations other than subject. There is however a crucial difference between the verb forms used for subject relativization and
those used for the relativization of other grammatical relations. As illustrated in (7a) below, where the square brackets show the boundaries of the relative clause, the verb forms used for non-subject relativization include an
initial agreement slot expressing subject agreement with exactly the same
possible person-number and gender-number values as the initial agreement
slot of independent verb forms. By contrast, as illustrated by (7b), the initial
agreement slot of the verb forms used for subject relativization can only
express gender-number agreement: with a first or second person antecedent,
the value expressed can only be 'class A' (i.e 'human singular') or 'class
BK' (i.e. 'human plural'). In other words, the forms used for subject relativization do not agree like independent verb forms with their subject, but rather like noun modifiers with their head. This constitutes clear evidence of
the deranked (i.e. participial) status of the verb forms used for subject relativization in Jóola Fóoñi, as opposed to the balanced status of the dependent
verb forms used in non-subject relatives.

(7) *Fóoñi (Jóola, Atlantic)* – pers. doc.
   a. **b-iit-a-b**   **[b-an**   *u-wañ-umi*]
      CLb-rice_field-D-CLb   CLb-which 1PL-cultivate-SBD
      'the rice field that we have cultivated'
   b. **úlí** **[*k-a-jamo-m***   **di**
      we   CLbk-PTCP-be_famous-SBD with
      ka-legen-a-k   **k-óolólí]**
      CLk-honesty-D-CLk CLk-our
      'we who are known for our honesty'

3 Relative Clauses Expressing Individual Properties of their Head

In the Atlantic and Mande languages spoken in Senegal, one commonly
finds relative clauses beginning with 'which you know that'. None of the
descriptions I have been able to consult signals this construction explicitly,
but in most of them, it can be found in some of the examples quoted in the
discussion of others points of grammar, or in the texts provided to illustrate
the description. It is immediately obvious from the contexts in which this
construction occurs that 'which you know that' must not be taken in its lit-

eral meaning, and this is confirmed by the reactions of speakers in elicitation.

At first sight, one may have the impression that, for the speakers of Senegalese languages, adding 'which you know that' at the beginning of relative clauses is just a kind of verbal tic that does not add or change anything in the meaning. However, a closer look at the contexts in which this expression can be found shows that 'which you know that' is never used to introduce relative clauses that specify the identity of an individual with reference to a particular situation in which this individual is episodically involved. By contrast, as illustrated by examples (8)–(13) (all extracted from naturalistic texts), it regularly occurs in relative clauses that characterize an individual or a kind with reference to a stable property.

(8) *Mandinka (West Mande)* – Creissels et al. (2015)
Sěejò mú bèn-dúlàa lè tí, mí
Sédhiou EQCOP meet-place.D FOC POSTP REL
í yé à lôŋ kó síi jámáa
2SG CPL 3SG know that ethnic_group many
lè bé jěe.
FOC LCOP there
'Sédhiou is a crossroad where many ethnic groups can be found.'
lit. 'which you know that many ethnic groups are there'

(9) *Wolof (Atlantic)* – Creissels et al. (2015)
ab dëkk-u kow boo xam
INDEF.CLb village-of upcountry CLb.REL.2SG know
né am mbey doŋŋ la dunde
that INDEF.CLm farming only FOC.3SG live.APPL
'a remote subsistance farming village'
lit. 'a remote village which you know that it lives on some farming only'

(10) *Keerak (Joola, Atlantic)* – Creissels et al. (2015)
ma-Ħus-am mɔ-nʊ-haasʊm kaanakʊ
CLm-sand-D.CLm REL.CLm-2SG-know that
m-ɔmɔ mʊ-hʊrʊm
CLm-COP CLm-salty
'the sand which contains salt'
lit. 'the sand which you know that it is salty'

(11) *Sereer (Atlantic)* – Creissels et al. (2015)
ox-e   and-oona   ee   ten   sinj-u
CL-REL   know-2SG.SBD   that 3SG found-FOC
saate fan-e
village CL-D
'the one who founded the village'
lit. 'the one you know that it's him who founded
the village'

(12) *Gubëeher (Ñun, Atlantic)* – Creissels et al. (2015)
taabl ə-gəni   u-na   buyɛnka ə-dej-i
table CLA-REL 2SG-know that   CLA-be_high-CPL
'a table which is high'
lit. 'a table which you know that it is high'

(13) *Ganja (Balant, Atlantic)* – Creissels & Biaye (2016)
bì-θásà   mà   ú-húr-ùn   yàa
CLbi-young_man D   2SG-know-SBD that
bégè   gî   ŋgì   à-nîn
CLbi.DEM be   with   CLha-woman
'the young men who are married'
lit. 'the young men you know that they have a wife'

In my fieldwork on Mandinka, I observed that, when asked to explain the meaning of a noun in Mandinka, speakers systematically use this kind of construction, as illustrated in (14).

(14) *Mandinka (Mande)* – Creissels et al. (2015)
Kòolêe,   wó lè   mú dùlâa   tí,
kòolée.D DEM FOC FOC place.D POSTP
dáa-mì   í   yé   à   lôŋ kó   kòo-báŋk-òo
place-REL 2SG CPL 3SG know that salt-soil-D
lè   bé   jěe.
FOC   LCOP there
'A *kòolée* is a place where the soil contains salt.'
lit. 'a place where you know that there is salted soil'

The grammaticalization of 'which you know that' is however not complete, in spite of the fact that 'which you know that' has lost its literal meaning. Relative clauses introduced by 'which you know that' can only be interpreted as referring to an individual-level property of the head, but the converse is not the case: constructions in which a relative clause interpreted as referring to an individual-level property of the head is not introduced by 'which you know that' are not considered ungrammatical by speakers. Unfortunately, large corpora that would make it possible to evaluate the frequency with which speakers use relative clauses explicitly marked as referring to an individual-level property are not available.

4 The Semantic Evolution Underlying the Use of 'which you know that' with Relative Clauses Referring to an Individual-Level Property of their Head

It seems reasonable to assume that the use of 'which you know that' to introduce relative clauses referring to an individual-level property of their head developed from the generalizing use of second person singular, rather than from second person referring specifically to the addressee. The use of 2nd person singular to express generalizations about humans is wide-spread in the languages of the world, and is particularly common in West African languages, including those that use 'which you know that' to introduce relative clauses referring to individual-level properties of their head.

According to this hypothesis, the original meaning of the construction 'N which you know that CLS' (N a noun, CLS a clause interpreted as expressing a property of N's referent) was 'N about which one knows that CLS', 'N about which it is well known that CLS'. Crucially, characterizing the referent of a noun by a property presented as common knowledge implies that the property in question is an individual-level rather than stage-level property.

However, it is clear that the notion of common knowledge is too restricted to account for the present-day use of 'which you know that' in Senegalese
languages. For example, it is obvious from the context in which (13) was found that the intended meaning was simply 'the young men that are married', not 'the young men about whom it is well known that they are married', and similar observations can be made about the other examples quoted above.

This means that, in the present-day use of 'which you know that', 'know' has been affected by a process of semantic bleaching. Formally, the verb 'know' is still present (and, as will be commented in the following section, still has the properties of the main verb of the relative clause), but the original meaning 'N about which it is well known that CLS' has evolved toward 'N having CLS as one of its individual-level properties'. The notion of common knowledge has been lost, and all that remains of the original meaning of the expression is the notion of individual-level property (originally implied by the notion of common knowledge).

5 Relative Clauses Introduced by 'which you know that' and the Syntax–Semantics Interface

Relative clauses introduced by 'which you know that' are an interesting case of apparent mismatch between syntax and semantics: semantically, a construction superficially glossable literally as 'N which you know that CLS' is interpreted as if CLS were simply a relative clause modifying N, with just the additional precision that the property it expresses is an individual-level property of its head.

For example, the original structure of Ganja *bójà mà úhúrùn yàa mméɛsɛ̀ ŋ hăj mà âttálânθ* 'a town where it is not easy to live' can be represented as indicated in (15), with 'know' as the main verb of the relative clause, and the clause expressing the property attributed to *bójà* 'town' embedded as a complement clause within the relative clause.

(15) *Ganja (Balant, Atlantic)* – Creissels & Biaye (2016)
    bójà mà [ú-húrù-n [yàa [m-mɛ́ɛsɛ̀ ŋ hăj
    town D 2SG-know-SBD that CLb-living GEN place
    mà ât-tálânθ]]]
    D NEG-be_easy
    'a town where it is not easy to live'
    lit. 'a town you know that living there is not easy'

This constituent structure is still consistent with the morphological details: crucially, the subordination marker suffixed to verbs in relative clauses in the completive aspect is found on the verb 'know', not on the verb of the clause that expresses the property 'Living in that place is not easy', whereas 'be_easy', as the main verb of a complement clause introduced by the complementizer *yàa* 'that', is in a form that could be used as the main verb of an independent clause. However, if one adheres to the view that the meaning representation of an expression is built in parallel with the construction of its syntactic structure (as assumed in non-Chomskyan formal grammar frameworks – see Partee 2014), the constituent structure indicated in (15) can hardly be maintained in a synchronic account of the 'noun + relative clause' construction of Ganja. In this perspective, in some way or other, 'be_easy' must be the main verb of a relative clause modifying 'town'.

Two possible solutions can be considered:

(a) *úhúrùn yàa mméesè ŋ hǎj mà âttálânθ* has been reanalyzed as a plain relative clause with 'be_easy' as the main verb, and 'you_know_that' is an unanalyzable block acting as a modifier of the main verb of the relative clause, adding the feature 'individual-level property' to its interpretation;

(b) *úhúrùn yàa mméesè ŋ hǎj mà âttálânθ* has been reanalyzed as a relative clause with 'be_easy' as the main verb, but of a distinct type, since 'which_you_know_that' has been reanalyzed as a relativizer occupying a complementizer position at the left periphery of the relative clause (recall that no relativizer occurs in the relative clauses of Ganja that are not marked as expressing an individual-level property – cf. example (6) above).

Solution (a) is ruled out by the mere fact that, in this construction, the verb acting as the main predicate in the construction of the property attributed to the head-noun (in this example, 'be_easy') cannot take the backgrounding marker it takes in the completive aspect in the relative clauses that are not marked as expressing an individual-level property. Moreover, in the relative clauses of Ganja that are not marked as expressing an individual-level property, a resumptive element occurs only if the relativized NP is not a term in the construction of the main verb (recall example (6) above), whereas in relative clauses introduced by 'which you know that', a resumptive element is obligatory (in example (15), *hǎj mà* 'the place'), because the relativized NP originally belonged to a clause complementing the main verb of the relative clause.

Consequently, the only possible solution is (b), according to which the grammaticalization of the stage-level vs. individual-level distinction in relativization has resulted in the emergence of a structurally distinct type of relative:

• the relative clauses of Ganja marked as expressing an individual-level property are introduced by the complementizer *úhúrùn yàa*, whereas no overt complementizer occurs with relative clauses unmarked for the stage- vs. individual-level distinction;

• the main verb of the relative clauses of Ganja marked as expressing an individual-level property is always in a form that could also be used in plain assertive clauses, whereas in relative clauses unmarked for the stage- vs. individual-level distinction, backgrounding marking is obligatory in the completive aspect;

- in the relative clauses of Ganja marked as expressing an individual-level property, the head noun must be resumed in some way or other, depending on the relativized function (subject index, object index, pronoun, or adverb), whereas in non-subject relative clauses unmarked for the stage- vs. individual-level distinction, resumptive elements occur only if the relativized NP is not a term in the construction of the main verb.

In other languages, the details may be different from those observed in Ganja, but similar observations can be made, leading in all cases to the conclusion that the grammaticalization of the stage- vs. individual-level distinction has led to the emergence of a structurally distinct type of relative clause.

For example, Wolof does not have special verb forms for relative clauses, but some of the verb forms that can be found in independent assertive clauses (and also in clauses complementing the verb 'know') are not allowed in relative clauses. For example in (9) (repeated here as (16)), *la dunde* |FOC.3SG|live.APPL| is a verb form expressing focalization of an object or oblique phrase. In Wolof, such verb forms can be found in independent clauses, or in clauses complementing verbs such as *xam* 'know', but cannot act as the main verb of relative clauses.

(16) *Wolof (Atlantic)* – Creissels et al. (2015)
    ab   **dëkk-u**   **kow**   **boo**   **xam**
    INDEF.CLb   village-of upcountry CLb.REL.2SG know
    né   **am**   **mbey**   **doŋŋ** **la**   **dunde**
    that   INDEF.CLm farming only   FOC.3SG live.APPL
    'a remote subsistence farming village'
    lit. 'a remote village which you know that it lives on farming only'

Similar observations can be made about the Fooñi example (1), repeated here as (17).

(17) *Fóoñi (Jóola, Atlantic)* – pers. doc.
    ka-jiil-a-k   **k-an**   **u-manj-umi**
    CLk-stump-D-CLk   CLk-REL 2SG-know-SBD
    k-oo-k-u   **tiitooraay**   **di**
    CLk-LCOP-CLk-DX in_the_middle LOC
    ba-ŋaan-a-b
    CLb-clearing-D-CLb
    'a stump which (you know that it) is in the middle of the clearing'

The point is that, in Fooñi,

- the use of the non-verbal locational copula *kooku* is possible in independent clauses, or in clauses complementing verbs such as 'know', but not as the main predicate of relative clauses, in which a verb 'be' must be used instead;

- the relativizer *kan* belongs to a paradigm of relativizers that can only introduce non-subject relative clauses, whereas subject relatives require the use of participial verb forms, as in (18), where *kammi* 'being' is a participial form of the verb 'be'.

(18) *Fooñi (Joola, Atlantic)* – pers. doc.
    ka-jiil-a-k   **k-a-mmi**   **tiitooraay**
    CLk-stump-D-CLk   CLk-PTCP-be.SBD   in_the_middle
    di   ba-ŋaan-a-b
    LOC   CLb-clearing-D-CLb
    'a stump being in the middle of the clearing'

6 Conclusion

In this article, I have analyzed the relative clauses introduced by 'which you know that', a construction which constitutes an areal feature of the Atlantic and Mande languages spoken in Senegal. In this construction, 'you know that' has lost its literal meaning, and just encodes that the clause superficially analyzable as the complement of 'know' expresses an individual-level property of the head noun. After putting forward a hypothesis about the semantic evolution underlying the present-day use of this construction, I have discussed the apparent mismatch between syntax and semantics that characterizes it, and concluded that, in the languages in question, the grammaticalization of the stage- vs. individual-level distinction has resulted in the emergence of a structurally distinct type of relative clause.

Abbreviations

APPL: applicative, BGR: backgrounding, CL: noun class, CLS: clause, COP: copula, CPL: completive, CTRP: centripetal, D: definite, DEM: demonstrative, DX: deixis marker, EQCOP: equative copula, FOC: focalization marker, GEN: genitive, INDEF: indefinite, LCOP: locational copula, LOC: locative, N: noun, NEG: negative, NP: noun phrase, PL: plural, PTCP: participle, POSS: possessive, POSTP: postposition, REL: relativizer, SBD: subordination marker, SG: singular

5

Non-Canonical Arguments and French Past Participle Agreement

Jesse Tseng

The formal analysis of French has received a lot of attention within the framework of HPSG, in large part thanks to the work of Danièle Godard and colleagues. Among the many proposals to be found in this work is a novel approach to past participle agreement in French compound past tenses, which has long been a major preoccupation of French normative grammar. This paper reexamines the HPSG analysis of past participle agreement in light of additional empirical data from French and related languages.

1 Introduction: The Traditional Rule

Compound or periphrastic past tenses in French consist of a tense auxiliary (*avoir* or *être*) and a past participle. Every time such a construction is used, the speaker/writer must decide whether the participle remains uninflected or if it should agree with one of its nominal arguments. The rules surrounding past participle agreement have been a subject of dispute for French grammarians for several centuries, and anyone who has had contact with French normative grammar knows that the standard rules are dismayingly complicated.

In this paper I will limit my attention to examples involving the auxiliary *avoir* and simple transitive verbs. The particularity of this syntactic configuration is that the normative rules sometimes call for the past participle to agree with the nominal direct object.[1] The stan-

---

[1]In contrast, when the auxiliary is *être*, the participle usually agrees with the

Constraint-Based Syntax and Semantics: Papers in Honor of Danièle Godard.
Anne Abeillé and Olivier Bonami (eds.).

dard rules in such cases are generally quite clear, but as we will see, a good deal of variation is observed even in these relatively straightforward situations.

The following examples illustrating the traditional rule all involve the transitive verb *détruire* 'destroy', whose past participle displays the following adjective-like paradigm, consisting of four distinct written forms corresponding to two distinct pronunciations:

(1)

	Masculine	Feminine
Singular	détruit [detʁɥi]	détruite [detʁɥit]
Plural	détruits [detʁɥi]	détruites [detʁɥit]

In each example, the direct object of the verb is the feminine plural NP *les maisons* 'the houses', or some coreferent nominal element. This potential agreement trigger for the participle will be indicated by italics.

According to the standard rules, in sentences with canonical VO order, the participle does not agree (in other words, it takes default masculine singular morphology).

(2) La tornade a **détruit** / *détruites *les*
the tornado AUX destroyed.MSG destroyed.FPL the
maisons.
houses.FPL

'The tornado has destroyed the houses.'

The past participle is supposed to agree with the direct object in three broad cases: when the direct object is realized as a pronominal proclitic (3), when it corresponds to a fronted *wh*-phrase (4), and when it is relativized (5):

(3) [ces maisons] La tornade *les* a
those houses the tornado PRO.3FPL AUX
détruites/%**détruit**.
destroyed.FPL/MSG

'[those houses] The tornado has destroyed them.'

---

subject, but there are several exceptions to this, particularly involving reflexive verbs.

(4) *Quelles maisons* la tornade a-t-elle
which houses.FPL the tornado AUX-PRO.3FSG
détruites/%détruit?
destroyed.FPL/MSG

'Which houses has the tornado destroyed?'

(5) *les maisons* que la tornade a **détruites/%détruit**
the houses.FPL that the tornado AUX destroyed.FPL/MSG

'the houses that the tornado has destroyed'

Despite usually having explicit metalinguistic knowledge of this normative standard, speakers routinely produce the MSG participle in examples like (3)–(5). This is why the non-agreeing form *détruit* is marked with '%', indicating non-standard status, as opposed to '*' for unacceptability. Indeed, most speakers perceive prescriptively incorrect non-agreeing participles in such contexts to be fully acceptable in all but the most formal registers, such as carefully edited writing. In fact, as we will see later in Section 3.1, it can be argued that using an active-voice participial form with audible agreement (such as *détruites* in the examples above) is the sociolinguistically marked option in informal spoken French.

The traditional rule calling for agreement with proclitic pronouns, illustrated in (3), makes an exception for the indefinite direct object pronoun *en*. With this pronoun, agreement is not strictly required, and in fact, most prescriptive sources recommend non-agreement:

(6) [ces maisons] La tornade *en* a
those houses the tornado PRO.3FPL AUX
détruit/?détruites.
destroyed.MSG/FPL

'[those houses] The tornado has destroyed some of them.'

In this case, the standard rule aligns with speakers' tendency to produce MSG forms, while audibly agreeing participles give rise to marginal or uncertain acceptability judgments.

2 Word Order vs. Canonicity

In traditional French grammar, the contrast between (2) and (3)–(5) is characterized in terms of word order: The past participle with *avoir* must agree with a preverbal direct object (other than the pronoun *en*), and must not agree if the direct object is post-verbal (which corresponds to the word order in the majority of sentences involving a transitive verb). Both native speakers and L2 learners are explicitly taught to look for a '*COD (complément d'objet direct) placé avant*' in compound tense constructions involving the auxiliary *avoir*, and to apply agreement accordingly if they find one.

2.1 HPSG Analyses of French

In syntactic analyses of French formalized in HSPG, the normative pattern above is not handled in terms of relative word order. Instead, past participle agreement with *avoir* is conditioned by the canonicity of the syntactic realization of the direct object argument: Canonically realized direct objects do not trigger agreement, while non-canonical direct objects do. Analyses along these lines are presented by Abeillé & Godard (1996: 52–53) and in more detail by Miller & Sag (1997: 586, 623ff.). Non-canonical arguments include pronominal clitics (which are formally analyzed as morphological affixes) and extraction gaps:

(7)

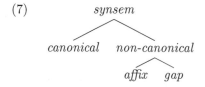

According to this analysis, the post-verbal full NP object in (2) is canonical, while the examples in (3)–(5) all involve non-canonical arguments. The pronominal object *les* in (3) is an affix, and the interrogative and relative constructions in (4)–(5) are both instances of argument extraction. A significant result of the HPSG analysis is that it provides a uniform formal treatment of extraction and pronominal affixation when it comes to phenomena like French past participle agreement.

The following pair of descriptions, adapted from Miller & Sag (1997), correspond respectively to past participles with a non-canonical direct object argument (the second item on the verb's ARGUMENT-STRUCTURE list), and past participles selecting a canonical direct object.[2]

---

[2]The descriptions in (8) and (9) do not constitute a complete analysis of past participle agreement in French. Additional descriptions are needed to account for the form of the past participle in other possible contexts (for example, when the second argument is non-canonical but not accusative, or when the verb has no second argument).

(8)
$$\begin{bmatrix} past\text{-}participle \\ \text{MORPH} \begin{bmatrix} \text{I-FORM} & F_\alpha(F_{pps}(\boxed{0})) \\ \text{STEM} & \boxed{0} \end{bmatrix} \\ \text{ARG-ST} \quad \langle \text{NP, NP } [non\text{-}canonical, \ acc, \ \alpha], \ \ldots \rangle \end{bmatrix}$$

where $\alpha \in \{[msg], [fsg], [mpl], [fpl]\}$

(9)
$$\begin{bmatrix} past\text{-}participle \\ \text{MORPH} \begin{bmatrix} \text{I-FORM} & F_{msg}(F_{pps}(\boxed{0})) \\ \text{STEM} & \boxed{0} \end{bmatrix} \\ \text{ARG-ST} \quad \langle \text{NP, NP } [canonical], \ \ldots \rangle \end{bmatrix}$$

Without going into the specifics of Miller & Sag's morphological analysis, we can simply note that in (8), the participle shares its agreement features α with its non-canonical direct object, while in (9), the participle takes the masculine singular form, regardless of the features of the canonical direct object. To take a couple of concrete examples, the non-agreeing participle *détruit* in example (2) above has the lexical description in (10), corresponding to (9), while the feminine plural participle *détruites* in example (3) has the lexical description in (11), corresponding to (8):

(10)   La tornade a **détruit** les maisons.
$$\begin{bmatrix} past\text{-}participle \\ \text{MORPH} \begin{bmatrix} \text{I-FORM} & F_{msg}(détruit) = détruit \end{bmatrix} \\ \text{ARG-ST} \quad \langle \text{NP, NP } [canonical, fpl] \rangle \end{bmatrix}$$

(11)   La tornade les a **détruites**.
$$\begin{bmatrix} past\text{-}participle \\ \text{MORPH} \begin{bmatrix} \text{I-FORM} & F_{\boxed{1}fpl}(détruit) = détruites \end{bmatrix} \\ \text{ARG-ST} \quad \langle \text{NP, NP } [affix, acc, \boxed{1}fpl] \rangle \end{bmatrix}$$

Although we are focusing here on constructions with the auxiliary *avoir*, it is important to point out that the descriptions in (8) and (9) make no reference to the auxiliary, because they are in fact valid whether the auxiliary is *avoir* or *être*. The only way a transitive participle can combine with *être* is if one of its arguments is a reflexive clitic, and in such cases the agreement rules are exactly the same as for participles combining with *avoir*: The participle remains invariable if the direct object argument is canonical (12a), but it agrees with a non-canonical direct object, i.e. an accusative pronominal affix (12b) or an extracted direct object argument (12c).

(12) a. Elle s'   est **construit/*construites** *ces*
          she REFL.3FSG.DAT AUX built.MSG/FPL   those
          maisons.
          houses

          'She has built those houses for herself.'

      b. Les maisons *se*   sont
          the houses REFL.3FPL.ACC AUX
          construites/*construit.
          built.FPL/MSG

          'The houses have been built (lit. have built themselves).'

      c. *les maisons* qu' elle s'   est
          the houses   that she REFL.3FSG.DAT AUX
          construites/%construit
          built.FPL/MSG

          'the houses that she has built for herself'

In traditional French grammar, completely separate sets of rules are formulated for *avoir* and *être*. The HPSG analysis presented above allows a unified treatment for all transitive participles, no matter which auxiliary they combine with.[3]

The HSPG analysis also accommodates the exceptional status of the pronoun *en*, illustrated above in (6). This pronoun is assumed not to carry accusative case, even when used as a direct object, but rather a special marking [CASE *de*] (Miller 1992, Miller & Sag 1997). The description in (8) is therefore not satisfied, so obligatory agreement is not triggered. A separate constraint would need to be formulated specifically for participles selecting *en* as their object, and this constraint can call for either no agreement or optional agreement, depending on the rule one chooses to model.

For the core cases illustrated by examples (2)–(5) above, the traditional rule referring to word order and the formal HPSG account based on canonicity make the same predictions. This is because the canonical position of the direct object NP in French is to the right of the

---

[3]For a detailed HPSG analysis of the syntax of the auxiliary + participle construction, see Abeillé & Godard (2002). Through argument composition, information about the verb's arguments is made available to both the auxiliary (in order to account for the morphosyntactic realization of affixes, i.e. clitic climbing) and to the participle (to account for agreement).

verb, and the three types of non-canonical direct objects considered thus far all correspond to a noun or pronoun realized to the left of the verb. It would be surprising if this were a systematic correlation and if canonicity and word order always lined up in this way in French. In reality, there are situations where they do not match and such constructions potentially provide evidence for preferring one or the other of the two criteria as the more accurate predictor of speakers' behavior and judgments about past participle agreement with *avoir*.

2.2 Preverbal Canonical Objects?

Abeillé & Godard (1996: 52) mention two possible test cases where an NP corresponding to the direct object is realized to the left of the verb, but nevertheless fails to give rise to agreement. The first test case involves *à*-marked unsaturated infinitives, as in the *tough*-movement example in (13a). Miller & Sag (1997: 626) also discuss such constructions, additionally providing an example of an infinitival relative (13b).

(13) a. *une lettre* difficile à avoir **écrit**/***écrite** pour
      'a   letter.FSG difficult to have written.MSG/*FSG for
      demain
      tomorrow'

    b. Il m'a donné *des*   *lettres*   à avoir
      'He gave me   (some) letters.FPL to have
      remis/***remises** aux   parents.
      delivered.M/*FPL to the parents.'

Both of these constructions are analyzed in detail within HPSG by Abeillé et al. (1997). It is argued, following Kayne (1975), that these constructions do not involve unbounded dependencies in French (unlike their English counterparts), so they are not analyzed in terms of extraction gaps in HPSG, but more or less as instances of locally governed object control.[4] To account for the agreement facts as presented in (13), given the analysis in (8)–(9) above, the controlled direct object argument must be typed as *canonical*, even though it is not syntactically realized as a local dependent of the verb.

    This analysis is counterintuitive, however, because the objects in (13) would clearly be considered non-canonical from a pre-theoretical point of view. It should be kept in mind that the types *canonical* and *non-canonical* in the hierarchy in (7) are formal objects whose names are meant to be suggestive, without necessarily matching up exactly

---

[4]See Bouma, Malouf & Sag (2001) for an HPSG analysis of adjectives like *tough* in English.

with any descriptive notion of (non-)canonicity. Still, there would be no technical obstacle to adding a third subtype of *non-canonical* alongside *gap* and *affix*, and using this new subtype for the direct object argument in examples like (13):

(14)

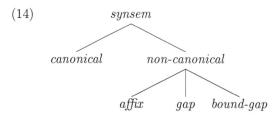

While this would correspond to a more intuitive descriptive classification, it would make the opposite prediction about past participle agreement, since arguments of type *bound-gap* are still non-canonical, and should therefore trigger agreement, according to (8). Of course the description in (8) can be modified to exclude *bound-gap*, but before doing this, we should consider the reliability of the judgments indicated in (13), which are based on informal introspection.

The traditional rule requires agreement in such examples, although they are only rarely addressed explicitly in prescriptive sources.[5] When explicit metalinguistic judgments are elicited, speakers seem to reject agreement in examples like (13), but there may be independent reasons for this.[6] A more nuanced picture emerges from Web corpus data. As a simple illustration, an exact string Google search performed in March 2017 returned the following results for the four ways of writing the infinitival relative 'things to have done [before getting married, before age 50, etc.]', where the noun *choses* 'things' is feminine plural:

(15) "choses à avoir **fait**"   MSG   74 hits
      "choses à avoir **faites**"   FPL   44 hits
      "choses à avoir faite"   FSG   1 hit
      "choses à avoir faits"   MPL   0 hits

---

[5]See, for example, the normative website Langue-fr.net, which says that agreement is obligatory in cases like *les cent sites à avoir vus* 'the one hundred sites.MPL to have seen.MPL' and *les cent choses à avoir faites avant de mourir* 'the one hundred things.FPL to have done.FPL before dying' (http://www.langue-fr.net/spip.php?article289).

[6]Agreement is disfavored if the participle is followed by additional material within the VP ('non-empty postverbal zone'). See Section 3.1 below.

The results show that speakers/writers do sometimes produce agreement in this construction in written French.

Abeillé (personal communication, January 2018) suggests that this variation in agreement may point to the existence of two competing syntactic structures among French speakers. As noted by Abeillé et al. (1997: fn. 3), some speakers do allow a certain degree of unboundedness in *à*-infinitival constructions, accepting complex VPs as in the following:

(16) a. %une ville difficile à aller visiter en ce moment
          'a city difficult to go visit at the moment'

      b. %un livre à devoir lire dès aujourd'hui
          'a book that one must read starting today'

The analysis of such examples may involve a non-canonical *gap* argument after all, as in the corresponding English constructions. Speakers of this dialect of French would then be expected to have agreement in examples like (13) above. It would be very interesting if this correlation between unboundedness and past participle agreement were to be confirmed, but the existence of two dialects is not the only explanation for the variation observed in (15). As we will see later in Section 3.1, this degree of variation is typical of past participle agreement with *avoir* in general, even in constructions where there is no reason to suspect any syntactic ambiguity.

The second test case mentioned by Abeillé & Godard (1996), where past participle agreement is absent despite pre-verbal expression of the direct object, involves non-clitic left dislocation:

(17) *Les surprises-parties*, je n'ai jamais **aimé/*aimées**.
      'Surprise parties.FPL, I've never liked.MSG/FPL.'

The absence of agreement in such constructions is also discussed by Leeman (2004), who shares the intuition that the participle should not agree, in apparent violation of the normative rule. It should be noted that the entire construction in (17) is considered non-normative, so one could simply say that past participle agreement is felt to be inappropriate in this register. But Leeman accepts agreement in other cases of topicalization that are similarly typical of informal registers:

(18) a. *Trois enfants* j'ai **eus**.
          'Three children.MPL I've had.MPL.'
                              (P. Istrati, *Les Récits d'Adrien Zograffi*)

      b. *Ma chemise* j'aurais **donnée** pour en être.
          'My shirt.FSG I would have given.FSG to be included.'
                              (M. Cerf, *Les Rois et les voleurs*)

According to Leeman, these last examples involve a true fronted direct object, while in examples like (17), the dislocated NP functions as a 'point of view' adjunct, with an interpretation along the lines of 'as for surprise parties...' The direct object of the verb is left unexpressed, but identified anaphorically (something like *pro*, in formal syntactic terms).

Abeillé, Godard & Sabio (2008) provide additional arguments for distinguishing these two types of fronted NPs, along with an HPSG analysis, although they do not specifically address the question of past participle agreement. As for the earlier examples in (13), the only way to account for the absence of agreement in (17) under the HPSG approach presented in Section 2.1 is to assume that the direct object argument is of type *canonical*, despite the fact that it does not have a canonical, local syntactic realization. On the other hand, one could also prefer a more descriptively-oriented analysis that adds a new subtype of *non-canonical* for the *pro*-like direct object in (17), along the same lines as the hierarchy in (14) above:

(19)

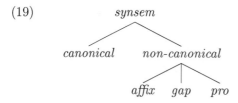

In fact, an anonymous reviewer suggests that the controlled object argument in the bounded dependency constructions discussed earlier could also be analyzed as *pro*, in which case the hierarchy in (14) could simply be replaced by (19). This move would need to be motivated by a fuller examination of the properties of the constructions, which at first sight appear to be rather different. In either case, extending the hierarchy of *non-canonical* subtypes in this way requires us to abandon the generalization formulated in (8)–(9), that past participle agreement is triggered by all *non-canonical* accusative arguments, since the empirical claim is that the *non-canonical* arguments identified here fail to trigger agreement.

The outcome of this discussion is thus rather inconclusive. Although the examples in (13) and (17) are presented in previous HPSG work as evidence that past participle agreement is triggered by non-canonicity (and not by word order), it seems that the choice to analyze the participle's object argument in such constructions as *canonical* (and not as some distinct subtype of *non-canonical*) is motivated in large part precisely by the agreement facts. And these facts themselves need to be established more firmly on empirical grounds.

2.3   Postverbal Non-canonical Objects?

In the previous section we failed to find convincing examples of *canonical* objects corresponding to an NP realized to the left of the verb. Another possibility for teasing apart word order and canonicity is to look for *non-canonical* direct objects realized to the right of the verb. The only candidate for non-canonical rightward realization in French is right dislocation. But in such cases, the object is always additionally realized as a pronoun within the clause (as in English):

(20)   a.   La tornade *(*les*) a **détruites/%détruit**, *ces maisons.*
             'The tornado has destroyed.FPL/MSG them, those houses.FPL.'

       b.   La tornade *(*en*) a **détruit/?détruites**, *des maisons.*
             'The tornado has destroyed.MSG/FPL some, some houses.FPL.'

The triggering effect of the right-dislocated object NP is therefore difficult to determine. The participle in (20a) shows agreement, but that is to be expected in any case with the clitic pronoun *les*. And the absence of agreement is expected with the pronoun *en*, because of the exceptional status of this pronoun (recall (6) above). Further empirical investigation is needed to determine if the presence of a full right-dislocated NP in examples like (20b) makes speakers more likely to produce agreement than with *en* alone.[7]

So while we might choose to analyze right-dislocated NPs as *non-canonical* elements, realized exceptionally to the right of the verb, this construction does not offer a good test case for comparing word order vs. non-canonicity as the relevant trigger of past participle agreement.

---

[7]One could also ask if agreement with *en* is facilitated by left-dislocated NPs, in examples like the following:

(i)   Des maisons, la tornade en a détruit/?détruites.
      'Houses, the tornado destroyed some of them.'

2.4 Syntactically Unrealized Arguments

We are left with one remaining class of cases to consider: Those where the direct object has no syntactic realization anywhere in the sentence. I will consider two types of object omission. The first can be described as an instance of pronoun cluster reduction, or affix fusion (Miller 1992: 178). The combination of a 3rd person accusative pronoun (*le/la/les*) and a 3rd person dative pronoun (*lui/leur*) normally gives rise to an ACC–DAT cluster, as in (21a). But in informal registers, the accusative pronoun can simply be left unrealized, as in (21b), with no change in interpretation:

(21)　a.　Je *la*　　　leur　　ai　**apportée/%apporté.**
　　　　　I　ACC.3FSG DAT.3PL have brought.FSG/brought.MSG
　　　　　'I have brought it to them.'

　　　b.　→ Je leur　　ai　**apporté[?e]**
　　　　　　I　DAT.3PL have brought

Past participle agreement is expected in (21a), given the presence of the accusative pronoun *la*. Preliminary Web corpus studies suggest that agreement is also attested in the reduced construction (21b), despite its informal character. For example, a Google search was performed in March 2017 looking for contexts discussing body temperature (e.g. of a child or a pet) and containing a version of the phrase 'I took it [his/her temperature]'. Some representative examples are given below:

(22)　a.　[Comment peux-tu savoir que ton chat n'a pas de température?] **Je la lui ai prise** tout simplement.[8]
　　　　　'[How do you know your cat doesn't have a temperature?] I took it, quite simply.'

　　　b.　Pour la température: **Je lui ai prise** pratiquement 30minutes après qu'elle soit sortit [sic] du bain.[9]
　　　　　'Concerning the temperature: I took it almost 30 minutes after she got out of the bath.'

　　　c.　[arreter de prendre la température pour rien!!!] **Je lui ai pris** souvent ces derniers temps à cause de sa gastro.[10]
　　　　　'[Stop taking [your baby's] temperature for nothing!] I have taken it a lot lately because of his gastroenteritis.'

---

[8] http://forum.doctissimo.fr/animaux/Chats/boite-semble-souffir-sujet_19608_1.htm

[9] https://www.mamanpourlavie.com/forum/sujet/ongle-arracha-fia-vre

[10] http://forum.doctissimo.fr/grossesse-bebe/bebes_annee/arreter-prendre-temperature-sujet_114280_1.htm

The search query was the exact quoted string in each case, plus the feminine singular noun *température*, and the results were inspected for the intended contextual interpretation and the correct syntactic configuration. Queries with dative plural *leur* ('I took their temperature') returned no results. For singular *lui*, with or without the accompanying accusative pronoun *la*, the results were as follows:

(23) | | | |
|---|---|---|
| "je la lui ai **prise**" | FSG | 6 hits (22a) |
| "je la lui ai prises" | FPL | 0 hits |
| "je la lui ai pris" | MSG/PL | 0 hits |
| "je lui ai **prise**" | FSG | 9 hits (22b) |
| "je lui ai prises" | FPL | 1 hit |
| "je lui ai pris" | MSG/PL | 3 hits (22c) |

With the explicit accusative pronoun *la*, the participle takes the appropriate feminine form, in accordance with the standard rule. But even when the accusative pronoun is left implicit in the informal reduced construction, the participle continues to show agreement in the majority of cases. The numbers are of course too low to draw any firm conclusions, and other suitable verbs/contexts should be tested.[11]

As far as the formal analysis is concerned, (21a) and (21b), or (22a) and (22b), can be treated as alternative realizations of the same underlying list of arguments (Bonami & Boyé 2007). In other words, the participle's direct object argument is a non-canonical 3FSG affix in both examples. Although this means that the participle satisfies the description in (8), and should therefore show agreement in both cases, it should be kept in mind that this analysis is only intended to model formal registers of standard French. Since the reduced construction is typical of informal registers, we might expect to observe more variation in speakers' behavior here, and results like table (23) suggest that this is the case.

The normative position on pronoun cluster reduction is simply that it is incorrect, and the full construction with both pronouns must be used, with obligatory agreement, as in (21a) an (22a). Taken at face value, the traditional rule prohibits agreement in a case like (21b), since

---

[11] A reviewer of this paper offered the following example (from the website https://www.sparadrap.org/enfants/piqures/):

(i) On a mis de la crème anesthésiante sur la peau de Daniel pour éviter qu'il sente la piqûre. Ça fait une heure qu'**on lui a mise**.
'We put some numbing cream on Daniel's skin so that he wouldn't feel the injection. We put it on him an hour ago.'

As in (22b), the participle shows feminine agreement even though the feminine pronoun *la*, referring to the noun *crème*, is omitted.

there is nothing in the sentence for the participle to agree with. On the other hand, the omission of the accusative pronoun may be considered such a superficial phenomenon that it continues to trigger agreement. In other words, it is difficult to say whether the traditional rule and the formal HPSG analysis make different predictions in this case.

The second type of object omission is simple object drop, which in fact covers a number of distinct phenomena, including lexicalized intransitives with existential or conventional interpretation of the direct object (the type 'I drink/eat'), and cases with anaphoric *pro*-drop:

(24) [... *la poésie* ...] J'ai toujours **adoré**[?e] / **détesté**[?e].
      (context: poetry.FSG) 'I've always loved/hated [it].'

This example is closely related to the dislocation structure already discussed in (17) in Section 2.2. Recall that speakers tend to reject agreement in cases of dislocation. This judgment is presumably even stronger in cases like (24), where there is no coreferential full NP anywhere in the sentence. This presents no problem for the traditional rule (although this is another non-normative construction that would be considered incorrect, regardless of the morphology of the participle). But as already discussed for example (17), object *pro*-drop is potentially problematic for the HPSG analysis in Section 2.1. In order to avoid predicting agreement via the description in (8), the missing direct object in a case like (24) would have to be assumed to be a *canonical* argument, which again seems unsatisfactory.

3   Empirical and Comparative Considerations

The constructions examined in the preceding sections suggest that French allows additional types of non-canonical argument realization beyond extraction and pronominalization, and they do not all necessarily pattern together as far as past participle agreement is concerned. So the claim that canonicity in general is the relevant triggering feature is too strong. But the HPSG analysis can still be seen as making a significant claim, which is that extraction and pronominalization form a natural class. Miller & Sag (1997: 623) speak of 'the unity of extraction and pronominal affixation'. In formal terms, this means that extracted arguments and pronominalized arguments belong to a common supertype present in the grammar, and that various phenomena in the language make reference to this supertype, instead of targeting the two specific subtypes separately. Concretely, if we accept that the inventory of non-canonical realization types in (7) must be expanded along the lines of (14) and (19), unbounded dependency gaps and pronominal affixes can still be subsumed under a privileged type, here labeled *non-canonical-core*:

(25)

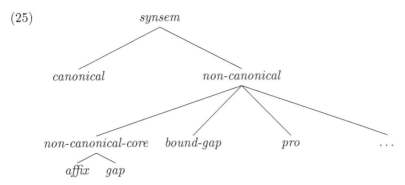

The description in (8) would then need to be modified to make reference to *non-canonical-core* instead of *non-canonical*, and additional constraints formulated for the new subtypes of *non-canonical* introduced here.[12]

Besides past participle agreement, other phenomena where extraction and pronominalization pattern together include floating quantifiers (26) and the complementation of certain raising verbs of thinking/saying (27):[13]

(26)   a.   *Paul a tous lu [ces livres].
            'Paul has read all those books.'

       b.   Paul les a tous lus.
            'Paul has read them all.'

       c.   ces livres que Paul a tous lus
            'those books that Paul has read all of'

(27)   a.   *Il croit [cette solution] convenir.
            'He believes this solution to be suitable.'

       b.   Il la croit convenir.
            'He believes it to be suitable.'

       c.   Quelle solution croit-il convenir?
            'Which solution does he believe to be suitable?'

In both cases, a canonically realized NP object is ungrammatical in present-day French (26a)–(27a), but the construction becomes possible

---

[12]Recall, as discussed at the end of Section 2.2, that it may be possible to identify *bound-gap* with *pro* and thus simplify the type hierarchy in (25).

[13]See Miller & Sag (1997) and Abeillé & Godard (1999) for HPSG analyses of floating quantifiers as in (26).

if the object is extracted or pronominalized.[14]

The distinction between using a common supertype like *non-canon-core* as indicated (25) vs. an explicit disjunction of types (*affix* ∨ *gap*) has formal consequences that do not concern us here. But the choice of formulation also makes empirical predictions, because we might expect speakers to behave differently if they are following one unified rule versus a disjunction of several distinct rules. In the rest of this section we take a closer look at the facts surrounding past participle agreement to see how closely pronominalization, relativization, and *wh*-movement pattern together in reality.

3.1 Variation in French Past Participle Agreement

Past participle agreement with *avoir* is typical of formal French, and this is the target variety for both the traditional normative rule and the HPSG analysis presented in Section 2.1. In fact there are very few situations where the normative rules for past participle agreement are reliably respected. Carefully edited written texts are the most abundant source of examples, although even there it is not uncommon to find instances of non-normative agreement and non-agreement. And while such texts can tell us about speakers' metalinguistic awareness, they reveal little about speakers' spontaneous linguistic behavior. In more naturalistic situations, past participle agreement with *avoir* is a much more variable phenomenon. We have already seen some examples of this variability in the Web data in tables (15) and (23), but these results are of course based on written French.

While writers are required to distinguish three or four orthographic forms for the past participle of every verb, in the majority of cases – specifically, for all past participles whose MSG form ends in an orthographic vowel (*-é*, *-i*, or *-u*) – these are all pronounced exactly the same, for all gender/number combinations. This means that for most spoken examples, there is no way to know what form of the participle the speaker is using. The only verbs that provide audible evidence of agreement are those that have a consonant-final past participle (in *-s* or *-t*). This subclass fortunately contains some very high-frequency members (*faire* → *fait* 'made', *prendre* → *pris* 'taken', *mettre* → *mis* 'put', etc.). But even with these verbs, most examples are unrevealing. In particular, all examples involving a masculine agreement trigger and a masculine participle must be discounted, since it is impossible in such cases to distinguish agreement and default inflection.[15]

---

[14]See also the complementation of 'control *faire*', as analyzed by Abeillé et al. (1997).

[15]Plural agreement is not audible with past participles, except in cases of liaison,

If we add to this the fact that the available corpora of spoken French are rather limited to begin with, it is not surprising that very few quantitative studies of past participle agreement have been carried out for spoken French. To give an idea of the data scarcity problem, the most recent study that I know of, by Gaucher (2013), starts with a combined corpus of 5.8 million words, and only ends up with 330 usable examples, with almost exactly half (164 examples) showing normatively correct feminine agreement, and half (166 examples) where the expected feminine agreement is missing.

Recall that our goal in this section is to determine whether speakers produce agreement in the same way, or to the same extent, with all triggers: pronouns, relativized objects, and *wh*-fronted objects. Previous studies have suggested that speakers produce agreement more frequently with pronouns (in particular 3rd person pronouns) than in relative clauses (Audibert-Gibier 1992). This is not confirmed by Gaucher's corpus data, since he actually observes 45% agreement with pronouns and 55% in relatives (the difference is not statistically significant). Note that these two constructions account for practically the entire corpus of examples, aside from just four *wh*-questions (of which only one shows agreement). No pertinent examples of *wh*-exclamatives were found, for example. We will need access to much larger spoken corpora if we hope to collect quantifiable, naturalistic data about some of the more exotic constructions discussed in the previous sections.[16]

At this coarse level of analysis, speakers do seem to show similar behavior with pronominal and extracted agreement triggers, although a more careful examination of the data should be carried out. A more significant result is the degree of variability: In compound tense constructions with *avoir*, speakers avoid producing the normatively correct audible feminine participle about half the time. The corpus data also shed light on a completely different criterion, which is the position of the participle itself. Audibert-Gibier (1992) observes that speakers are more likely to produce agreement if there is nothing following the participle (in her terms, if the 'postverbal zone' is empty), and less likely if the participle is immediately followed by additional material within the VP (e.g. a complement or modifier of the verb, or a postverbal subject):

---

which is rare and marginal in compound tense constructions with *avoir*.

[16]A reviewer suggests that written corpora might be used for this purpose, if limited to informal genres, and large-scale corpora of this type are increasingly available. It is certainly worth looking at past participle agreement in informal written texts, and comparing the results with what happens in spontaneous spoken French.

(28) *Empty postverbal zone (agreement more likely)*
Pourquoi tu *les*   as   pas **mise(s)**? (p. 13)
why   you PRO.3FPL AUX NEG put.F

'Why have you not put them on?'

(29) *Non-empty postverbal zone (agreement less likely)*
L' évolution, je *l'*   ai   **fait**   avant (p. 14)
the evolution I PRO.3FSG AUX done.MSG before

'Evolution, I did it before.'

This is in fact an intuition that several grammarians in past centuries (such as Vaugelas in the mid-17th century) have tried – without success – to incorporate into the normative rule about past participle agreement. Gaucher's study confirms that speakers are indeed sensitive to this criterion: They produce agreement 60% of the time when the participle is VP-final (or followed by a pause), but only 36% of the time when the 'postverbal zone' is non-empty.

These results have no real consequences for the traditional rule. It will continue to be taught, and speakers will continue to ignore it much of the time. In informal contexts, missing agreement with *avoir* is not preceived as an error; in fact it usually goes completely unnoticed. Using the normative agreement in such registers often stands out as stilted or unnatural, especially in cases where the feminine participle has a more salient, homophonous use as a noun or adjective, as in the following examples from Blanche-Benveniste (2006: 38):

(30) a. C'était *une institutrice* que nous avons tous **crainte**.
          'She was a schoolteacher.FSG that we all feared.FSG.'

      b. Cela fait partie des *voitures* que je n'ai jamais **conduites**.
          'That's one of the cars.FPL that I've never driven.FPL.'

For linguistic analysis, if the goal is to model speakers' behavior, this type of empirical data should be taken into account. The HPSG analysis presented earlier had a somewhat different goal, as it was only ever intended to account for a specific, rather artificial variety of French. As mentioned above, this variety does actually exist, in the form of formal written French, so an analysis of this type can be useful in this domain. For less formal varieties of French, however, the analysis must be modified or perhaps totally overhauled.

3.2 Comparative Considerations

In this final section, we take a brief look beyond French at some related languages that also have (or had) past participle agreement in compound tenses with the auxiliary HAVE.

First of all, from a historical perspective, the compound past with HAVE in Romance developed out a Latin construction involving a passive participle:

(31) Habeo *litteras* **scriptas.**
      have   letters.FPL written.FPL

      'I have [the] letters [that are] written.'

In this initial stage, the passive participle is a modifier of the direct object of HAVE, so it naturally shows adjectival agreement, no matter what the word order or the morphosyntactic realization of the object. This structure underwent several changes to become the Romance compound past, one of which was that the passive participle lost its modifier status and became the main lexical verb, in the active voice.

Despite this significant change, the participle continued to agree with its (now) direct object in the Romance languages well into the medieval period and beyond. In fact, there are Romance varieties where this is still the case today, for example in some dialects of Southern Italian and of Occitan. In these varieties, unlike in modern French, the participle agrees even with a direct object NP realized in its canonical postverbal position:

(32) a. *Rouergue Occitan* (Stroh 2002: 9)
          Aviàm **ganhada** *la guèrra.*
          'We had won.FSG the war.FSG'

      b. *Dialectal Italian*
          %Ho **mangiata** *una pesca.*
          'I have eaten.FSG a peach.FSG'

Agreement is also found with pronominal objects and in relative clauses, etc., just as in French, but in these varieties, there is no special rule for these constructions. The direct object argument simply triggers agreement in all syntactic configurations, as long as the auxiliary is HAVE.

At the other extreme, we can mention Spanish and Portuguese, where agreement has been eliminated altogether; the past participle only appears in the MSG form in periphrastic tenses with the auxiliaries *haber* and *ter*. Other Romance varieties are at an intermediate stage in this process of grammaticalization, and they retain traces of past participle agreement in certain cases. French is of course one example, and standard Italian is another.

In Italian, the normative rules for past participle agreement in compound tenses with *avere* only require agreement in one case: with 3rd person direct object pronouns (33). Recall from (6) in Section 1 that the rules requiring agreement with proclitic pronouns in French make an exception for the indefinite pronoun *en*. In Italian, the corresponding pronoun *ne* does not have any such exceptional status: It triggers agreement just like definite 3rd person pronouns (34).

(33) *Li*   ho   **visti**   / *****visto**   alla   stazione.
      PRO.3MPL AUX seen.MPL *seen.MSG at.the station

'I have seen them at the station.'

(34) *Ne*   ho   **visti**   / *****visto**   alla   stazione.
      PRO.3MPL AUX seen.MPL *seen.MSG at.the station

'I have seen some (of them) at the station.'

In stark contrast with French speakers, Italian speakers' behavior seems to be generally consistent with this standard, across all registers, and in both spoken and written language. But there is wider variation in other syntactic contexts, in particular with 1st and 2nd person pronouns, where the normative rule says that agreement is optional (35):

(35) Maria,   non *ti*   ho   **visto**   / **vista**.
      Maria.FSG NEG PRO.2SG AUX seen.MSG   seen.FSG

'Maria, I didn't see you.'

Agreement in other contexts, including with full postverbal NP objects (recall (32b) above) and in relative clauses (%*la pesca che ho mangiata* 'the peach.FSG that I have eaten.FSG'), represents regional or archaic usages that are considered stylistically marked, but not incorrect, according to the normative rule (Salvi 1991).

The agreement rule in Italian is sometimes formulated in terms of word order, just as in French traditional grammar: Agreement is possible when the direct object precedes the verb, which means it is either a proclitic personal pronoun or a relative pronoun.[17] But for the majority of speakers, agreement is only acceptable with clitic pronouns. Unlike in French, then, pronominalization and extraction do not pattern together in Italian with respect to past participle agreement. In fact, not all pronouns pattern together, since agreement is only systematic with

---

[17]I have not come across any sources for Italian that explicitly mention *wh*-interrogatives.

3rd person forms, and many speakers do not produce agreement with 1st and 2nd person direct object clitics. So there is no generalization to be made in terms of canonicity of argument realization to account for Italian past participle agreement.

4 Conclusion

Our initial goal for this study was to revisit formal syntactic proposals in HPSG for analyzing certain cases of past participle agreement in French, traditionally characterized in terms of word order, by introducing a formal notion of canonicity of argument realization. The main types of non-canonical realization in French are pronominalization and argument extraction, and it is exactly in these cases that the past participle is supposed to show agreement in normative French.

An examination of other constructions potentially involving non-canonical arguments, such as bounded dependencies and *pro*-drop, leads us to call into question the strong generalization that all non-canonical arguments trigger past participle agreement in French. Once we go beyond the core cases of agreement that speakers are explicitly taught, judgments quickly become uncertain. And even in the most common cases (with clitic pronouns and in relative clauses), outside of the most formal situations of edited writing or prepared speech, the phenomenon of past participle agreement is observed to be highly variable.

While the original HPSG proposals were an ingenious recharacterization of the traditional normative rule, a different approach is needed if we want to model the agreement patterns that speakers actually produce. In this regard, it is interesting to note that the syntactic and prosodic context to the right of the participle (Audibert-Gibier's 'postverbal zone') plays an important role in conditioning agreement. Speakers are more likely to produce agreement if this context is empty, and more likely to ignore the normative rule and leave the participle uninflected if the postverbal zone is filled. It is somewhat surprising for agreement to be sensitive to a contextual criterion of this nature, but then past participle agreement with *avoir* is already unusual, as the unique case of objet agreement in the language.

Acknowledgements

I would like to thank Anne Abeillé, François Mouret, and an anonymous reviewer for many helpful comments on earlier versions of this paper.

6

'Pure' Indexicals vs. True Demonstratives

FRANCIS CORBLIN

1 Introduction

In the most widely accepted terminology, 'indexicals' applies to a set of context-dependent referential terms. Typical members of the set in English are: *I*, *here*, *now*, *we*, *you*, *tomorrow*, *he*, *they*, *this*, *that*, *this guy*, etc. Within this set, there is a classical (Kaplan 1989a) distinction between *pure indexicals* and *true demonstratives* as shown in Table 1.

Table 1 Types of indexicals: The starting point (Kaplan 1989a).

Pure indexicals	(True) demonstratives
Prototype: *I*	Prototype: *this woman*

The bases of the distinction are not made fully explicit by Kaplan, who gives only few examples. Perry (1997) introduces a related distinction between *automatic* (pure indexicals) and *intentional* (true demonstratives) indexicals, and proposes an explicit repartition of a larger set of indexicals between the two classes.

The alleged property which leads to introducing this distinction is roughly that some indexicals ('pure' indexicals) get their reference automatically when uttered ('pure indexicals' like *I*, *here* and *now*), while others ('true demonstratives' like *this woman*) require taking into account actions or intentions of the speaker in order to find the intended referent. Although

Constraint-Based Syntax and Semantics: Papers in Honor of Danièle Godard.
Anne Abeillé and Olivier Bonami (eds.).

this observation may sound correct at first, it raises serious problems when considered more closely. Scholars have shown, for instance, that if so defined, the class of 'pure' indexicals is empty (Mount 2008), or almost empty (Recanati 2001). Moreover, some expressions (e.g. *now* and *here*) may count as typical members of both classes, if the classes are so-defined, and no such approach can work without admitting 'demonstrative uses' of (otherwise pure) indexicals, which undermines a clear distinction between the two categories.

The main problem with the classical distinction is that subsequent studies convinced us that neither a mere utterance (of a 'pure' indexical) nor an auxiliary action like a pointing (for a true demonstrative) gives us by itself the intended referent without any extra inference (Lücking, Pfeiffer & Rieser 2015).

But this does not prove that the classical distinction has no substance. In this paper, I will introduce a crucial distinction between the *anchor* of an indexical and its denotation, a distinction which helps to realize what is insightful and what is wrong with the classical opposition between pure indexicals and true demonstratives, and leads to a better definition of these two classes of indexicals. The work of Nunberg (1993) will be of particular relevance for this enterprise, not only because his notion of *index* of an indexical is the source of what I call its anchor, but also because his study makes room in the assignation of a referent to an indexical for the ontological sort of entity (e.g. *person*, *plurality*, *space*, *time*, etc.), an indexical has to denote. I will try to explain on these bases why different items of the same basic semantic category (indexicals or demonstratives) may seem to have different behaviors.

2   The Classical Distinction and its Inadequacies

A basic idea supporting the classical distinction is that for some indexicals, their mere utterance 'fully determines their reference' (Kaplan 1989a: 491) although for others the reference of the indexical can be rather freely chosen by the speaker, provided that some conventions or some actions (like a Kaplanian *demonstration*) help the hearer to find the intended referent. This is clearly reflected in Perry's terminology 'automatic/discretionary' (Perry 2001) or 'intentional' (Perry 1997), as Table 2 illustrates.

Table 2 Types of indexicals (Perry 1997: 11).

	Narrow	Wide
Automatic	*I*, *now**, *here**[1]	*tomorrow*, *yea*
Intentional	*now*, *here*	*that*, *this man*, *there*

Another relevant distinction is the contrast between what Perry (1997) calls the 'constitutive facts about the utterance' (agent, time position), the *narrow* context, and these facts 'plus anything else that might be relevant', the *wide* context.

Perry's presentation makes explicit the main issues such an approach has to face. First, it does not give a unique category to some indexicals (*now* and *here*), an issue noted by Perry 1997: 12) himself, which legitimates the asterisk in Table 2. Perry (1997: 13) insists that, depending on the stretch of space or time denoted by such indexicals, they can be analyzed as *automatic* (nothing more than their utterance is relevant) or *intentional* (the intentions of the speaker matter). In addition, this typology has to be completed by the notion of 'demonstrative use' of 'pure' indexicals.

> One can point to a place on a map and refer to it as "here" [Kaplan 1989a]. *Now* and the present tense can be used to draw attention to and confer immediacy on the time of a past or future event, as when a history teacher says "Now Napoléon had a dilemma ..." [Smith 1989]. (Perry 1997: 13)

But the notion of demonstrative use does not receive any precise definition although it appears clearly as a threat for both contrasts (automatic/intentional and narrow/wide). Last but not least, note that there is no cell in the table for demonstratives, although someone may find items in each of the four cells she may want to label 'demonstrative' (e.g. *here*, *yea*, *this man*).

It is not surprising, then, that most scholars exploring more carefully this way of drawing a line among indexicals have to conclude that all indexicals, except possibly *I*, are demonstrative, or 'impure' indexicals, or discretionary indexicals. Recanati (2001) provides a convincing set of examples showing that neither *here* nor *now* are pure indexicals in the classical sense, and Mount (2008) argues that it is not even impossible to challenge the thesis that *I* is a pure indexical since in some cases it does not denote the speaker of the utterance, but some object related to her (as in the famous example *I am parked outside*).

---

[1] The asterisk is used by Perry to signal that *now* and *here* can be either automatic or intentional, depending on their denotation. See infra for more on this.

Although there is an intuitive basis supporting the division of indexicals in two classes under the prototypes *I* and *this woman*, the classical way of grounding the distinction on the opposition between automatic vs. intentional indexicals leads mostly to question the validity of the intuition. It is easy to show that for none of them does their utterance fully determine their reference, and that, for each of them, it is necessary to rely upon conventions, gestures, and intentions to decide what the intended referent is.

3 A More Sophisticated View of Indexicals: Nunberg (1993)

Nunberg (1993) accepts the classical view that 'the meaning of indexicals provides a rule which determines the referent in terms of certain aspects of the context' (Kaplan 1989a: 490), but tries to go further by 'zooming in' on the way indexicals actually get their reference. Nunberg distinguishes three components in the semantics of indexicals.

3.1 The Deictic Component

A key part of Nunberg's approach is what he calls 'index': 'the contextual element picked out by the linguistic meaning of an indexical expression like *you*, as well as ... the thing picked out by a demonstration associated with the use of a word like *that*' (Nunberg 1993 : 4). This index is not the intended referent, but a clue for finding it, an argument of a complex function returning the referent itself. In a nutshell, the intended referent is supposed to have some distinctive relation to this index, a relation which helps to separate it from other individuals of the same sort. For instance, if the index of the demonstrative *this chair* is the dot of a laser pointer, the referent of this utterance is the closest chair w.r.t. that dot.

Nunberg admits that this is not the way the term 'index' has been used in semantics, and justifies his terminological choice by arguing that it is consistent with Peirce's original usage of the term. For both reasons, and others (it looks rather tautological to say that an indexical has an index!), I will make a terminological move and use the term 'anchor' instead. In my opinion at least, the notion is not different from Nunberg's index: the idea remains that an indexical must be anchored (= to find its intended referent by relation to some part of its context of use) and this anchor, is *not* the intended referent, but the argument of some function returning the intended referent.

3.2 The Classificatory Component

According to Nunberg (1993: 8), indexicals also have a *classificatory component*, a constraint on the sort of entity denoted by the indexical. As examples of classificatory features, Nunberg mentions semantic sorts like *person*, *time*, *space*, *animate*, *male*, *plurality*, and the descriptive content of demonstratives (*that car*). I will argue later that these sortal differences, in combination with the view that indexicals are 'anchored' on their index, can explain many differences of behavior between the indexicals of the same category (e.g. many differences between *I*, *here*, and *now*).

3.3 The Relational Component

The third component of the meaning of indexicals in Nunberg's theory is called relational. It is defined as a constraint on the relation 'between the index and the interpretation [denotation]' (Nunberg 1993: 9). This component plays a role in distinguishing *we* from *I*: both indexicals are anchored on the same index (the speaker), but *we* must denote a plurality (descriptive component) including its index (relational component).

In Nunberg's text, the relational component is used for formulating a property distinguishing 'pure' indexicals and demonstratives: in his own words, 'indexical uses of the third-person pronouns ... have no explicit relational component' (Nunberg 1993: 9), in contrast to pure indexicals (e.g. *we*). We will return to this as a weak point of the theory in Section 4.2 below.

4 Partitions of Indexicals in the More Sophisticated Theory

In the classical approach, there is no way to identify some indexicals as 'pure' because they would target their referent by themselves, 'automatically'. In the more sophisticated theory, the referent is always under-specified by the deictic-anchoring component and any indexical can denote something very different from its mere referential anchor. Nunberg uses two oppositions for making differences among indexicals. He distinguishes, without comment, 'participant terms' and 'non-participant terms', and makes explicit claims about indexicals having a relational component and indexicals having no relational component.

4.1 Participant Terms vs. Non-participant Terms

Under the heading *participant terms*, Nunberg deals with *we*, *I*, *you*, *today*, *yesterday*; under the heading *non-participants terms*, he includes as paradigmatic examples 'demonstratives and demonstrative uses of third person pronouns like *he*' (Nunberg 1993: 23). This looks close to Perry's distinction between narrow and wide contexts (see Section 2 above). Perry's contrast is based on the denotation[2] of the indexicals: either the denotation is one of the necessary ingredients of any utterance (speaker, time, location) or it is an entity which is not within this small set. In my view of Nunberg's approach, the relevant contrast supporting the difference between participant terms and non-participants terms is a matter of anchor (Nunberg's *xi*), not of denotation: either the anchor is defined as a necessary parameter of its utterance, or the anchor has to be stipulated by some special action concomitant to the utterance like a demonstration.

But Nunberg's approach is more complex, since he claims that a second distinctive property of participant *terms* is that they have a relational component whereas 'nonparticipants terms 'simply have no relational component' (Nunberg 1993: 25).

4.2 Having vs. not Having an (Explicit) Relational Component

According to Nunberg (1993: 25), 'non-participant terms simply have no relational component; used indexically, they can contribute any individual or property that corresponds to their indices in some salient way'.

What this claim intends to capture is the case of *we*, which takes as index the speaker, but has to denote a plurality including, or 'instantiating', as Nunberg puts it, the index. Roughly speaking, Nunberg claims that only participant terms impose specific relations between their index and their denotation whereas non-participant terms impose no such relation. In the present context, it is not necessary to discuss details of this proposal, since Nunberg himself does not take it as the distinctive property setting apart true indexicals from demonstratives, but more as an interesting difference between the two classes.

This opposition raises many issues: first, it is difficult to make precise the notion of having a 'specific' relationship to some index (as opposed to having any relationship); secondly, it requires a special layer of the theory (relational component) which may look ad hoc; and, thirdly, it is not obvious that the other parts of the theory cannot deal with the facts motivating it, like the interpretation of *we*[3] as opposed to the interpretation of *they*. My

---

[2] Perry's distinction would be difficult to apply to cases like *we* or *yesterday*. *We* denotes not only a necessary ingredient of its utterance but also entities which are not necessary; *yesterday* and *today* might be considered as members of different categories since *yesterday* is not part of the narrow context as defined by Perry, although *today* is.

[3] It does not seem impossible, for instance, to take as a property of the classificatory component the constraint that *we* must denote a plurality including the speaker-index.

impression is that once one considers as crucial the different nature of anchors for indexicals (pure indexicals taking as anchors the parameters of their utterance vs. true demonstratives taking as anchors the product of a dedicated action), as I do in this paper, one paves the way to making the relational component of Nunberg dispensable. However, for the present purposes, it does not seem necessary to take a definite position on this.

4.3 Indexicals: Types of Anchors and Ontological Sorts

Thus, there are some reasons to consider that the distinctive property which sets apart pure indexicals from true demonstratives is that pure indexicals take as their anchor constitutive parameters of their utterance (speaker, time, place), while true demonstratives must be given their anchor by some dedicated action.[4] The distinction between the index (my anchor) of an indexical and its denotation is crucial for clarifying what is insightful and what is wrong with the classical approach: if there is something 'automatic', always defined, with pure indexicals, it is not their denotation, but their anchor; there is something correct in the distinction between narrow and wide indexicals, but, again, it is not a matter of denotation, but a matter of anchoring.

What is best explained on the basis of Nunberg's notions is why, within the set *I*, *here*, *now* and *we*, some indexicals may be said to be more 'pure' than others. Recall that, in Kaplan's approach, only *I* is pure, along with the asterisks on *here* and *now* in Perry's Table 1 above.

Leaving aside the issue of the relational component (see Section 3.3 above), Nunberg's approach provides for each indexical a sort (classificatory component) and an anchor (deictic component), as shown in Table 3 below. The denotation has to be found with the help of the anchor, by general mechanisms,[5] and has to be of the ontological sort stipulated by the classificatory component.

---

[4] To take this distinction as a crucial feature distinguishing pure indexicals from true demonstratives is also well represented in the literature following Kaplan's work as well as in this work itself. I follow on this Corazza (2002, 2004), who takes this opposition as the first of three properties distinguishing the two categories: 'I argued in favor of three main features that distinguish them: (i) The use of a pure indexical, unlike the use of a demonstrative, never requires a pointing gesture to fix the reference; (ii) The use of a pure indexical, unlike the use of a demonstrative, is not perception-based; and (iii) Pure indexicals, unlike demonstratives, are never vacuous terms' (Corazza 2002: 446). The two other distinctive features retained by Corazza would deserve a more detailed discussion and look subordinate to the first one.

[5] The same mechanisms are supposed to be relevant for all indexicals, i.e. they are supposed to lead from the anchor (e.g. the dot of a laser pointer target of a demonstration) to the intended referent of the demonstrative.

Table 3 Some pure indexicals in the spirit of Nunberg (1993).

	Classificatory component (Sort)	Deictic component (Anchor)
I	Speaker	Speaker
here	Place	Place of utterance
we	Plurality including the speaker	Speaker

This gives us a plausible basis for explaining why *I* may be seen as less under-specified (more 'pure' in the classical Kaplan–Perry's sense) than *here*, *now* and *we*): there is one and only one speaker that knowing that a given speaker is the referential anchor identifies, namely herself,[6] but there are many places, time points and pluralities that knowing that a given entity is the referential anchor might identify.

This is so first of all because place, time, plurality, are of a different ontological sort than speaker: speaker being usually defined as a person, is a countable discrete entity, whereas time and space are non-countable 'mass-like' entities. This is confirmed by using a laser pointer and asking people to interpret *this person* (*this glass*, *this table*) vs. *this place*, *this group of students*, etc.

Suppose that for *I*, *here*, *now*, the referential anchor is provided by the utterance itself (speaker, place, time) and for *this man*, *this place*, the referential anchor is the dot of a laser pointer:[7] it is interesting to observe that the classificatory constraint will lead to the same kind of opposition. *I*, *this man* will most often target their intended referent rather easily (often without any other clue), but *here* and *this place* will typically need the help of extra-factors in order to know which place exactly the speaker intends to focus on, just because considering their ontological category (*space*), it is not the case that standard relations like proximity or inclusion w.r.t. a referential anchor are enough for separating one stretch of space from the others. The stretch of space one intends to denote with *here* is notoriously imprecise and extensible, as noted by Perry (see Section 2 above).

If we locate a part of the referential imprecision in the ontological constraint imposed by the representational component of indexicals, we can explain two things:

---

[6] There is no other person that is closer or more strongly related to the speaker than her/him-self.

[7] For the purposes of the present paper we admit that a pointing gesture interpreted as a demonstration is correctly realized as a laser pointer and its dot (a point or region of the visible environment), and in the discussion we consider only special cases in which a real pointing occurs. For more on the complexity of real pointings, see Lücking et al. (2015).

1. We expect the same kind of imprecision for all indexicals referring to non-countable entities: space, time, plurality, etc. A referential anchoring can never help to distinguish one such entity from the others, just because there is a huge number of such entities in relation to the anchor. And we do observe this for *here*, *now*, *you*, *they*, *these people*, *this group of persons*.

2. A Kaplanian demonstration cannot help solve the problem when the imprecision is ontological in nature. When using *here* with an explicit demonstration, one shifts the referential anchor from the utterance place to the dot of the pointer (I will return to this in Section 7 below), but there are many places including the pointer's dot.

My interim conclusion is as follows: In my own view of Nunberg's approach, maybe more explicitly than in Nunberg's text itself, the main feature setting apart pure indexicals from true demonstratives is the nature of their referential anchor. By using another component of Nunberg's approach, namely the classificatory content of indexicals, and the classical opposition between discrete countable entities and non-discrete ones, it seems possible to explain why indexicals of the same postulated category may behave differently, for reaching their intended referent, as a matter of 'ontological imprecision'.

5   The Nature of Referential Anchors

What makes indexicals special *per se* is that they reach a denotation as the result of a complex function taking as argument an anchor, that is some specific part of the real world, and that each indexical specifies, as a part of its lexical definition, how to find its denotation on the basis of its anchor. Each indexical being lexically associated to a sort, once anchored, it remains to find which individual of the relevant sort is intended by the speaker by means of general principles (i.e. valid for all indexicals) which help to distinguish one and only one individual of the sort by relation to the anchor.

What makes *we* and *they* different is that they use different referential anchors: *we* takes as referential anchor a parameter of its utterance (its speaker), whereas *they* takes as referential anchor a part of the context which has to be made salient by some special action of the speaker targeting some part of the context, or by some special property of the context itself dispensing the agent of such an action. This leads to distinguish two kinds of referential anchors.

(i)   Automatic reflexive anchors

Any utterance provides a set of potential anchors, its agent, time, and location;[8] part of the conventional meaning of some indexicals (pure indexicals) is that they use these anchors – *I*, *here*, *now*, *we*, etc. are typical examples. Considered as potential anchors, the parameters of use of an utterance have interesting properties: they are always defined (no utterance without an agent, a time and place), and in face-to-face communication, they are accessible to the participants.

(ii)   Contingent external anchors

It is possible to accompany any utterance of a referential expression by a Kaplanian demonstration, like a laser pointing. If understood as a demonstration, a pointing is supposed to provide an anchor for the utterance of the expression. Pointing is a process which has been largely documented and discussed in the literature (see for instance Lücking et al. 2015 for a short recent review). For the purposes of the present discussion, we adopt a pretheoretical simple conception, and the typical example of using a laser pointer to help the audience to see what we mean. In a nutshell, our simplistic conception is the following: if an action distinguishing a specific part of the context is associated by the speaker with the utterance of a referential expression, there is a good chance that she is doing so for helping the audience grasp what exactly she is talking about. This provides an anchor (a specific part of the real world targeted by the pointing) by relation to which the intended referent is supposed to be found out.

Let us assume that the selection of the relevant anchor is lexically specified as a part of the deictic component of indexicals. This is illustrated in Table 4.

Table 4 Two classes of indexicals and their respective anchors.

	I, *here*, *now*, *we*, ...	*she*, *this woman*, ...
Anchor	The utterance itself Reflexive Necessarily defined	E.g. the dot of a pointer External Contingent
Classical denomination	(Pure) indexical	(True) demonstrative

---

[8]   This is so on the basis of general postulates for actions sentences : there is no uttering action without an agent and a time and place of occurrence. So any utterance provides an anchor, a part of the real world which can be used for finding a denotation the speaker intends to share with the hearer.

It follows from this that the mere utterance of *I*, *here*, *now* is fine in any context, but that the mere occurrence of *this man* requires a special context, some special action or some specific property of the context isolating some part of the environment as a potential anchor for a demonstrative. This looks like a difference between a total function (pure indexicals) and a partial function (true demonstratives). Note that 'to be fine' just means to get a referential anchor, not at all to identify the intended referent without any extra-help. For instance, *we* and *this group of persons*, once anchored (respectively on the speaker, and to the dot of a pointer), remain both imprecise concerning the delimitation of the intended plurality. As already noted (see Section 4 above), one source of imprecision comes from the fact that both expressions denote a mass-like entity (a plurality of persons) whereas the anchor provides an individual, the speaker, for *we*, and the dot of the pointer, a restricted area of the visible context, for *this group of persons*. On the sole basis of the anchor, it is impossible to decide what the extension of the plurality the speaker intends to denote is. The main difference is that for *we*, the inclusion of the anchor (*me*) in the plurality is obligatory, whereas for *this group of persons*, the anchor may be anything closely related to the group of persons I intend to denote. In my view, this is so because *we*, by virtue of its classificatory component can only denote a plurality including the speaker, although for the demonstrative *this group of persons*, any place I point to can be an anchor, and the inclusion of this anchor in the denotation is only possible and frequent: I can point to a place close to a group of persons in order to denote them.

A short passing comment on Nunberg's 'relational component' (Section 4 above) is in order here. It does not seem completely right to say that demonstratives can denote 'any individual or property that corresponds to their indices' (Nunberg 1993: 25). It is very difficult, for instance, to use true demonstratives to denote any person or plurality that can be denoted by a pure indexical anchored on the speaker, i.e. to use, say, *this person* or *this group of person*, for denoting, respectively, the speaker or addressee, or a plurality including them: only *I*, *you* and *we* can be so used. This should be made part of the theory at some point, but I do not think that Nunberg's relational component, as it is, can do the job since, as I understand it, it formulates a positive constraint on all pure indexicals (their index must 'instantiate' their denotation), although I have in mind a negative constraint on some demonstratives (true demonstratives cannot denote individuals when these individuals are in the denotation of pure indexicals anchored on the speaker).

6   From Anchors to Denotations

The distinction between the anchor of an indexical and its denotation, which I consider a good point of Nunberg's approach as compared to the classical presentation may also be seen as a weakness, because the precise way leading from anchors to denotation remains to be made fully explicit and is only covered in my own presentation by the rather vague expression 'general principles'.

In my view, the distinction anchor/denotation opens a field of investigation, which is not accessible from the classical theory, by 'zooming on' the referential process, and leads to much fruitful research, empirical as well as theoretical: it would be rather unfair to ask the initial distinction itself to say the last word on the topic before deserving any consideration. It seems to me that the results of some recent works on pointing by means of gaze and gestures (Kranstedt et al. 2006, Lücking et al. 2015) tend to establish that the material target of a pointing gesture, whatever it is, never gives automatically the intended referent without the help of some extra-inferences which remains to be described explicitly.

I would just like to give some brief speculative comments on the way leading from anchors to denotations of indexicals. I see anchors as part of the utterance environment, identified either by the speech act *per se* (for pure indexicals) or by some dedicated action (like a Kaplanian demonstration). They are interpreted as clues for finding which individual of the associated sort the speaker wants to say something about. This sort plays a crucial role for isolating the referent, and the issue is: 'which x (sort associated with the indexical) a relation to a (the anchor) helps to distinguish as the intended referent from any other conceivable x'. Again, the idealized case of using a laser pointer may help. When interpreting 'this vase' in front of a window display with the help of the laser dot, we ask our partner to consider a vase that a relation to the dot separates from others; this would be in the general case a relation of proximity: 'take the individual I intend to speak about as the closest vase w.r.t. the dot'. This allows, for instance, pointing on any part of the window display if there is only one vase in it, or using a very large or badly defined dot. In contrast, if there are more than one vase in the window display, the relative proximity vases/dot will be relevant for deciding which vase is the referent: as a rule, the intended referent will be the closest vase w.r.t. the dot: if there is no such vase (imagine some vases on a circle and a dot on the center of the circle) then no referent can be chosen on the basis of this clue.

For indexicals associated to sorts covering non-discrete entities (like spaces, times and pluralities), there is no relation to a punctual anchor which might separate one individual of the sort from others. Let us consider 'these vases' (a window display) again. A natural interpretation is 'all the vases of the window display'. We can derive this interpretation in the following way: there is a unique collection of vases which are the closest vase w.r.t. the dot, namely all the vases of the visible display containing the dot (all other vases would be less close). But *these vases* can also be used for any collection of vases closer to the dot than others, especially if other properties of the display help to separate collections of vases. Suppose for instance there are three vases on the left of the display and four on the right, with a large space between without any vase: then a dot on the left part of the display will be interpreted as denoting the three left vases, and a dot on the right part as denoting the four right vases.

These brief comments are just a very schematic view of a field of investigation which has to be considered in its own right but may be of some interest for the discussion of the so-called 'demonstrative uses' of pure indexicals.

7   On Demonstrative Uses of Pure Indexicals

The notion of 'demonstrative use' of an indexical is very often used at some point in the discussion about the typology of indexicals (Bennett 1978, Kaplan 1989a, b, for instance) but never discussed in great detail. The main claim of the present paper is that the classical distinction of two classes of indexicals is correct, even though it can only be defended once a clear distinction is made between the anchor and the denotation of an indexical, and once the role of the sort lexically associated with an indexical is acknowledged. A brief discussion of the notion of demonstrative use of indexicals is in order, just because the notion itself may be interpreted as an argument in favor of the view that there is not, after all, a clear-cut difference between indexicals and demonstratives.

7.1 Generalizing the Notion of Demonstrative Use

Let us begin by a working definition: an utterance of a referential term (e.g. indexical, proper name) accompanied by a dedicated action understood as a demonstration (e.g. a laser pointing) is a demonstrative use of this term.

One has, first, to clarify the relation of a demonstrative use of a term with genuine demonstratives as conceived in the approach introduced above. In my view, a genuine demonstrative requires to be anchored by means of an associated action (a Kaplanian demonstration) or by taking into consideration some specific features of the situation directing the attention of the participants towards some part of the discourse situation. Suppose for instance two injured persons, unable to move any part of their body except their phonatory organs and aware that they share the perception of their immediate environment. Imagine that the wind suddenly breaks one of the windows of the room in which these persons are lying on their hospital bed. One of them might say 'This window must be fixed' and be correctly understood by her room-mate. In this sentence, *this window* is a standard demonstrative because its anchor is contingent, although it is not associated with any specific *action* of pointing. Keeping in mind that what is required by a true demonstrative is not necessarily a genuine action of pointing, it will be easier to limit the discussion of demonstrative uses of referential terms to cases in which they are used with an explicit pointing. In this restricted sense, the injured persons previously mentioned would be able to use demonstratives, but unable to make demonstrative use of demonstratives (and of any other referential term), just because they are unable to accomplish any action except speaking.

Once admitted that some actions are recognized as the typical complement of true demonstratives because these actions provide the anchor demonstratives need as a basis for finding their intended referent, nothing prevents one from using similar actions of pointing with other categories. Let us briefly take an example outside the scope of the present discussion, namely proper names. Proper names do not require to be anchored (in the sense that indexicals do), probably because they are associated with another kind of recipe for finding their intended referent. But one can use a proper name and point to some person present in the discourse situation. It would be conceived, in my terms, as a demonstrative use of a proper name. The proper name does not cease to be a proper name, but the pointing, for what concerns the intended referent of the proper name, is much more relevant than any other possible concomitant action (say, rubbing one's nose when pronouncing it). If I point to some part of the environment with a laser pointer when pronouncing 'Mr Smith', there are great chances that the hearer is invited to use the dot, roughly as she would have done if I had said 'this person', namely: 'consider this dot as an anchor helping to separate the entity I intend to refer to from others because it is more closely related to this dot than any other'. Now, I am also using the proper name *Mr Smith* to let my hearer know which individual I intend to denote. There are very interesting topics to discuss about this particular example, but I will not go into them. The main point I would like to focus on is that things work only if both determinations of the intended referent are compatible. A typical situation is the following: the hearer has never met Mr Smith, and does not know the name of the person picked up by the demonstration. She will thus accommodate that this person is the one I call 'Mr Smith'. This is a frequent way of learning how to fix the reference of a proper name. But any divorce between the proper name and the demonstration will lead to failures. For instance, my hearer knows a person we both call *Mr Smith*, and is convinced that the person I point to is another person. Or my hearer knows the proper name of the person I point to, and knows that his proper name is not *Smith*.[9] If the two determinations of the denotation are compatible, a demonstrative use will either add information for the hearer ('I intend to speak of Mr Smith, and here is how you have to fix the reference of this name') or will be a confirmation acknowledging the presence of Smith in the context.[10]

7.2 Pure Indexicals in Demonstrative Use

A similar process is open for any other referential term which does not require an associated demonstration like pure indexicals: one is free to use them with a demonstration, if the demonstration is not incompatible with what would happen without it, and especially if it gives a better clue for finding the intended referent. When a pointing, if interpreted as a demonstration, would lead to a denotation incompatible with the canonical interpretation of the pure indexical, it is not interpreted as a demonstration, and there is no demonstrative use at all; for instance, if I point to you while saying 'I'. But, in any case, it is not impossible to take the pointing as an additional clue for finding the intended referent compatible with the canonical interpretation of the true indexical, a demonstrative use can be accepted. The emerging view of demonstrative use of 'pure' indexicals is as follows: interpret the 'pure' indexical as usual; try, then, to interpret it as a true demonstrative anchored by the concomitant pointing (try to interpret it as 'this entity' on the basis of the pointing); if so-doing returns a denotation compatible with what you got, accept the pointing as a demonstration anchoring the expression: either it will denote the same entity in another way, or it will contribute to be more precise about the intended denotation (to eliminate alternatives compatible with the interpretation of the 'pure' indexical qua-'pure' indexical).

Let us consider for the sake of illustration demonstrative uses of *I*, *you* and *we*. If I point to you when saying *I*, you will never interpret it as a demonstrative use, because the pointing and *I* are incompatible. You will think my pointing has other motivations. If I point to you when saying *you*, you will take my pointing as a demonstrative use: the canonical interpreta-

---

[9] Such cases of divorce between the two ways of finding the intended denotation would be interesting to discuss by themselves, but they are beyond the main focus of this paper and have already been discussed at length in the literature.

[10] In a sense, the speaker, by using the demonstration, makes clear to her hearer that she might have use 'this person' for targeting the intended denotation, even though she uses a proper name.

tion of *you* (singular, like French *tu*) as a 'pure' indexical can denote any of my interlocutors; a concomitant utterance of 'this person' would have denoted *you*, because you are one of my potential interlocutors, the demonstrative use can be interpreted as eliminating alternatives compatible with the canonical use, and is thus accepted as anchoring the denotation on you. If I point to you by saying *we*, this may count as a demonstrative use anchored by my pointing. Used as a 'pure' indexical, *we* can denote any group of persons including me; to use a concomitant pointing on any person of the environment (you or anyone else) has to be interpreted as if I had used a demonstrative bound to denote a set so-defined (a plurality including me) anchored by the dot of the pointing (for instance you): this derives correctly what is observed: in such a situation, if one takes my use of *we* as a demonstrative use, she will understand that I intend to denote a plurality of persons including me, and anchored on the dot of the pointer, exactly as a use of a true demonstrative like 'these persons' would have been, that is, in the most general case, a group of persons including also you.

7.3 Pure Indexicals in Demonstrative Use Are not True Demonstratives

When considering the triplet of pure indexicals (*I*, *here*, *now*), one can observe interesting differences about what happens when their utterance is accompanied by an explicit pointing towards some part of the context, as shown in Table 5.

Table 5 Demonstrative uses of some 'pure' indexicals.

True indexical	Supplemented by a demonstration
I	'irrelevant or for emphasis' (Kaplan 1989a)
here, now[11]	The demonstration provides a new anchor (Bennett 1978)

Some implicit views of what happens when one supplements *here* with an explicit demonstration rely on the idea that *here* is no longer a pure indexical (anchored on its place of utterance) and becomes a true demonstrative (anchored on the demonstration target) similar to a genuine demonstrative like (at/in) *this place*.

But this idea faces theoretical as well as empirical issues. First, there are some reasons to think that *here* remains anchored on its place of utterance, in some way or other, and is not free to denote any place identified by

---

[11] Although *here* and *now* are rarely discussed separately, and are thus supposed to share most of their properties, there are interesting differences concerning their demonstrative use; I will come back to this below.

any pointing as a true demonstrative like *this place* is. It is not easy to document this affirmation with fully convincing written examples, probably because in narrative prose, what is considered as the place of utterance, is often relative to the point of view of the characters. My main point is that a pure indexical like *here* cannot be used to denote some spatial entities accessible by pointing, when these entities are considered as spatial entities disjoint from the place of utterance, although a true demonstrative like *this place* would work correctly. I just give an invented example involving French data for the sake of illustration. Suppose a mother speaks to her young daughter about her dead father:

(1)　Mother:　Ton père n'est plus avec nous, il est au ciel maintenant.
　　　　　　　'Your father is no longer with us. He is in the heaven now.'

(2)　Daughter: Et pourquoi est-il *ici (là-haut/là-bas/à cet endroit)?
　　　　　　　'And why is he *here now (up there/over there/in this place)?'

Such examples indicate that when a pure indexical enters a demonstrative use, it does not become a true demonstrative and preserves its inherent properties, that is a strong relationship to its place of utterance. The problem with (2) seems to be that once the first sentence has asserted that the father's place is not part of the world accessible from the discourse situation, it becomes impossible to refer to this place with the indexical *ici* (even if the speaker uses a concomitant pointing towards the sky), although most true demonstrative and definite NPs are able to do so. To be brief, the pure indexical *ici*, even in its demonstrative uses, can only have access to a spatial entity conceived as being part of the discourse's location.

　　The second issue with the view that *here* would become a demonstrative when used in association with a pointing is theoretical. It is rather difficult to explain how a term denoting its place of utterance can be transformed into a term denoting any *other* space when associated to a demonstration.

　　It might be even more natural to assume that *here* is a demonstrative, like *this place*, and that there is a default interpretation of true demonstratives used without any demonstration, namely that for so-used demonstratives, it is the basic necessary anchors of the utterance which are used. This assumption has to be made anyway for dealing with a frequent interpretation of true demonstratives like 'this place' (= here), or 'these days' (= now). One might be tempted then to explore the view that *here* is a demonstrative, and that its pure-indexical-like uses are just the 'non-demonstrative' uses of demonstratives (Bennett 1978: 15). Of course this does not account for the empirical evidence mentioned in the previous paragraph, but this remains an option to be considered. I will try to explore later this view and try to show it leads to the same results and requires the same additional assumptions regarding the special properties of time and space, as the sorts associated to *now* and *here*.

7.4 Contrasting the Demonstrative Uses of here and now

The line I will follow is that *here* and *now* are pure indexicals, which have the demonstrative uses they have because of the *sort* they are associated with (i.e. space and time, respectively).

The demonstrative *this place* receives as its anchor the dot of the pointer. In the sophisticated approach, the anchor *is not* the intended referent, but just a clue for finding it. Consider how it works for *this man* used with a laser pointing. The dot of the pointer is some spatial entity of the environment, and the intended referent is the closest man w.r.t. this anchor. You can point on him, under him, over him, etc. If there is something special with *this place*, it is possibly that the anchor and the referent are of the same sort: both are spatial (non discrete) entities. How can a place (anchor) be a clue for helping to find another place (referent)? Is it true that *this place* will always denote a spatial entity *including* the anchor? Although true in most cases, I think that this no more than a default option, something we will assume in the absence of more specific information. A typical situation is one in which the discourse context provides independent ways of distinguishing different spatial entities in the context. Consider for instance a shell game (French bonneteau): one can use 'Where is the coin? In this place?' (pointing under, over, etc. the place where the coin might be). Let us assume that for a demonstrative like *this place*, the inclusion of the anchor in the intended denotation is assumed in the absence of more specific information regarding the kind of space you intend to refer to. In the shell game, the default does not apply because the context gives information about which kind of spaces are intended, namely spaces hidden by the vases.

Assume that *here* is a pure indexical, not a demonstrative. It is anchored on the utterance location, and will denote a spatial entity 'related' to the anchor (close to it), and in the absence of more specific information (default) including it. Like any other referential term, it can be accompanied by a demonstration, pointing to some location of the accessible context. This use is accepted when the demonstration can be interpreted as a way of being more precise about what is intended, an extra-help. Such an action is, undoubtedly, a specific piece of information, which cancels the default. Thus, we identify the intended referent as a space related to the *demonstratum*, and by default including it. Roughly speaking, *here*, is in such cases, a pure indexical taking advantage of a demonstration to specify more precisely its referent, as illustrated in Table 6.

Table 6 Demonstrative use of the pure indexical *here*.

	Pure indexical	Demonstrative use
Anchor	Place of utterance (l.ut).	Demonstratum (l.dem.)
Referent	A space related to l.ut.	A space related to l.dem.
Default	A space including l.ut.	~~A space including l.ut.~~
		A space including l.dem.

This way of deriving the demonstrative uses of *here* manages to explain how the demonstrative is a way of being more precise, by eliminating some alternatives for the intended referent, as in the other demonstrative uses considered before.

It is rather easy to explain why this demonstrative use option is open for the spatial indexical *here*, and why it is less accessible for other pure indexicals. I have already claimed that a demonstrative use is accessible if it is useful, which is possible only if the indexical interpretation leaves alive many alternatives, leaving open the possibility to interpret the demonstration as eliminating some of them. This explains directly that *I* has no demonstrative use, although *you* has many (see Section 7.3 above).

This predicts also that indexicals denoting non-discrete entities will easily have demonstrative uses, and this is true for terms denoting pluralities like *we* and *you*, as it is for terms denoting spatial and temporal entities like *here* and *now*.

There is a difference between *here* and *now* that is related to the sort they are bound to denote – space and time, respectively. This is probably why *here* is often considered as a true demonstrative (to be included in the same grammatical category as *this place*), which is less frequent for *now*. An obvious difference is that it is easy to create spatial anchors by pointing on some part of the visible situation (e.g. with a laser pointer), but impossible to create temporal anchors by so doing. Things work as if, in a discourse situation, the only accessible anchor for interpreting temporal demonstratives were the time of the discourse itself and if it were impossible to use some equivalent of a Kaplanian demonstration for pointing to other temporal entities to be used for anchoring demonstratives. Recall that we distinguished (Section 7.1 above) two ways for providing anchors for demonstratives: either the speaker executes a dedicated action like pointing with her finger (a Kaplanian demonstration), or the discourse situation itself makes salient some entity used as anchor. For temporal demonstratives, only the second option would be open, just because it is not possible to isolate temporal entities by pointing to them. This explains why there are no demonstrative use of the temporal indexical *now* comparable to the uses of *here* based on a contingent anchor and helping to make more precise its intended demonstration. This is just because there is no temporal demonstrations. But, if we are correct, *now* being a *pure* indexical, it will not be easy either to use it in narrative fragments and to anchor it on time events made salient by the ongoing discourse, as one can use freely true demonstratives like 'this day', 'this time'.[12]

The result is that the main alleged demonstrative uses of temporal *now* one can find involve narration and are of the kind: 'Now Napolén had a dilemma'.[13] There are important differences between *now* and true demonstratives like *this day*, *this moment* ('At this moment, Napoléon had a dilemma'). Although true demonstratives can be used freely for referring to time entities made salient in narrative discourses, *now* looks rare and marked, evoking in many cases reported speech (actual or interior). This contrast is not unexpected in the present approach: if *here* and *now* are pure indexicals and not true demonstratives, their interpretation remains anchored to their utterance parameters. In order to take them as demonstrative uses, an explicit signal is expected, like a Kaplanian demonstration. This is different from true demonstratives, which exploit either a dedicated action like a pointing, or the salience properties of the situation. If Kaplanian demonstrations can only provide spatial anchors (a laser pointing can only focus on spatial entities), and if temporal entities cannot be demonstrated, then temporal indexicals will not have demonstrative uses based on demonstrations (in contrast to spatial indexicals), and the alleged examples of demonstrative uses of *now* (as those of *here*) require another analysis, possibly confirming the intuition that they might be reported uses of true indexicals.[14]

7.5 Indexicals Interpretation of True Demonstratives vs. Pure Indexicals

The conclusion of the above approach is that *here* is a true indexical which is very easy to complement by a Kaplanian demonstration in order to get the so-called 'demonstrative uses'. Another way of telling the story would be to claim that *here* is a true demonstrative, and that true demonstratives when deprived of any explicit demonstration are supposed to take as anchors the parameters of the utterance situation. This option has been evoked above, in Section 7.3.

---

[12] We made similar observations for *here*.

[13] See Section 2 above.

[14] See e.g. Predelli (1998).

Consider (3), for instance:

(3)   This country met this year many issues.

A natural interpretation, out of the blue, is 'the country (I am presently in) met the year (we are presently in) many issues'. This means that the basic necessary anchors provided by any utterance, in particular its time and place, can be used for anchoring demonstratives of the corresponding sort, if there is no other signal for finding contingent anchors.[15] It might be tempting then, to try an analysis of *here* and *now* as true demonstratives, and to see the cases in which they are anchored on the parameters of their utterance as the regular default behavior of all true demonstratives deprived of any demonstration. Again the different status of temporal and spatial anchors would play a role: for *now* the anchoring on moments distinguished by pointing being impossible, there will be very few genuine demonstrative uses; for *here*, the anchoring to locations distinguished by pointing being standard, genuine demonstrative uses will be as regular as pure indexical-like uses. This analysis would offer the picture of Table 7.

Table 7 A radically simplified picture of indexicals.

Anchoring	Pure indexicals	True demonstratives
	I, you, we	*this place, here, now*
Basic anchors of ut.	Obligatory	Default
Contingent anchors	Possible if informative	Regular

Although this picture meets the criteria of simplicity and of one-to-one correspondence from items to categories, the main argument for not preferring it and preferring the idea that *here* and *now* are pure indexicals having demonstrative uses is empirical. The picture of Table 7 does not account for some empirical differences between *here/now* and true demonstratives like *this place/this moment*, namely that to use them for entities disjoint from the spatio-temporal anchors of their utterance is much more marked than a full status of demonstratives would have predicted. For instance, true demonstratives, can be easily used as anaphors to a previously introduced entity, as in (4):

(4)   They entered the park. At this moment, they no longer had any protection.

If *now* were just a demonstrative, it would be as easy to use it in anaphoric uses than it is to use 'at this moment', but it is not, and its use is

---

[15] Imagine, for instance, the considered sentence in a historical essay about France in 1989.

marked, as noted above. The approach defended in this paper predicts these differences, by viewing *here* and *now* as native pure indexicals and this is one reason for preferring it.

8 Conclusions

This paper argues that what makes indexicals indexical is that they must be anchored, and that what supports their splitting in two classes, 'pure' indexicals and 'true' demonstratives, is the nature of their anchor: either their anchor is provided by the necessary defined basic parameters of the utterance (speaker, place and time), or it is provided by a contingent action (like a Kaplanian demonstration), or by some contingent property of the discourse context making some entity salient.

This paper claims then, that the classical distinction among indexicals between pure indexicals and true demonstratives can be defended against criticisms once one adopts a slightly more sophisticated framework for describing the process by which indexicals get their reference. The difference between the anchor of an indexical and its intended denotation, and the relevance of the sortal constraint each indexical imposes on its denotation have been shown to be crucial for defending the thesis that the classical distinction is basically correct: pure indexicals and true demonstratives are mutually exclusive categories distinguished by the nature of their respective anchors. Moreover, the paper attempts to argue that some differences of behaviour between indexicals, which might be invoked against the claim, can be explained as a consequence of the sort associated to each indexical. It also attempts to go a little bit further in the analysis of the so-called 'demonstrative use' of pure indexicals, arguing that the notion of 'demonstrative use' is not *ad hoc*, and can be used without weakening the clear-cut difference between pure indexicals and true demonstratives.

Two sources of complexity have been encountered but not considered in the paper: (i) The complex processes leading from anchors to intended denotations. On this topic, we think the detailed work on pointing reported in Lücking et al. (2015) opens up a very interesting and promising field of research. (ii) The precise delimitation and internal complexities of the two postulated categories. For instance, we discussed the pure indexical *here*, without taking into account that *there* might be analyzed as another pure indexical. But this analysis in itself would be a threat for the claims of this paper because, at first glance, the empirical arguments we gave for supporting the view that *here* is a pure indexical (not a true demonstrative) do not extend to *there*, which can be used, roughly, in the same contexts as the true demonstrative expression *in this place* In a joint paper with Tijana Asic (Corblin & Asic 2016), we argue that the French lexical item *là*, which has some common properties with the English *there*,[16] is neither a pure indexical nor a true demonstrative, but an instance of a third semantic class of indexicals, i.e. *definite* expressions, exemplified in French by short definites like *la femme*, *l'homme*, *le chien*, etc. So if the present paper attempts to provide a neat separation of a set of typical indexicals in two disjoint classes (pure indexicals/true demonstratives), it is likely that this distinction is too coarse for covering the whole set of indexicals, and that more fine-grained distinctions are necessary for covering indexical expressions which does not fall strictly in one or the other category, although they may appear to share some properties of both.

Acknowledgements

Many thanks are due to the editors and anonymous reviewers of this volume. Their questions, criticisms and suggestions were very helpful for improving the last version of this paper.

---

[16] There are many differences as well between the French *là* and the English *there*. One of them, pointed to me by Olivier Bonami (p.c.) is that *there* looks more strongly *distal* that *là*. I share the intuition and I think that trying to deal with it in depth is a fruitful direction for research, not only in order to document the contrast between the two items, but also because it focuses on the opposition *proximal/distal* which may play no role for grounding the basic distinction between pure indexical and true demonstratives, but will come into play once the precise delimitation of the class of indexicals and its internal complexity will receive attention.

7

Presupposition Projection and Main Content

MATHILDE DARGNAT AND JACQUES JAYEZ

1 Introduction

The problem of *projection* has attracted much attention from linguists. In addition to constituting a kind of enigma, it has exposed the collaboration or (sometimes) tension between semantics and pragmatics. Put simply, projection corresponds to a set of observations which share a common feature: operators like negation, interrogation or possibility modals seem to affect only a part of the semantic content of a sentence. For instance, in (1a) there are two pieces of information, the *main content* and the *presupposition*. The former is the proposition that Paul does not smoke and the latter the proposition that he has been smoking. When the sentence is negated, as in (1b), the presupposition remains untouched whereas the main content is negated. (1c) illustrates the same configuration with an expressive (Potts 2005). The proposition that the speaker's neighbour is stupid is not questioned but remains in effect. In (1d), the speaker's hesitation conveyed by *well* (Ajmer & Simon-Vandenbergen 2003: 1124) escapes the possibility modal.

(1) a. Paul stopped smoking.

    b. Paul didn't stop smoking.

    c. Did my stupid neighbor buy a new car?

    d. It might be the case that, well, Paul is a sort of double agent.

Although projection is not limited to presuppositions (Potts 2005), it is most frequently studied on the basis of presupposition triggers like

Constraint-Based Syntax and Semantics: Papers in Honor of Danièle Godard..
Anne Abeillé and Olivier Bonami (eds.).
Copyright © 2020, CSLI Publications.

stop, know, only, too or clefts. In this context, the main question has been to derive the projection properties of complex sentences such as (1b) from those of elementary sentences like (1a). This *projection problem* (Langendoen & Savin 1971) has received several solutions, which we will not review. We will only note two aspects of this research domain, which are directly relevant to our concerns.

First, the role of context and pragmatic interpretation has been highlighted on several occasions. In general, it seems that projection does not occur whenever it would lead to an implausible interpretation. Two well-known examples are the hypothetical status of the presupposition in an *if*-clause, as in (2a), and certain so-called *factive* verbs, as in (2b), copied from Karttunen (1971: ex. (25c)).

(2) a. If Paul has ever smoked before, then he has stopped.

　　 b. If I discover later that I have not told the truth, I will confess it to everyone.

Concerning (2a), if the presupposition that Paul has smoked projected, it would create a conflict with the *if*-clause, since the same proposition, that Paul has been smoking before, would be both entertained by the speaker (projection) and contemplated as a simple possibility (*if*-clause). Similarly, with (2b), projection would create a conflict with the possibility that the speaker does not know for sure that she has not told the truth (*if*-clause), see (Stalnaker 1974). This may sound pretty trivial, except for the fact that, in such cases, the projection does not 'resist' but gives way, thus avoiding an interpretation problem.

Second, as already apparent from (1c, d), projection is not limited to standard examples of presuppositions. It occurs also with what Potts characterizes as *conventional implicatures*. It is not clear whether projection is the common symptom of a set of actually different mechanisms or rather an homogeneous and general mechanism, whose manifestations are modulated by more local differences (lexical semantic content, for instance).

In this paper, we discuss a recent approach to projection (Simons et al. 2011, 2017; Beaver et al. 2017), which argues for the latter perspective, making projection essentially a side-effect of the management of the *Question Under Discussion* (QUD) à-la Roberts (2012). We call this theory the *QUD-based approach*.

Summarizing, the QUD-based approach predicts that a presupposition projects (= is not affected by a truth-inversion/suspension operator) if and only if either (i) it does not address the current topic of conversation (the QUD) or (ii) has no *Obligatory Local Effect*. The intuition behind this equivalence can be described as follows. For (i), when a piece of information does not address the QUD, it is somehow 'kept off the track', that is, kept at a distance from the main flow of discourse. In this respect, it is not impacted by operators like negation, question, or possibility modals, which target precisely the main information. The Obligatory Local Effect, introduced in Tonhauser et al. (2013), corresponds to the fact that a projective piece of information is captured by a belief operator. For instance, a sentence like *Mary thinks that Paul stopped smoking* implicates that Mary believes that Paul does not smoke but also that he has been smoking before. In other terms, the belief operator captures the presupposition of the complement clause. When some content has no Obligatory Local Effect, this means, roughly speaking, that it can be detached from the main flow of discourse without major damages, most notably without affecting the truth-conditional status of a sentence. This idea, highlighted in Potts' (2005) book, but anticipated by Frege, can be illustrated by non-restrictive relative clauses. So, in *Mary thinks that Paul, who is her neighbor, stopped smoking*, the fact that Paul is Mary's neighbor is not necessarily part of Mary's belief state. Here the intuition is that, when a piece of information is not obligatorily captured by a belief operator, it can 'float around' and, as a result, escape the truth suspension/inversion operators.

In this paper, we argue that this view is only partially correct. Our precise reasons for this claim are stated in the relevant sections, but we can motivate our reservations from a more general point of view. The QUD-based approach is, to a large extent, a radical pragmatics approach, that is, it makes presupposition projection essentially revolve around the interpretation of speakers' intentions as to the discourse topic. While emphasizing the role of pragmatics has been an influential and successful trend in theoretical linguistics for years, it seems that the time has come for a more balanced view, which makes room for *learning* linguistic usages. People certainly react to contexts and adjust their contribution to discourse interaction, but they no less certainly learn *preferences* of usage. When these preferences are 'strong', that is, strongly context-independent, they can conflict with 'soft', that is, context-dependent, pragmatic pressures. In that case, delineating the equilibrium between the different forces cannot always be done in a crisp and clear way, by applying elegant principles to derive a robust solution. We have to accept the possibility that things are murkier than one may wish. With respect to presupposition projection, we argue that lexical preferences (strong), discourse attachments (strong) and QUD-relevance (soft) interact in a number of ways, some of which we describe in the last section (4).

The structure of the paper is as follows. We present the QUD-based approach in Section 2, before discussing it in Section 3. In Section 4, we advocate a different approach, based on a distinction between *at-issue content* and *main content*. We will use English as our reference language but turn occasionally to French when it provides interesting contrasts between lexemes or constructions.

2 Projection under the QUD-based Approach

The QUD-based approach is partly grounded on the following idea: a piece of information can project only if it is not interpreted as relevant to the QUD, that is, to a set of plausible alternatives among which the participants in the linguistic exchange seek to discriminate.[1] For instance, in (3), answers A1 and A2 entail that the responder believes that Paul broke the window pane. A2 answers the question via the presupposition that Paul broke the pane, a possibility which is analyzed at length by Simons (2007). Examples like (4) are even more interesting because they suggest that projection does not occur in certain configurations where the presupposition is relevant to the QUD (did Paul break the pane?). It is crucial to note that assuming that the presupposition projects in (4-A) below results in a somewhat infelicitous answer, insofar as the speaker not noticing that Paul was around is an irrelevant fact, with respect to the explicit QUD. Changing the context can make this fact relevant under a projective interpretation, as illustrated in (5), where the answer aims at alleviating the responsibility of the responder.

(3) Q: Who broke the window pane?
    A1: It's Paul.
    A2: Anna noticed it's Paul.

(4) Q: Is it Paul who broke the window pane?
    A: I didn't notice that Paul was around.

(5) Q: Is it Paul who broke the window pane? I thought I had asked you to keep an eye on the little scamp!
    A: I'm sorry, I didn't notice he was around.

In contrast to (2b), (4) does not make the belief set of the speaker inconsistent when the presupposition projects. Instead, in that case,

---

[1] We assume the standard definition of alternatives as exhaustive mutually exclusive possibilities ($A_i \Rightarrow \neg A_j$ for every $i \neq j$ in the set of alternatives). The implementation of this constraint depends on the ontology at hand. For instance, in a classical modal frame with a set of worlds W, a set of alternatives is any $\mathcal{A} \subset \mathcal{P}(W)$ such that the members of $\mathcal{A}$ (information states) are pairwise incompatible.

the main content would be either partly irrelevant to the explicit QUD or relevant to a different QUD. This shows that, at least in some cases, there is an interaction between the QUD and presupposition projection. In the QUD-based approach, this interaction is extended to projection in general and systematized in a way that makes examples like (3) and (4) particular cases of more general principles. For simplicity, we will divide our presentation of the approach into two parts, following mainly the neat expositions given in Beaver et al. (2017) and Simons et al. (2017).

2.1 QUD and Focus

The QUD can be characterized formally as a set of restricted alternatives. The restriction comes from the available contextual cues, which allow one to exclude theoretically possible but otherwise implausible answers. For instance, with a question like *Who paid for the car?*, the QUD is any set of alternatives of the form *X paid for the car*, where *X* is a plausible candidate, given the context. For instance, *X* could be a member of the family, a friend, a business partner, or a group thereof, etc. The most recent QUD is called the *Current Question*. So, the Current Question is by definition a set of plausible alternatives.

The *focus* is a set of unrestricted alternatives (no plausibility restriction applies). For QUD and focus to be *congruent*, it is required that the focus be a superset of the QUD (Beaver & Clark 2008). This accounts for the fact that dialogs like (6) can be felt as odd. As with (4), we can 'repair' the exchange by assuming that a different QUD is accessible. For instance, if Paul has a reputation of being a destructive child and is likely to have broken the pane, the answer is interpreted as correcting the possible belief that Paul broke the window and the question might sound rhetorical.

(6) Q: Who broke the window pane?

A: Paul broke [a vase]$_F$.

The central feature of the relation between QUD and focus is the *Current Question Rule* of Beaver & Clark (2008), expressed in (7). (7.2) is straightforward: it prevents a question to be already resolved.[2] (7.1) accounts for the fact that, in general, questions 'presuppose' that some answer is true.

---

[2]The status of rhetorical questions is not a problem under this view. They can be considered as special speech acts, where the goal is not to get information but to elicit a public assertion, or as more or less strongly biased questions, where the prior probability distribution of answers for the speaker favors certain elements of the set of formally possible answers.

(7) *Current Question Rule*

1. The Current Question must contain at least one true alternative.

2. The Current Question must contain at least two alternatives which are not true or false in the common ground.

The Current Question Rule interacts with focus as follows. When (i) the set of alternatives determined by focus is congruent with an explicit or reconstructed Current Question and (ii) a subset of alternatives is excluded (by negation, for instance), the Current Question Rule still requires that one alternative be true, which amounts to projecting an existential presupposition. For example, in (8), in addition to the standard correspondence between Q1 and A, the Current Question could be Q2. Assuming that A has a form $\neg([\text{Paul}]_F \text{ came})$, the expression in the scope of the negation is congruent with a Current Question of the form $\{X : X \text{ came to the meeting}\}$, for any contextually plausible agent X. The Current Question conveys the existential presupposition $\exists X (X \text{ came to the meeting})$. The proposition that Paul didn't come eliminates those alternatives in which Paul came, thus constituting an answer to the Current Question. The negation does not eliminate the existential presupposition, since the latter depends on the Current Question (recoverable from the focus structure and the context), not on the answer.

(8) Q1: Who didn't come to the meeting?

    Q2: Who came to the meeting?

    A: $[\text{Paul}]_F$ didn't come.

For simplicity, in what follows, we will ignore the distinction between QUD and Current Question (the most recent QUD). Unless otherwise indicated, the QUD will always be the Current Question.

2.2 QUD and Projection

In Simons et al. (2011), it was argued that a piece of information p can project whenever the question whether p is not intentionally relevant to the QUD. The definition in Beaver et al. (2017) is different and we will focus on the latter, because it clarifies the claims in Simons et al. (2011) on at least one crucial point. The authors use the notion of *Obligatory Local Effect*, introduced in previous work Tonhauser et al. (2013) and illustrated in (9). In (9), the belief that Bill has been smoking, which is the presupposition of the clause *Bill has stopped smoking*, is necessarily attributed to Jane. Generalizing, we observe an Obligatory Local Effect whenever a projective content is obligatorily attributed to the agent of a belief operator. The original definition in Tonhauser et al. (2013) is reproduced in (10).

(9) Jane believes that Bill has stopped smoking.

(Tonhauser et al. 2013: ex. (38a))

(10) *Obligatory Local Effect*
A projective content m with trigger t has obligatory local effect if and only if, when t is syntactically embedded in the complement of a belief-predicate B, m necessarily is part of the content that is targeted by, and within the scope of, B.

In contrast to (9), a sentence like *Jane believes that the stupid Bill has stopped smoking* does not entail that Jane believes that Bill is stupid (the local effect is not obligatory). The Obligatory Local Effect is a component of the constraint on projection. In a nutshell, a piece of information projects if and only if its does not address the QUD or is not subject to the Obligatory Local Effect. In the following constraint on projection, condition 1 makes sure that the non-projecting content has at least minimal relevance to the QUD, by preventing it from being compatible with all the alternatives in the QUD. We abbreviate the projection constraint in the *Projection Equation* (11.3):

(11) *Projection Constraint*
A piece of information projects if and only if:
1. it does not entail that some possible answer to the QUD is false, or
2. it has no Obligatory Local Effect.
3. *Projection Equation*:
Projection $\equiv$ QUD-Irrelevance $\vee$ $\neg$OLE.

If a presupposition trigger gives rise to a presupposition with Obligatory Local Effect, the Projection Equation predicts that, in a projective environment, such as negation, interrogation, embedding possibility modal construction, projection will not occur if the presupposition is interpreted as relevant to the QUD. We already saw an illustration of this mechanism with (4). The possibility that Paul was or was not around eliminates certain alternatives. If Paul was not around, he cannot have broken the window pane. If he was around, it eliminates alternatives in which he was too far to have broken the pane.[3] Intuitively, the answer in (4) is biased towards a negative factual or epistemic judgment: Paul didn't break the pane or, at least, the speaker has no evidence that it might be the case.

---

[3]The second possibility calls for a more liberal, probabilistic, view, which we adopt in Section 4.2.

Finally, we come to focus structures where presuppositions project systematically. In the case of factive verbs, Beaver et al. (2017) and Simons et al. (2017) use again the QUD-based approach to predict projection whenever the focus structure is as in (12). The set of alternatives has the form {Paul knows that p : p is a proposition}. Whatever the restrictions on the set of plausible propositions are, they must include the fact that they are *knowable*, which entails that they are true. So, in the case of (12), the proposition that Mary solved the problem is considered as true, and, in this respect, 'projects'.

(12) Paul doesn't know that [Mary solved the problem]$_F$.

3   Discussion

The QUD-based approach provides a tight connection between projection and the management of information in discourse. In the spirit of Stalnaker (1974), it offers an alternative to purely lexical theories, which see presupposition projection as a mere effect of lexical instructions attached to presupposition triggers.[4] In contrast to Stalnaker, it adopts a broader perspective because it deals with conventional implicatures as well, and because it accounts for non-projection. In this section, we discuss in turn the Obligatory Local Effect and the predictions of the QUD-based approach with respect to presupposition triggers.

3.1   The Obligatory Local Effect and Anaphoric Triggers

It is intuitively clear that many lexemes trigger information that (i) does not address the QUD and (ii) is not presented as being common ground. Such lexemes fall into the general category of conventional implicatures, as identified in Potts (2005). Given the Projection Equation (11.3) above, we would expect that, if conventional implicatures robustly project, as suggested in Jayez (2015) and Beaver et al. (2017), they also robustly escape the Obligatory Local Effect or are not relevant to the QUD. Beaver et al. (2017: 281) also consider the case of presupposition triggers that lack Obligatory Local Effect and mention in this regard anaphoric triggers.

Before discussing this point, let us note that the literature on such matters is confusing. What has been labeled *conventional implicatures* by Grice includes certain anaphoric triggers, a fact which has been mostly overlooked. Grice (1975, 1978) classified *therefore* and *but* as conventional implicature triggers. In this subsection, we look at some consequence, concession and additive triggers, like *therefore, as a re-*

---

[4]However, we doubt that, in the current state of the literature on presuppositions, such theories exist.

sult, so, however, yet, too, etc. Summarizing, we show (i) that all these triggers are very probably presupposition triggers and not conventional implicature triggers in the sense of Potts (2005) and (ii) that they raise a problem for the QUD-based approach. More precisely, we show that the mentioned discourse markers, like a number of presupposition triggers, (i) are anaphoric, (ii) can be backgrounded, (iii) clearly tend to project and, in addition, (iv) have Obligatory Local Effect and (v) can address the QUD, even if they project. We briefly explain these five points in turn, mentioning *too* only for the last two points, since its status as a presupposition trigger is already well-established.

(i) It is markedly odd to use *therefore, yet*, etc. without referring to an antecedent provided by the previous discourse or the context. So, all these items are anaphoric.

(ii) If we adopt Potts' (2005) idea that presuppositions are presented as being in the common ground, in contrast to conventional implicatures, which are presented as new, examples like those in (13a, b) suggest that the triggers under review behave like presupposition triggers. (13ab) reproduce a pattern used by Potts (2005: ex. (2.41)) in order to show that conventional implicatures are *antibackgrounding*, i.e. they resist previous mention in the discourse. No effect of this type is observed with *therefore* (13b). In (13c, d) the consequence and concession relations are relativized to the antecedent of an *if*-conditional, exactly as the presupposition of (2a) or similar examples. Altogether, (13) suggests that the discourse markers under consideration are presuppositional. This could be expected under a view of presupposition triggers as elements that describe their antecedent in a particular way. For instance, *stop smoking* refers to a previous state described as satisfying the property of smoking. This is the gist of the *anaphoric* theory of presupposition (van der Sandt 1992, Geurts 1999). With *therefore*, for example, one refers to a proposition which somehow entails the proposition expressed by the sentence or clause to which *therefore* adjoins: *therefore P'* refers to some P such that P' is a consequence of P.

(13) a. ??Paul is the committee chairman. As a result, Paul, **who is the chairman**, cannot be a counselor.

b. Being the committee chairman is not compatible with being a counselor. Paul is the chairman, **therefore** he cannot be a counselor.

c. If, really, being the committee chairman is not compatible with being a counselor, Paul, who is the chairman, cannot, **as a result**, be a counselor.

d. If, really, being the committee chairman is not compatible with being a counselor, I am surprised that Paul is the chairman and **yet** also a counselor.

(iii) The contents that correspond to the consequence or concession relation are *not* part of the main content. Compare their status with that of *because*, which is genuinely part of the main content. In (14a, b) the causal relation between the two propositions is negated or questioned. In (14c, e) the consequence or concession discourse relation associated with *so* or *yet* escapes the negation or question operator, which bears only on the propositions connected by the discourse relation.

(14) a. I don't think that Paul resigned because he didn't get along with his boss.

b. Did Paul resign because he didn't get along with his boss?

c. I don't think that Paul didn't get along with his boss and, so, resigned.

d. Did Paul disagree with his boss and, so, resign?

e. Did Paul disagree with his boss and, yet, decided to stay?

(iv) The mentioned discourse markers have Obligatory Local Effect. In (15), the only possibility to make the markers escape the belief operator is to interpret the sentences as coordinating two beliefs of Mary (*Mary believes that p and as a result/yet she believes that p'*), but this does not fit with the syntactic structure, which is a coordination of two complement clauses under the belief operator (Mary believes that A and B).

(15) a. Mary thinks that Paul is the committee chairman and, as a result, cannot be a counselor.

b. Mary believes that Paul is the committee chairman and, yet, is a counselor.

Additive markers like *too*, *again* or *still* behave similarly. In a context where Susan and Paul have been given a problem to solve, (16b) sounds contradictory because Mary's thoughts include the fact that

Susan solved the problem, see Tonhauser et al. (2013: ex. (46a)) for a similar case.

(16)   a. Mary doesn't know that Susan has solved the problem. She thinks that Paul solved it.

   b. #Mary doesn't know that Susan has solved the problem. She thinks that Paul solved it too.

(v) This part is slightly trickier. Imagine the following situation: two physicists discuss some problematic observation about two particles, p_1 and p_2. The physicists cannot determine what happened to the particles. They only know that the disintegration of either one automatically causes the disintegration of the other. The two answers in (17) are felt as odd or are reinterpreted as metalinguistic. In the latter case, the responder corrects the questioner by signaling that the use of *therefore* or *too* is inappropriate, due to the non-satisfaction of the presupposition (that p_1 disintegrated). This is normally only possible through a special prosodic focus marking, such as a rise in pitch and loudness on *therefore* or *too*, see Beaver et al. (2017: ex. (19)) and Jayez (2015), Simons et al. (2017) for similar examples. In the former case, the oddness of the answers comes from the fact that the presuppositions tend to project, which is not compatible with the final assertions. In (17-A1), the negation must apply to the main content, giving the reading 'I don't think that p_2 disintegrated'. If *therefore* did not project, it would be affected by the negation, giving the –complex but normal– reading 'I don't think that p_2 disintegrated as a result of p_1 disintegrating because, in fact, neither p_1 nor p_2 disintegrated'. Since *therefore* and *too* have Obligatory Local Effect and their presupposition is relevant to the QUD ('What is the responder's opinion about p_1 and p_2?'), the dualized version of Projection Equation (11.3), i.e. OLE ∧ QUD-relevance ⇒ non-projection, predicts that it should not project. It is not clear how the projection constraint (11) deals with such cases. The fact that *too* and similar markers robustly project is not a novel observation, see Jayez (2015) for discussion and references. The data sketched here reinforce the possibility that it is not a limited phenomenon.

(17)   Q: p_1 probably disintegrated and p_2 followed, do you agree?

   A1:   #Well, I don't think that, therefore, p_2 disintegrated. Neither one did.

   A2:   #Well, I don't think that p_2 disintegrated too. Neither one did.

3.2 Projection

Projection Equation (11.3) predicts in particular that projection does not occur when the presupposition addresses the QUD. Some observations have been mentioned as direct counter-examples to this claim. They are listed below.

(18) Q: Does Paul have a strong will?
    A: Well, he didn't quit smoking for instance.

(Adapted from Jayez 2010)

(19) Q: Did you go shopping?
    A: I didn't realize that the store was closed today.

(Koev 2017: ex. (15))

(20) Q: Which neighbor kid keeps ringing John's doorbell and running away?
    A: John is beside himself with frustration. He hasn't figured out it's Billy.

(Peters 2016: ex. (32))

(21) Q: When did Finland become independent?
    A: It must have been after the Bolsheviks came to power in Russia but before Lenin died in 1924.

(Karttunen 2016: ex. (28))

In this sequence of examples, the various relevant presuppositions seem to address the QUD and nonetheless project. However, some qualification is in order. Concerning (19), the intended interpretation of the answer is somewhat unclear. Does it mean (a) 'I went shopping because I had not realized the store was closed' or (b) 'I could not go shopping because the store was closed'? In case (b), the presupposition ('The store was closed today') addresses the QUD but the main content seems to be partly irrelevant and it is not clear whether the interpretation is quite natural. In case (a), the projected presupposition is not relevant to the QUD because the latter is something like 'did you try to get something at the store' and *not* 'did you get something at the store' (this would be case (b)). To get a more convincing example, one could modify the dialog in (19) as in (22), where the two pieces of information in A contribute an explanation for the complex event mentioned in Q: the responder accounts for her going to the store by the fact that she did not think that the store was closed (main content) and for her quick return by the fact that the store is closed (presupposition).

(22) Q: Why on earth did you do a round trip in ten minutes with the car?

A: I had not realized the store is closed today.

(21) too is problematic as a purported counterexample. The two presuppositions do not address the QUD in themselves, as evidenced by the oddness of (23).

(23) Q: When did Finland become independent?

A: #The Bolsheviks came to power in Russia and Lenin died in 1924.

To make sense of (21), the temporal relations have to be taken into account, but they are part of the main content and do not project. In (24), the existence of a complex event where, first, the Bolsheviks came to power and, afterwards, Finland became independent, is negated. So, the general form of such examples is $\neg AFTER(e_1, e_2)$ and what possibly projects is just e_1 or e_2.

(24) It is not the case that Finland became independent after the Bolsheviks came to power in Russia.

It is in general difficult to construct counterexamples based on negative operators. However, there is a natural class of counterexamples illustrated in (25). The general idea behind such examples is to have a dialog where the responder accounts for some fact by contemplating the possibility for an agent of being aware of some pleasant or unpleasant state of affairs.[5]

(25) Q: Why is Paul happy/depressed?

A1: He might have realized that Mary is going to marry/leave him.

A2: Did he realize that Mary is going to marry/leave him?

So, it seems that the systematic connection between addressing the QUD and not projecting is, at best, a statistically dominant feature, but not an intrinsic characteristic of projection phenomena. Three other kinds of objection have been raised against the QUD-based approach.

The first one concerns the interpretation of dialogs like (26). Simons et al. present that example as an illustration of the fact that a non-addressing QUD content can project. The presupposition that raw vegetables are edible is not an explanation of the responder's surprise and, as a result, it can project. Karttunen (2016) notes that replacing *know* by *believe* or *think* gives exactly the same result because the proposition that one can eat raw vegetables is common ground (in our

---

[5]The A2-type answers are subquestions in the sense of Roberts (2012).

culture) and will project no matter what. He argues that the original example does not in itself provide support to the authors' thesis. Elaborating on this, let us consider (27-A1). Since the proposition that the earth is flat is irrelevant to the QUD, it should project, which, of course, creates a conflict with the common ground proposition that the earth is not flat. So, the difference between (27-A1) and (27-A2) is correctly predicted. However, in order to demonstrate that the prediction depends exclusively on the non-relevance to the QUD and not, for instance, on a strong preference for projection with *know*, one has to show that, when the embedded clause *does* address the QUD, non-projection is systematically, or at least preferentially, observed for the same verb. This type of problem leads us to the next question, which concerns the class of verbs called *factives*.

(26) Q: What most surprised you about the first graders?
     A: They didn't know that you can eat raw vegetables.

(Simons et al. 2011: ex. (15))

(27) Q: What most surprised you about the first graders?
     A1: #In contrast to many children of the same age, they didn't know that the earth is flat.
     A2: In contrast to many children of the same age, they didn't believe that the earth is flat.

Karttunen (1971) had identified a subclass of *semi-factive* verbs where projection is less systematic than with emotive factives (*regret, be surprised that*, etc.) or epistemic factives (*know, realize*, etc.). Semi-factives include for instance *observe, see, be aware, notice, remember*. There is a rather sharp contrast between full factives and semi-factives in certain types of configuration mentioned in the QUD-based approach.

(28) Q: Was Paul at work yesterday?
     A1: Probably not. His boss did not observe/see/notice he was in his office.
     A2: Probably not. His boss (is not aware/doesn't remember) he was in his office.
     A3: ??Probably not. His boss doesn't know/regret he was in his office.
     A4: Probably yes. His boss didn't realize he was in his office.

In contrast to A1 and A2, where the most likely interpretations exclude projection, projection is obligatory with A3 and A4, resulting in a hardly interpretable answer in A3.[6] It is difficult to reconcile this kind

---

[6]See also examples (38) and (39) in Peters (2016).

of observation with the reasoning proposed by Simons et al. (2011: ex. (24)) that, in an appropriate context, projection can be blocked with 'x does not know that p' because, if p was the case, x would know it.[7] Although the inference makes perfect sense, it cannot override the preference for projection with full factives. French is interesting because it marks the difference in projection with mood and register. In (29), the indicative version A1 is strongly deviant whereas the subjunctive version A2 is possible but quite formal.[8] The subjunctive marking is clearly related to ignorance or uncertainty, as attested by cognate constructions like *que je sache*$_{\text{PRES-SUBJ}}$, meaning *to my knowledge, as far as I know* and *pour autant que je sache* (lit. 'as much as I know$_{\text{PRES-SUBJ}}$'). This a well-known association in many languages (Godard 2012, Giannakidou 2016) and it is striking that languages like French exploit it to *conventionalize* projection for full factives, which indicates that projection cannot be reduced to pragmatics.

(29) Q: Est-ce que   Paul était au travail hier?
         INTERROG-MARKER Paul was at work yesterday
         'Was Paul at work yesterday?'

   A1: *Je ne   sais   pas qu' il était
        I EXPL-NEG know-PRES-IND not that he was
        dans son bureau.
        in   his office
        'I don't know he was in his office.'

   A2: Je ne   sache   pas qu' il était
        I EXPL-NEG know-PRES-SUBJ not that he was
        dans son bureau.
        in   his office
        'I have no evidence that he was in his office.'

The last problem concerns the 'knowability' property of the complement of factives. First, one might argue, like Karttunen, that such a property involves some circularity. If we can only know knowable, hence true-to-fact, contents, the veridical character of such attitudes seems to derive from the very concept of knowing, independently from the linguistic term. Otherwise, we would have to assume that the relation between truth and knowledge is conventionalized in language, which would amount to saying that *know* presupposes the truth of the

---

[7]Note also that the reasoning makes crucial use of the main content.

[8]The subjunctive is also possible in the embedded clause with semi-factives and excludes projection: *Je n'ai pas observé qu'il [ait été]$_{\text{PAST-SUBJ}}$ dans son bureau*, 'I didn't observe he was in his office'.

known content, and drive us back to the phenomenon we are supposed to explain. If language just provides a label for the concept of knowing, and this concept entails the truth of the object of knowledge, we have to posit a difference in some dimension between knowing and observing, seeing, etc., possibly on the basis of semantic differences between the verbs, a program which has yet to be carried out, see Turri (2013) for a related problem.

4 The Role of the Main Content

Taking stock, we have seen that the QUD-based approach faces two kinds of problems: (i) The attempt to predict projection on the basis of the absence of Obligatory Local Effect is not (entirely) successful (see *too* and similar discourse markers) and (ii) the claim that QUD-addressing content cannot project is not supported by certain observations.

However, rejecting the QUD-based approach altogether is not the move we would recommend, because the approach offers two important ideas that advance our understanding of projection. There is indeed a strong connection between Local Effect and projection as well as between QUD-addressing and projection properties. In this section, we propose to diagnose the source of the difficulties of the QUD-based approach and to reconfigure it accordingly, in order to preserve the major insights on which it is based.

4.1 When is Projection 'Obligatory'?

The operators that apply to sentences containing presupposition triggers and make projection manifest (negation, interrogation, possibility modals) can target two different types of semantic form. For convenience, we represent the main content-presupposition combination as a pair of the form ⟨ main content,presupposition ⟩. When a trigger combines with its complement (modulo argument structure) or target (for modifiers), there are basically two possibilities: either the 'logical' form (= combinatory potential) of the trigger puts semantic constraints on the main content or it does not.[9] To illustrate, consider the forms associated with *stop*, *know*, *only* and *too* as NP modifiers. Superficially, they are similar, i.e. they are functional lambda-terms expecting a property (P) or a proposition (p) at some point and returning a (possibly quantified) main content-presupposition pair where the property or proposition occurs on the left and on the right. So, they have a general form: $\dots \lambda X \dots \mathcal{Q} \langle \phi(X), \psi(X) \rangle$, where X is of type P or p and $\mathcal{Q}$

---

[9]We follow here Jayez (2015) but we modify his criterion of *separation*.

is a (possibly empty) sequence of quantifiers. We present the forms in a simple (syntax : semantics) categorial format.

(30) a. **stop**: $(NP\backslash S)/VP : \lambda P\lambda x \cdot \exists t\langle after(t, \neg P(x)), before(t, P(x))\rangle$

b. **know**: $(NP\backslash S)/that\text{-}S : \lambda p\lambda x \cdot \langle is\text{-}certain(x, p), p\rangle$

c. **only-NP**: $(S/VP)/NP : \lambda x\lambda P \cdot \langle \forall y((y \neq x) \Rightarrow \neg P(y)), P(x)\rangle$

d. **too**: $NP\backslash(S/VP) : \lambda x\lambda P \cdot \langle P(x), \exists y\,(y \neq x \wedge P(x))\rangle$.

On closer look, the structure for *too* is different because there is no constraint on P in the main content part. The constraint $\exists y\,(y \neq x \wedge P(x))$ is in the presupposition part. We get a similar picture with a discourse marker like *therefore*, for which the consequence constraint is in the presupposition part (31).

(31) **therefore** : $S/S : \lambda p \cdot \langle p, \exists p'\ Consequence\text{-}of(p, p')\rangle$

Empirically, it seems that non-projection is difficult whenever the main content part does not contain any particular semantic constraint.[10] If this is on the right track, we would expect that, if there are triggers that lack any information 'about' the main content, they strongly tend to project. Indeed, such triggers exist and can help us to clarify the notion of aboutness we need.

A particularly striking case concerns *hic et nunc particles* (HNPs) studied for French in Dargnat (forthcoming). HNPs are those discourse markers that refer to circumstantial information only available at utterance time, such as mental events affecting the speaker, external events or discourse events. They signal mainly emotional reactions or epistemic stages of the speaker, action scheduling, hesitations and reformulations. They have specific prosodic features, which help identify them automatically in speech corpora (Dargnat, Bartkova & Jouvet 2015). Standard examples are *Aïe!, Ouille! (Ouch!), bon (≈well), hein (≈ right?), tu parles! (You bet!), Zut! (Oops!)*, etc. HNPs fall in the more general category of *use-conditional* items, that is, items that must be characterized by their usage, not by their contribution to the truth conditions of the sentence (Gutzman 2015).

Like most conventional implicature triggers, HNPs systematically project but, in addition, they cannot be embedded in a non-immediate perspective, in contrast with some expressives, like those in (32). In this respect they could be considered as Anti Local Effect items, which occupy the endpoint of the scale shown in Table 1.

---

[10]We ignore here the metalinguistic cases, where one manipulates the focus, as noted in Section 3.1(v).

(32) a. A l'époque,   Paul pensait   que son fichu métier
At that time Paul thought   that his damn job

finirait   par le   tuer.
would end up   by   him kill-INF.

'At that time, Paul thought that his damn job
would end up killing him.'

b. #A l'époque,   Paul pensait   que son métier
At that time   Paul thought   that his job

finirait   par le   tuer   merde!
would end up   by   him kill-INF shit!

'At that time, Paul thought that his damn job
would end up killing him shit!'

Table 1 A (very partial) scale of projection.

Category	Main Content	Presup.	Conventional Impl.	HNP
Obl. Loc. Eff.	—	Yes in general	Variable	No
Projection	—	Variable	Robust	Obligatory

In order to illustrate more concretely the inner workings of HNPs, we describe the case of the particle *quoi* in sentence-final position. *Quoi* signals that the speaker has no better option than to use the sentence to which the particle is adjoined. This is illustrated in (33).

(33) Et puis je commence à chanter des trucs un peu hyper cul-cul **quoi** et genre euh j'écris le texte et je le regarde je le lis je dis putain mais c'est trop cul-cul **quoi** (...) Mais mon dieu la meuf c'est une psychopathe **quoi**
(Izia Higelin, interview on France Info, 11 July 2012)
'Next, I start singing things that are a bit corny QUOI and like uh I write the lyrics I look at them and I say fuck! it's too corny QUOI Oh my God, the chick, she is a psychopath QUOI'

It is often associated with an implicature of reluctance: although the speaker is not spontaneously willing to say that p, for instance because she is afraid of sounding blunt, rude or somehow offensive, she nonetheless resolves to do so because she is unable to find a more adequate characterization. One might assimilate *quoi* to a standard conventional implicature trigger, assigning to it a structure like (34), where we use a triple $\langle$ main content, presupposition, conventional implicature $\rangle$ and a scale σ of relative adequacy for propositions.

(34) **quoi**: S\S : $\lambda p \,.\, \langle p, NIL, \forall p'(p \geq_\sigma p') \rangle$

However, this puts *quoi* on a par with expressives like *the damn* N, evaluative/epistemic adverbs like *fortunately* or *unexpectedly*, or German epistemic modal particles like *ja, doch*, etc. (Karagjosova 2003), and fails to capture its *hic et nunc* specificity. Actually, although *quoi* is syntactically a sentential adjunct, it is not a direct modifier of the proposition expressed by S, and, so, is not reducible to (34) or similar forms. *Quoi* communicates that the speaker *decides* to use the clause she uses and does not draw attention to the content of the clause per se but to the *process* of selection of the clause. This is what makes *quoi* an HNP, an element which refers to an event of mental elaboration in the spatio-temporal immediate vicinity of an utterance. More generally, having HNPs bearing on utterance-proximal events accounts for a pervasive intuition in the literature on interjections, namely that interjections encode reactions to the situation and not (just) judgments (Ducrot 1984, Wharton 2003, Świątkowska 2006).

We assume that HNPs are associated with 'objective' updates. Standard updates are usually partitioned into different types. The main content is associated with an update of the information state representing the common ground, the non-main content with an update of another type of information state. These differences can be related to different intentions, an intention to influence the addressees and make them modify the common ground vs. an intention of publicizing some piece of information, speaker-centered (expressives, evaluative adverbs) or not (non-restrictive relative clauses, presuppositions).[11] HNPs do not correspond to communicative intentions. They are not 'invisible', though. They are part of the linguistic code and can be processed by addressees but they are not conventionally associated with a communicative intention, although intentions of obtaining some effect can be inferentially ascribed to a speaker in a given context. In terms of update, HNPs are comparable to external events, observable phenomena produced and possibly controlled by the speaker, accessible but not addressed to the hearers. We propose that HNPs give rise to automatic updates of the common ground, like any other mutually manifest event and can be described by their conditions of use (which keeps them in the category of conventional markers).[12]

---

[11]We remain agnostic as to whether a rendition in terms of particular (non-propositional) updates (see e.g. Murray 2014) or communicative intentions, along the lines of Ginzburg (2012), is to be preferred.

[12]To wit, for *quoi*, the semantics would be:
$\lambda p.\langle p, NIL, utter(speaker, p, t_u) \wedge BEL(speaker, \forall p'(p \geq_S p'))\rangle$, where t_u is utterance time. The conventional implicature includes the action of voicing p at utterance time as well as a belief about the relative value of p.

To sum up, there are at least two cases. (i) A part of the meaning of the form affects the main content and non-projection can occur, (ii) the meaning does not affect the main content and non-projection is strongly restricted or virtually impossible (HNPs).

4.2 Skipping the Main Content?

In this section, we argue that some of the difficulties noted for the QUD-based approach stem from an absence of distinction between the *at-issue* content and the main content. As its name indicates, the at-issue content corresponds to that part of the content which addresses the QUD. It is perfectly true, as already acknowledged in (Ducrot 1972), that the presupposition can address the QUD. More importantly, it is perfectly true, contra Ducrot, that the presupposition can be in such cases the more important piece of information (Simons 2007), as in (3-A2), repeated below. Finally, it is also perfectly true that, in many cases, a presupposition that addresses the QUD does *not* project because this would conflict with the most plausible interpretation of the conversational exchange, as in (4).

(3) Q: Who broke the window pane?

   A1: It's Paul.

   A2: Anna noticed it's Paul.

(4) Q: Is it Paul who broke the window pane?

   A: I didn't notice that Paul was around.

However, in Section 3.2 we mentioned some examples where the presupposition is at-issue and projects. We can account for them in exactly the same terms as for (4): assuming that the presupposition projects delivers the right interpretation. At first sight, this suggests that all that matters is pragmatics. Whether projection or non-projection is preferred depends on which one contributes to the most plausible scenario for addressing the QUD. In fact, this simple approach has to be seriously qualified.

First, as noted in Section 3.2 with respect to Karttunen's (1971) observations on factives, lexical preferences can complicate the picture and pragmatics does not override them. Second, as argued in Jayez (2015) from a different perspective, QUD-addressing is subject to Ducrot's (1972) *Linking Law* (*loi d'enchaînement* in French), which says, roughly speaking, that one cannot attach a constituent to the presupposition *alone* through a causal or opposition discourse relation, or, equivalently, that one cannot 'shunt' the main content with such relations. For example, whereas (35a) is a perfectly normal sentence where not having caviar (the main content) is explained by the price of caviar, (35b) is obscure and cannot mean that Paul had caviar because he liked it.

(35) a. Paul stopped having caviar for breakfast because it's expensive.

b. #Paul stopped having caviar for breakfast because he liked it.

The function of any relevant answer to the QUD is to influence the probability of some subset of alternatives. In the spirit of Ducrot, we assume that, whatever the contextual conditions are, (i) the main content *must* play some role in this process and (ii), in contrast, this involvement is not obligatory for the non-main content, in particular the presupposition. This difference is apparent in examples like (36). Answer A1 entails that the responder is not subscribed and presupposes that she was subscribed four years ago. The presupposition is not relevant to Q. It is not felt as totally irrelevant (a *non sequitur*) because it could address a potential question (when did you stop your subscription?) about a super-topic (the general status of the addressee's subscription). However, it is not connected to the explicit topic (the existence of a current subscription) or any other explicit piece of information and constitutes a sort of supplement. Replacing A1 with *I am not subscribed* is possible without altering the question-answer relation. A2 is more difficult to interpret because, although the presupposition addresses the QUD, the main content is not easily related to Q. A possible interpretation is that, for some reason, the responder adds a supplemental indication of her state of mind about the situation, but this could be perceived as peripheral with respect to the QUD. A3 sounds irrelevant. The presupposition addresses the QUD but the main content hangs around without contributing to making a possible answer to the QUD more or less plausible.[13]

(36) Q: Are you currently subscribed to the journal? It would get you a discount for the proceedings.

A1: I stopped my subscription four years ago.

A2: I am glad I am not subscribed.

A3: #My friends don't know/know I am subscribed.

---

[13]Spelling out what 'plausible' means requires that one develop a notion of (probabilistic) dependence. Probabilistic dependence could be analyzed for instance in the framework of *confirmation theory* (Fitelson 2001), which states that p is positively (resp. negatively) relevant to p' with respect to some function ϕ over probabilities iff $\phi(\mathsf{Pr}(p), \mathsf{Pr}(p')) > 0$ (resp. < 0). Classic examples for ϕ include $\mathsf{Pr}(p'|p) - \mathsf{Pr}(p')$ or the log-likelihood difference $\log(\mathsf{Pr}(p|p')/\mathsf{Pr}(p|\neg p'))$. We will not discuss the different limit conditions and possible options here.

(37) *Generalized Linking Law* (GLL)
> If a constituent A is attached to another constituent Q by a Question-Answer relation, the main content of A must be relevant to a subset of the alternatives associated with Q.

This asymmetry between main content and non-main content distinguishes between a purely pragmatic approach, which would predict –correctly– that the network of probabilistic dependencies varies with context, and a semantic approach, which makes room for context, but posits a fundamental asymmetry between main content and non-main content. What are the consequences for projection? Along the lines of Ducrot and given the GLL, the main content is always at issue (relevant to the QUD) and, given the Projection Equation (11.3), never projects. The presupposition can address the QUD. In that case, it can project or not, depending on the plausibility preferences (pragmatics), the lexical constraints (semantics, see the case of full factives) and the general requirement that the main content must address the QUD (GLL). In particular it is possible for a presupposition to address the QUD and project when the main content-presupposition combination is relevant to the QUD, see the examples discussed in Section 3.2. However, when a non-main content content does not address the QUD, it *must* project because there is nothing to interfere with the default projective behavior of non-main content. So, at-issueness determines the necessity of non-projection, not the necessity of projection: QUD-irrelevance entails projection but QUD-relevance does not entail non-projection.

5   Conclusion

In this paper, we have provided a critical examination of a recent and influential theory about projection, the QUD-based theory. Our goal in carrying out this task was not to evaluate the theory in itself but rather to contribute to an analysis of pragmatics-driven approaches, which the QUD-based approach illustrates in a powerful and articulate way.

We have reached the conclusion that the main claim of the QUD-based approach, i.e. an equivalence between non-projection and QUD-addressing, has to be weakened and replaced by an entailment from not addressing the QUD to projecting. In other terms, the content which does not address the QUD *must* project and that which addresses the QUD *can* project, depending on a set of (sometimes complex) factors.

In doing so, we have retained a fundamental insight of the QUD-based theory, the importance of context and, more precisely, of the relation to the QUD in predicting projection. In a nutshell, a presupposition projects or not according to what the most plausible QUD-addressing scenario is. We have also claimed (Section 4.1) that projection is strongly preferred or obligatory whenever the trigger makes no specific contribution to the main content in addition to the minimal compositional structure (see the case of HNPs analyzed in Section 4.1). Taken together, this aspect and the equivalence between not-addressing the QUD and necessarily projecting suggests that semantic material that has no direct (addressing) or indirect (via lexical content) access to the QUD projects most of the time. More work is needed to assess the robustness of this hypothesis. This entails, in particular, extending the empirical observations to include more complex conversational exchanges and a richer notion of QUD, see Ginzburg (2012).

Acknowledgements

We gratefully acknowledge the contribution of an anonymous reviewer and those of Olivier Bonami and Robert Reinecke, whose many perspicuous questions and remarks helped us to improve this text in a (hopefully) significant way.

8

Quantification in Oneida

JEAN-PIERRE KOENIG AND KARIN MICHELSON

When writing a comprehensive grammar of a language, there is a set of structures or phenomena one is expected to talk about: argument structure, relative clauses, coreference and binding, unbounded dependencies and extraction, negation, and so on. One is also expected to discuss semantic notions, chief among them being quantification. But oftentimes, and inevitably, the analysis of the language follows from what is most common or best known. In some cases the typical has been reified into the universal, and it is assumed that the syntactic structures, the mapping between syntax and semantics, or the meaning expressed by lexical items or constructions are the same across languages. Even in typologically oriented studies, the deck is stacked against finding truly unusual structures, since the descriptive vocabulary presumes universality of the vocabulary's applicability, sometimes without that presupposition being explicit. In this chapter we discuss a case in point, quantification in Oneida (Northern Iroquoian), against rather standard assumptions in the literature on quantification. Two questions are at the forefront of our investigation into the Oneida grammar of quantification:

1. What is the range of ways that languages encode quantification over entities?

2. Does the particular choice that a language makes limit non-periphrastic expressiveness?

Early cross-linguistic research in the 90s by Bach, Jelinek, Kratzer, Partee and others (see Bach et al. 1995) suggested that how much quantification over entities is done via something like determiners (so-called

Constraint-Based Syntax and Semantics: Papers in Honor of Danièle Godard.
Anne Abeillé and Olivier Bonami (eds.).

D-quantification) or indirectly via something like adverbs (so-called A-quantification) varies across languages. But it is widely believed that this division between D- and A-quantification does not affect expressibility. In other words, languages may vary to the extent they make use of D- or A-quantification, but critically they all include quantifiers that denote relations between sets, what has come to be known as generalized quantifiers after the pioneering work of Barwise & Cooper (1981). As Peters & Westerståhl (2006: 12) put it:

> So far as is known, all languages have expressions for type $< 1, 1 >$ quantifiers, though some languages have been claimed not to have any expressions for type $< 1 >$ quantifiers.

The sentence in (1) and the two possible semantic representations of (1) in (2) illustrate $< 1, 1 >$ quantifiers. (2a) is a simplified representation of the meaning of (1) if *three* is treated as a generalized quantifier. *Three* denotes a relation between the set denoted by what *three* combines with (a set of women) and the meaning of the VP (a set of entities that left). Note that this analysis of number names as denoting relations between sets differs from what we learn in basic arithmetic, where number names denote numbers (themselves defined as properties of sets). (2b) provides a simplified representation of the meaning sentence (1) would receive under this alternative view.[1]

(1)   Three women left.

(2)   a.   *Generalized Quantifiers*: $|W \cap L| = 3$
      b.   *Basic Arithmetic*: $\exists s(s \subset W \wedge |s| = 3 \wedge L(s))$

The difference between D- and A-quantification does not exhaust morphosyntactic variation in the expression of quantification, though. In particular, Oneida almost exclusively uses clauses headed by count verbs to express quantification over entities. A few other languages have been reported to use morphological verbs (sometimes defective verbs) to express quantification (e.g. Chickasaw, Munro 2017; Chocktaw, Broadwell 2006; Kallalisut, Bittner & Trondhjem 2008; San Lucas Quaviní Zapotec, Lee 2008), but the extent to which verbs are used in

---

[1]Several scholars have proposed a different analysis of the meaning of cardinal numbers in English and some other languages, see Landman (1996) and Krifka (1999), among others. It is not critical to the point of our paper to decide which analysis is correct, as long as *some* determiners are analyzed as generalized quantifiers. We illustrate our point with cardinal quantifiers, as these are present in both Oneida and English whereas there do not seem to be proportional quantifiers in Oneida, as we discuss below.

Oneida seems rather unique, as it is almost the exclusive way to express quantification over entities, with one semantically circumscribed exception we discuss below. The questions we ask in this paper are the following:

1. How do we compose the right quantificational meaning when quantification is expressed by clauses headed by count verbs?

2. Does the expression of quantification over entities with count verbs and count clauses make a difference in the kind of quantification notions that can be expressed?

The gist of our answers to these questions is that the mode of composition in Oneida is constructional and conjunctive; consequently Oneida uses the basic arithmetic strategy to express quantification and this strategy leads to some restrictions on expressibility. Before providing detailed answers to these questions, in the next couple of sections we describe in some detail (but for reasons of space leaving out material not relevant to this paper) how quantification is expressed in Oneida.

1 Overview of Quantification in Oneida

1.1 (Mostly) Exact Cardinality

To understand better how quantification over entities is expressed in Oneida, in (3) is given the basic structure of verbs.[2] (3a) represents the structure of Oneida verbs (see Lounsbury 1953). The verb base is the output of derivational processes, including noun incorporation. To a verb base is suffixed an aspect suffix, and the resulting structure is inflected with a pronominal prefix, which can reference up to two animate arguments. The pronominal prefix may be preceded (optionally) by a sequence of up to five prepronominal prefixes. (There are eleven prepronominal prefixes in all, and their distribution and form is quite complex.) The structure of the base is given in (3b). It is not uncommon for a base to include an incorporated noun as well as several derivational (or "root" suffixes) and a (semi-)reflexive prefix. Both incorporated nouns and three prepronominal prefixes (the repetitive, dualic or duplicative, and partitive) figure prominently in expressions of quantity.

---

[2]We use the traditional terms *verb* and *noun* throughout this paper for ease of understanding. But as mentioned in Koenig & Michelson (2014), we know of no evidence for syntactic parts of speech in Oneida; moreover the necessary morphological classification of roots and stems in Oneida does not fit the standard notions of verbs or nouns. So we will use the terms *verb* and *noun* as shorthands to mean a lexical item describing a situation and entity, respectively (whether a base, stem, or word).

(3)   a.   [$_{\text{WORD}}$ prepro-pro-[$_{\text{STEM}}$ base-asp]]

     b.   [$_{\text{BASE}}$ refl-base$_{\text{N}}$-root$_{\text{V}}$-inch-caus-rev-instr-ben-distr-disloc]

It is interesting that the expression of cardinality in Oneida, despite being expressed through verbal means, nevertheless varies with animacy and number, i.e. morphological restrictions on verbs are like grammatical number on nouns (singular, dual, plural) in other languages.

One entity. To count a single entity the root *-t-* '(be) one' is used, together with the repetitive prepronominal prefix *s-* or *ts-*. What is being counted is expressed via an incorporated noun: *-yaʔt-/-yá·t-* 'body' for animates in (4) and (5), and *-lʌn-* 'song' in (6).[3] A "joiner" (JN) vowel *a* occurs between a consonant-final noun root and a consonant-initial verb root. In addition the verb selects the Agent category of pronominal prefixes.[4] In examples (4) and (5) what is being counted are animate entities; animate arguments are referenced via pronominal prefixes, and so the verb forms express typical ϕ properties of what is being counted, i.e. person and number, as well as gender—masculine, feminine-indefinite, or feminine-zoic—for third

---

[3] Abbreviations used in this paper are A agent, BEN benefactive, CAUS causative, CSL cislocative, DISLOC dislocative, DISTR distributive, DL dualic (or duplicative), DP dual-plural or non-singular, DU dual, EX exclusive, FACT factual, FI feminine-indefinite, FUT future, FZ feminine-zoic, HAB habitual, INCH inchoative, INSTR instrumental, JN joiner vowel, M masculine, NEG negative, NSF noun suffix, OPT optative, P patient, PART partitive, PL plural, PNC punctual, POSS possessive, REFL reflexive, REP repetitive, REV reversative, SG singular, SRF semi-reflexive, STV stative, TRL translocative. Feminine-zoic is a gender, used for some females and animals (see Abbott 1984, Michelson 2015). The 3rd person feminine-zoic singular pronominal prefix serves as a default whenever a verb does not reference any animate semantic arguments; the default prefix is abbreviated Z/N. The symbol > indicates a proto-agent acting on a proto-patient; for example, 3M.SG>1SG should be understood as 3rd person masculine singular acting on 1st person singular. A bare numeral 3, unaccompanied by any number or gender, can reference 3rd person feminine singular, 3rd person indefinite, 3rd person masculine dual or plural, and 3rd person feminine-zoic dual or plural semantic arguments. In the interlinear glosses of excerpts from texts, not every particle is glossed separately. ʌ is a low-mid, central unrounded nasalized vowel, and u is a high or (for some speakers, close to mid) back mildly rounded nasalized vowel. A raised period indicates vowel length. Underlining indicates segments which are devoiced due to a set of phonological changes that take place at the ends of utterances. Excerpts are drawn from a collection of texts published in Michelson, Kennedy & Doxtator (2016). Unattributed examples come from Michelson's notes with the late Mercy Doxtator and the late Norma Kennedy.

[4] Pronominal prefixes are either transitive, referencing two animate arguments, or intransitive. Intransitive prefixes belong to two paradigm classes, Agent and Patient. These two categories are semantically motivated but also, at times, semantically unpredictable and an idiosyncratic property of verbs. See Michelson (1991) and Koenig & Michelson (2015b) for discussion.

person prefixes. Since what is being counted in (6) is inanimate, a default feminine-zoic/neuter singular pronominal prefix occurs. Note that he occurrence of the name for the number one, *úska*, is not allowed.

(4) s-ha-yá·t-a-t
REP-3M.SG.A-body-JN-be.one[STV]
'one male person'

(5) ts-ye-yá·t-a-t
REP-3FI.A-body-JN-be.one[STV]
'one female person, one person'

(6) s-ka-lʌ·n-á-t
REP-3Z/N.SG.A-song-JN-be.one[STV]
'one song'

Two entities. Two entities are counted with the verb roots *-ke-* 'amount to' and *-yashe-* 'be together', plus the dualic (duplicative) prepronominal prefix. The root *-ke-* is used mostly for inanimate entities, as in (7), and *-yashe-* is used exclusively for animate entities, as in (8). What is being counted is expressed via an incorporated noun with *-ke-* and with an independent nominal (but only if that much detail is needed) with *-yashe-*. Note again that the occurrence of the number name, *tékni* 'two', is not allowed.

(7) tahnú· oyá·   te-ka-hu·w-á-ke
and   another DL-3Z/N.SG.A-boat-JN-amount.to[STV]
t-u-t-u-táyaht-e?,
DL-FACT-CSL-FACT:3Z/N.SG.A-enter-PNC
'and another two boats [filled with tobacco leaves] came in,'
    (Olive Elm, Learning to Work in Tobacco, recorded 1998)

(8) Te-hni-yáshe   ni-hwánhak-s,
DL-3M.DU.A-together[STV] 3M.DU.A-tie-HAB
'Two (persons) are tying (tobacco leaves),'
    (Mercy Doxtator, All About Tobacco, recorded 1998)

Three or more entities. Three verb roots are used for counting three or more entities: *-ke-* 'amount to', used only for inanimates (9) and (10); *-i-* 'make up the total of', used only for animates (11); and *-u-* 'be a certain amount', used for both animates and inanimates.[5] All three require the partitive prepronominal prefix. The precise number of entities is expressed externally to the verb form by a number word or

---

[5]For inanimates, the defective, and frozen, verb form *nikú* is used. It includes the partitive prefix *ni-* and a defective pronominal prefix *k-*.

the vague term *tóhka?* 'a few'. The structure used to express a quantity that exceeds two entities, i.e. a root plus the partitive prefix, differs from the structure for expressing a quantity equal to one or two entities in that those roots, with either the repetitive or dualic prefix, disallow the external expression of number.

(9)   Áhsʌ ni-ka-lʌ·n-á-ke
      three PART-3Z/N.SG.A-song-JN-amount.to[STV]
      ʌ-w-at-lʌn-o·t-ʌ́·,
      FUT-3Z/N.SG.A-SRF-song-stand-PNC

      'It (the Nickelodeon) will play three songs,'
                          (Olive Elm, Friday Nights, recorded 2005)

(10) Tóhka? s kwí· ni-ka-ya·l-á-ke
      a few   PART-3Z/N.SG.A-bag-JN-amount.to[STV]
      wa?-akwa-yʌ́t<u>ho-?</u>.
      FACT-1EX.PL.A-plant-PNC

      'We planted a few bags [of potatoes].'
              (Georgina Nicholas, An Oneida Childhood, recorded 1981)

(11) áhsʌ se?   né·   ni-hat-í
      three emphatic assertion PART-3M.PL.A-total[STV]
      t-a-hʌ·<u>n-é·</u>.
      CSL-FACT-3M.PL.A-come:PNC

      'three (Santa Clauses) are coming.'
          (Verland Cornelius, A Lifetime of Memories, recorded 1995)

The count verb *-ke* 'amount', with the translocative and dualic (and optionally partitive) prepronominal prefixes, and usually preceded by the emphatic particle *kwáh*, is used to express what is closest in Oneida to 'every'.

(12) Kwáh   n-y-a?te-ka-núhs-a-ke
      emphatic PART-TRL-DL-3Z/N.SG.A-house-JN-amount.to[STV]
      o?slu·ní·   tho   lat-í·<u>tlu-?</u>.
      white person there 3M.PL.A-reside-STV

      'Every house there's a white person living there.'

1.2 Vague Quantifiers

The equivalent of 'many' is expressed by verb stems, including *-eʔtowanʌ-* 'big pile' and *-ityohkwanʌ-* 'big group' (both based on the root *-owanʌ-* */-kwanʌ-* 'big, large'), and *-nakl(e)-* 'be plentiful'. Since the quantity involved is always larger than two, these stems combine with the partitive prepronominal prefix *ni-*. The sentence in (13) exemplifies the first stem.

(13) Né·   kiʔ   ok   thikʌ́ ké·yale?   tsiʔ
     assertion actually only that I remember that
     ni-yaw-eʔt-owanʌ́   osahé·taʔ ísiʔ
     PART-3Z/N.SG.P-pile-large[STV] bean(s)   yonder
     y-aʔ-on-áti-ʔ.
     TRL-FACT-3FZ.DP.P-throw-PNC

'I only remember what a large amount of beans they [my sister and her friend] threw away.'

(Norma Kennedy, Worms in the Soup, recorded 2009)

1.3 Expression of Quantity with Possession

In all the cases we mentioned above, quantification is expressed by a verb and a pronominal prefix. Interestingly, the presence of a count verb is not required to quantify over the number of entities when the entities are possessed. (14) illustrates the expected pattern where the root *-yashe-* '(be) together' plus the dualic prepronominal prefix is used to quantify over two animate beings. (15) exemplifies a pattern specific to possession; in this case the number word *tékni* 'two' combines directly with the verb of possession *-yʌ-*. Note that whereas (14) follows the usual ban on the external expression of a number name with the repetitive or dualic prefix when one or two entities are involved, in (15) *tékni* 'two' co-occurs with the dualic prepronominal prefix *te-* in the possession-specific pattern.

(14) te-hni-yáshe   kʌs
     DL-3M.DU.A-together[STV]   habitually
     wak-nʌskw-a-yʌ-t-áhkweʔ   é·lhal.
     1SG.P-animal-JN-have-STV:PAST   dog(s)

'I used to have two pet dogs.'

(Mercy Doxtator, My Dog Blackie, recorded 1995)

(15) Né·   ki?   uhte wí· aolí·wa? tékni ok
assertion in fact probably why   two   only
te-yako-wi·l-á-y$\land$-?.
DL-3FI.P-child-JN-have-STV

'It's probably why she has only two children.'
(Pearl Cornelius, Family and Friends, recorded 1993)

There is also a verb root -ka?te-/-ká·te- 'have many' whose meaning entails both possession and quantity.

(16) Tahnú· k$\land$s   aksótha
and   usually my grandmother
yako-tsi?tsy-a-ká·te-?   k$\land$s.
3FI.P-flower-JN-have.many-STV usually

'My grandmother used to have a lot of plants.'
(Verland Cornelius, A Lifetime of Memories, recorded 1995)

1.4 Comparison

To talk about a relatively greater state or condition, Oneida uses particles (sáha? 'more' in both "positively oriented" or "negatively oriented" direction, i.e. 'more' or 'less' in English, e·só· 'many, much, lots, very', só·tsi? 'very much, too much') as well as a construction with a verbal prepronominal prefix, the cislocative (CSL) t-, as illustrated in (17) and (18).

(17) Sáha? la-hn$\land$·yés   tsi? ní·
more 3M.SG.A-tall[STV] than me
ni·-y-ót.
PART-3Z/N.SG.A-be.a.way/kind[STV]

'He is taller than I am, as compared with me.'

(18) Tahnú· t-yukwa-nuhs-atho·lé·   sá·,
and   CSL-1PL.P-house-cold:STV also

'And our house was so cold, the coldest,'
(Clifford Cornelius, A Lifetime Working, recorded 1994)

The particles sáha? 'more', só·tsi? 'very much, too much' can also be used to compare numbers of entities, as shown in (19). A particle sequence, which consists of ísi? 'yonder, right there' and nú·, which occurs commonly in combination with other particles involving location, can also be used to express comparison (20)–(21); in this case the verb of the main clause usually has the partitive prefix, as is common with verbs that occur in a locative or temporal context.

(19) Te-ka-naʔtal-a-ké   sʌhaʔ e·só·
      DL-3Z/N.SG.A-bread-JN-amount.to[STV] more lots
      waʔ-k-atu·ní·   tsiʔ nisé· ni·yót.
      FACT-1SG.A-make:PNC than you how it is
      'I made two pies more than you did.'

(20) Ísiʔ nú· n-aʔ-k-ahy-a-hni·nú·   tsiʔ nisé·
      further PART-FACT-1SG.A-fruit-JN-buy:PNC than you
      ni·yót.
      how it is
      'I bought more apples than you did.'

(21) Úska ísiʔ nú· n-aʔ-k-ahy-a-hni·nú·
      one   further PART-FACT-1SG.A-fruit-JN-buy:PNC
      (oʔnhúhsaʔ).
      (egg)
      'I bought one too many (eggs).'

The notions 'less' and 'too little' are rendered with *sʌhaʔ* 'more' together with the form *nikúha*, which consists of *nikú* 'amount' plus the diminutive ending *-ha*, and a a particle *kʌʔ* that otherwise means '(right) here' but in this case has been lexicalized with *nikúha* in the expressions *sʌhaʔ kʌʔ nikúha* 'less, fewer', and *só·tsiʔ kʌʔ nikúha* 'too little' (22).

(22) s-anúhte-ʔ   kʌ   úhkaʔ ok náhteʔ sʌhaʔ kʌʔ nikúha
      2SG.P-know-STV QUES someone   more small amount
      lo·-yʌ́·   Grade 6 education,
      3M.SG.P-have:STV Grade 6 education,

      'do you know (of) someone who has less than a Grade 6 education?'

                (Clifford Cornelius, A Lifetime Working, recorded 1994)

2   Analysis

The previous section described in broad outlines how to quantify over entities in Oneida. The overall descriptive generalizations are: (1) quantification over entities involves count verbs plus prepronominal prefixes and, in some cases, externally expressed number or quantity names, and (2) clauses expressing possession are exceptional in that a count verb is not needed (although allowed). In this section, we provide our analysis of these two generalizations and argue that Oneida does not have $< 1, 1 >$ quantificational expressions, i.e. expressions that denotes relations between two sets.

2.1   Some Relevant Major Constructions of Oneida

To better understand our analysis, it will be useful to have a brief
outline of the major syntactic constructions of Oneida. Since we have
discussed these in previous work (see Koenig & Michelson 2014, 2015b),
we provide only the bare bones of our analysis, glossing over details.
Readers are invited to consult the work we cite for more details. First,
there seem to be no formal features beyond the word level in Oneida.
That is to say, the attribute SYN, which in HPSG gathers together formal features relevant to model syntactically-restricted distribution of
expressions, is absent in the representation of Oneida signs. There is
an attribute MORPH, with a rich internal structure, within lexical signs
since Oneida has a very rich inflectional morphology (see Koenig &
Michelson 2015a, Diaz, Koenig & Michelson 2019). But morphological
features are the only formal features that are included in the representation of Oneida signs and they are appropriate only for lexical signs.
Other than MORPH, Oneida signs bear only semantic and pragmatic
properties, and their representations thus only include SEM and CON-
TEXT attributes. Because of the absence of syntactic features, the work
of putting together words or phrases is entirely left to constructions.
Two constructions are of particular relevance here, the predicate (and
dependents) construction and the internally-headed relative clause construction. We describe both of these below.

The predicate (and dependents) construction.   The *pred-cx* construction is described in (23). Because the structure of clauses is flatter
in Oneida than in English and because in principle a clause can consist
of just a verb (leaving aside the rather rich set of discourse particles that
occur in almost all main clauses in Oneida), there are quite a few antecedents in the conditional in (23). We only mention two here as they
are the only relevant ones (see Koenig & Michelson 2014 for a fuller
list). The obligatory daughter corresponds to what is a verb in English;
the second set of optional daughters corresponds to entity expressions
that, typically, further specify an argument of the head of clauses; the
third set of optional daughters corresponds to various scopal particles.
We assume here that the ordering of scope-sensitive operators in Oneida
is strictly left-to-right. It should be borne in mind though, that there
is often no clear evidence in Oneida for syntactically-determined scopal
relations. But to the extent there is, it seems to match a left-to-right
order. We use Lexical Resource Semantics to represent the meaning
of expressions (see Richter & Sailer 2004) and divide an expression's
semantic content into its internal context (the value of ICONT) and external content (the value of ECONT). For our purposes, and simplifying

somewhat, suffice it to say that the value of a clause's ECONT represents the scope-resolved meaning of the clause whereas the ICONT of each daughter in (24) represents its semantic contribution to the clause it is part of (e and s are sorts for indices that correspond to entities and situations, respectively). (Note that whenever possible, we will simplify semantic representations and only include one CONT attribute for ease of presentation.)

(23) A situation expression can consist of a situation-describing word (the semantic head) preceded by zero or more expressions and followed by zero or more expressions. The index of the whole is that of the situation-describing word and the semantic content of the whole is determined as follows:

    1. If a non-head daughter describes an entity, a location, a number ..., its index must be included in the content of the semantic head (co-indexed with one of the head's arguments or an argument of an argument ... of the head), and the content of the whole includes the conjunction of the content of the non-head daughter and (part of) the content of the head.

    2. If a non-head daughter is a scopal operator (e.g. negation) its argument must include the content of all expressions to its right that are scope sensitive.

    3. If ...

(24)
$$\begin{bmatrix} \text{IND} & \boxed{1}s \\ \text{ECONT} & \alpha \end{bmatrix} \rightarrow \left(\begin{bmatrix} \text{IND} & none \\ \text{ICONT} & Op(\beta) \end{bmatrix} \right)^* , \left(\begin{bmatrix} \text{IND} & \boxed{2}e \\ \text{ICONT} & \boxed{3} \end{bmatrix} \right)^* , \begin{bmatrix} \text{IND} & \boxed{1} \\ \text{ICONT} & \boxed{4}P(\boxed{1}, \ldots) \end{bmatrix}$$
$$\boxed{2} \lhd \boxed{4}; \ (\boxed{3} \wedge \boxed{5}) \lhd \alpha; \ \boxed{5} \lhd \boxed{4}; \ \alpha = leftmost(Op(\beta))$$

(*leftmost* selects the semantic content of the leftmost daughter that contributes a scope-sensitive operator)

Example (25a) illustrates the *pred-cx*, and its semantic representation is provided in (25b) (for simplicity we omit the semantic contribution of the non-bolded particles; we use sans-serif font for semantic representations). The oval boxed semantic representation corresponds to the semantic contribution of the entity expression, whereas the unboxed semantic representation corresponds to the semantic contribution of the predicate; shadowed boxed variables correspond to the index of semantic heads.

(25) a. **Lakeʔkʌ́ha Leo**, né·   kʌs   né·
my brother   Leo   assertion usually assertion
wa-h-atkátho-ʔ   thikʌ́ tsiʔ niwahsu·tés,
FACT-3M.SG.A-see-PNC that   during the night
'My brother Leo saw it during the night,'
(Rose Antone, What My Brother Leo Saw, recorded 2011)

b. $\left[\text{brother}'(\text{'I'}, \boxed{\text{x}}) \wedge \text{Leo}'(\boxed{\text{x}})\right] \wedge \text{see}'(\boxed{\text{s}}, \boxed{\text{x}}, \text{y})$

A few remarks on the subterm constraints included in (24) are in
order, as they affect scopal relations. Because nouns that specify properties of a semantic argument of a verb need not be a sister of the verb
(the semantic dependency can be unbounded), we use underspecification to model unbounded identification of entity variables (values of
IND) and the argument of the predicate they specify properties of. The
subterm constraint $\boxed{2} \triangleleft \boxed{4}$ in (24) only requires the index of the entity
expression to be a subterm of the meaning of the situation expression,
not an immediate argument of its meaning, thus accounting for the
unbounded semantic dependency that can exist between a noun and a
verb. The use of underspecification avoids the need to percolate indices,
the more conservative approach taken in Koenig & Michelson (2015b).
As we argue below, universal quantification also involves a verb and semantically all variables that are part of the semantic representation of
verbs are, implicitly, existentially quantified: They introduce into discourse an entity or set of entities. We thus treat the HPSG index of all
arguments of verbs and all nouns as free variables that are implicitly
existentially quantified via their anchoring to a model (à la DRT, see
Kamp & Reyle 1993). (24) is incomplete, particularly when it comes
to the relation between scopal operators and nouns, but, as the data
we have does not yet unambiguously choose among several competing
hypotheses, we cannot say more. At a minimum though, (24) suggests
that, leaving aside scopal operators, semantic composition in Oneida
consists in binding variables together (see Koenig & Michelson 2015b
and 2019 for qualifications on the binding of variables) and conjunction of semantic contents. (26) represents the various configurations of
combinations of semantic contents we have seen to date.

(26) a. $P(\ldots \boxed{\text{x}} \ldots) \wedge Q(\ldots \boxed{\text{x}}, \boxed{\text{y}}, \ldots) \wedge R(\ldots \boxed{\text{y}} \ldots)$
b. $P(\ldots \boxed{\text{x}}, \ldots) \wedge (\neg (Q(\ldots \boxed{\text{x}} \ldots)))$
c. $(\neg (P(\ldots \boxed{\text{x}}, \ldots))) \wedge Q(\ldots \boxed{\text{x}} \ldots)$

We end this overview by pointing out the role that variable identification plays in semantic composition in Oneida, i.e. in a language where semantic embedding of the kind found in English is less ubiquitous and a 'flatter' mode of semantic composition (conjunction of contents) is more prevalent. The importance of variable identification is something Quine stressed in his algebraic rethinking of predicate calculus.

> [T]he essential services of the variable are the permutation of predicate places and the linking of predicate places by identity. (Quine 1976: 304)

Internally-headed relative clause construction. The second major syntactic construction of Oneida relevant for this paper is the internally-headed relative clause construction. (There are other kinds of relative clauses in Oneida, in particular free relatives, but they are not of relevance in this paper.) The construction is informally stated in (27) and illustrated in (28a) (as mentioned earlier, shadowed box variables correspond to the index or discourse referent of semantic heads). The semantic content of the relative clause in (28a) is provided in (28b). The sole purpose of internally-headed relative clauses in a language with no syntactic features is to semantically type-shift an expression that would otherwise describe a situation (or a proposition, or a fact, ...) into an expression that describes an entity, location, ..., i.e. whatever the relevant argument (or adjunct) of the predicate of the clause describes. When applied to the bolded clause in sentence (28a), the *ihrc-cx* construction ensures that the clause describes the person that is small, i.e. an expression whose index can then be identified via the *pred-cx* construction with the person that does not want to eat.

(27) $\begin{bmatrix} \text{IND} & \boxed{1}e \\ \text{CONT} \boxed{2} \end{bmatrix} \rightarrow \begin{bmatrix} \text{IND} & s \\ \text{CONT} \boxed{2} P(\dots \boxed{1} \dots) \end{bmatrix}$

(28)   a.   yah né·   té·-yʌ-lh-eʔ?   a·-yu-tekhu·ní·
             not assertion NEG-3FI.A-want-STV OPT-3FI.A-eat:PNC
             kʌʔ niyaká·,
             she is little

             'the little one doesn't want to eat,'
                   (Olive Elm, Visits to My Auntie's, recorded 1993)

      b.   small′(s, $\boxed{x}$)

As we will see in the next section, the type-shifting effected by internally-headed relative clauses is what Oneida uses to encode quantification (see (29) and Koenig & Michelson 2012). It is the *ihrc-cx* construction that ensures that the index of the count clause *áhsʌ nikanláhtake* is the argument 'leaves' of the count verb *-ke-* in (29).

(29) Áhsʌ ni-ka-nláht-a-ke
      three PART-3Z/N.SG.A-leaf-JN-amount.to[STV]
      ʌ-té-s<u>k-u-</u>ʔ.
      FUT-CSL-2SG>1SG-give-PNC

      'The [tobacco] leaves that amount to three, you are to hand them to me.'
             (Olive Elm, Learning to Work in Tobacco, recorded 1998)

(30) a. **Áhsʌ nikanláhtake** ʌtés<u>k-u-</u>ʔ.
          'The [tobacco] leaves that amount to three, you are to hand them to me.' [You are to hand me three leaves]
          (Olive Elm, Learning to Work in Tobacco, recorded 1998)

      b. leaf′($\boxed{x}$)∧amount′(s, $\boxed{x}$, y)∧three′(y)

2.2 How to count in Oneida

With these syntactic considerations out of the way, we turn to the central question addressed in this paper, namely how quantification over entities is expressed in Oneida and whether the way it is expressed has expressive consequences. Our answers are summarized below.

Claim 1 *Quantification is expressed as in mathematics. The quantity expression is an argument, not a relation (*cardinality(s, 3)*).*

Claim 2 *Because of the structure of Oneida clauses and because number names and other expressions denoting quantities are arguments of count verbs, truly proportional quantification cannot be expressed in Oneida.*

Quantification over entities in Oneida has two parts. First, there is a count clause headed by a verb meaning something like 'amount to', 'be together', 'total'. Second, the count clause is adjoined to a main clause with a verb, one of whose arguments is what is being quantified over. Both parts of quantificational structures are described in more detail in the rest of this section, which is devoted to the mechanics of how meaning composition of quantified clauses in Oneida works. The next section justifies the claims that the semantic representations we propose in this section embody.

The count clause. Three properties of count clauses are relevant to our discussion. First, the count verb for cardinal quantification may (and sometimes must) incorporate a noun root that indicates the category of what is being counted.

Second, the quantity expression can be expressed externally (*áhsʌ* 'three' in (29) above), via a prepronominal prefix (the dualic in (31)), or as part of the verb stem's meaning (*akwekú* in (32)). Consider, for example, the count clause in (29). The verb *nikanláhtake* consists of the count root -*ke*- 'amount to', which encodes the notion of cardinality but which does not restrict the number of entities being counted, the incorporated noun -*nlaht*- 'leaf', which indicates the category of what is being counted, the default feminine-zoic/neuter singular pronominal prefix *ka*-, and the partitive prepronominal prefix *ni*-, which indicates that more than two leaves are involved. The number word *áhsʌ* indicates that the number of leaves involved was actually three.

(31) Né·n, ka?ikʌ́ wahsuta·té· kʌ́·,   ohna·kwáli? nú·wa?
      so it's this   night   y'know, rubber   then
      te-ka-hna·kwál-a-ke   kʌ́·
      DL-3Z/N.SG.A-tire-JN-amount.to[STV] eh
      w-a?t-yakw-átsha?ah<u>t-e?</u>.
      FACT-DL-1EX.PL.A-burn.up-PNC

      'So then this one night, we burned up two tires.'
                (Barbara Schuyler, Wintertime, recorded 2008)

(32) Thó·nʌ? akwekú thikʌ́ tho   wa?-é-ta-ne?
      then   all   that   there FACT-3FI.A-put.in-PNC
      káksaku.
      in the dish

      'Then someone put it all in the dish.'
                (Mercy Doxtator, After a Loss, recorded 2000)

Third, the internal structure of the count clause is licensed by the *pred-cx* we discussed in the previous section; it includes a predicate and optionally expressions that describe entities and numbers. (33) is a simplified representation of the root -*ke*- 'amount to', which contributes an amount relation. We use s and e to sort indices into indices that refer to or otherwise correspond to situations and indices that refer to or otherwise correspond to entities. For simplicity, we treat numbers as entities here.

(33)
$$\begin{bmatrix} \textit{-ke-base} \\[4pt] \text{SEM} \begin{bmatrix} \text{CONT} \begin{bmatrix} \textit{amount-rel} \\ \text{COUNTED} & e \\ \text{COUNT} & e \end{bmatrix} \\ \text{IND} \quad s \end{bmatrix} \end{bmatrix}$$

The noun incorporation construction is stated in (34) below. It concatenates a base describing an entity and a base describing a situation in that order. Morphological properties are shared between the resulting base and the situation base and, semantically, the resulting base describes the same situation as the component situation base and its semantic content is the conjunction of the two bases' content.

(34) $\textit{NI-base} \Rightarrow$
$$\begin{bmatrix} \textit{base} \\ \text{PHON} & \boxed{2} \oplus \boxed{3} \\ \text{MORPH} & \boxed{1} \\[4pt] \text{SEM} \begin{bmatrix} \text{IND} & \boxed{4} \\ \text{CONT} & \boxed{5} \wedge \boxed{7} \end{bmatrix} \\[12pt] \text{SIT-DGHTR} \begin{bmatrix} \text{PHON} & \boxed{3} \\ \text{MORPH} \boxed{1} \\ \text{SEM} \begin{bmatrix} \text{IND} & \boxed{4} \ s \\ \text{CONT} \boxed{5} P(\ldots \boxed{6} \ldots) \end{bmatrix} \end{bmatrix} \\[14pt] \text{ENT-DGHTR} \begin{bmatrix} \textit{noun} \\ \text{PHON} \boxed{2} \\ \text{SEM} \begin{bmatrix} \text{IND} & \boxed{6} \ e \\ \text{CONT} \boxed{7} \end{bmatrix} \end{bmatrix} \end{bmatrix}$$

Turning now to the last piece of the morphosyntax of count clauses, which is the requirement that count verbs co-occur with certain prepronominal prefixes, the constraint stated in (35) ensures the appropriate co-occurrence restriction between any base that includes an amount relation in its meaning and the presence of the relevant prepronominal prefixes. It requires any base that includes an amount relation to occur with either the repetitive, dualic, or partitive prepronominal prefixes (see Diaz et al. 2019 on the morphology of prepronominal prefixes). The constraint $\textit{amount-rel} \lhd \alpha$ states that the amount relation must be *part of* the meaning of the verb, since in many cases the verb's meaning also includes the meaning of an incorporated noun.

(35) $\textit{base} \wedge \begin{bmatrix} \text{SEM|ICONT}|\alpha \end{bmatrix} \wedge \textit{amount-rel} \lhd \alpha$
$\Rightarrow \begin{bmatrix} \text{MORPH|MORPH-FEAT|PREPRO|REP} + \end{bmatrix}$
$\vee \begin{bmatrix} \text{MORPH|PREPRO|DL} + \end{bmatrix} \vee \begin{bmatrix} \text{MORPH|PREPRO|PART} + \end{bmatrix}$

Finally, the constraints in (36)–(38) match the occurrence of the appropriate pronominal prefix with the right constraint on the number of entities, one for (36), two for (37), and more than two for (38).

$$(36) \quad \begin{bmatrix} amount\text{-}rel \\ \text{COUNT} \quad \boxed{1} \end{bmatrix} \triangleleft \alpha \ \wedge \ \begin{bmatrix} lexeme \\ \text{SEM} \quad \begin{bmatrix} \text{ICONT}\,\alpha \end{bmatrix} \\ \text{MORPH} \begin{bmatrix} \text{PREPRO} \begin{bmatrix} \text{REP} + \end{bmatrix} \end{bmatrix} \end{bmatrix} \Rightarrow \begin{bmatrix} eq \\ \text{COUNT}\,\boxed{1} \\ \text{BOUND}\ 1 \end{bmatrix} \triangleleft \alpha$$

$$(37) \quad \begin{bmatrix} amount\text{-}rel \\ \text{COUNT} \quad \boxed{1} \end{bmatrix} \triangleleft \alpha \ \wedge \ \begin{bmatrix} lexeme \\ \text{SEM} \quad \begin{bmatrix} \text{ICONT}\,\alpha \end{bmatrix} \\ \text{MORPH} \begin{bmatrix} \text{PREPRO} \begin{bmatrix} \text{DL} + \end{bmatrix} \end{bmatrix} \end{bmatrix} \Rightarrow \begin{bmatrix} eq \\ \text{COUNT}\,\boxed{1} \\ \text{BOUND}\ 2 \end{bmatrix} \triangleleft \alpha$$

$$(38) \quad \begin{bmatrix} amount\text{-}rel \\ \text{COUNT} \quad \boxed{1} \end{bmatrix} \triangleleft \alpha \ \wedge \ \begin{bmatrix} lexeme \\ \text{SEM} \quad \begin{bmatrix} \text{ICONT}\,\alpha \end{bmatrix} \\ \text{MORPH} \begin{bmatrix} \text{PREPRO} \begin{bmatrix} \text{PART} + \end{bmatrix} \end{bmatrix} \end{bmatrix} \Rightarrow \begin{bmatrix} sup\text{-}eq \\ \text{COUNT}\,\boxed{1} \\ \text{BOUND}\ 3 \end{bmatrix} \triangleleft \alpha$$

As mentioned in Section 1.3, verbs of possession can combine with number names without the need for count verbs. We hypothesize that verbs of possession can optionally undergo a lexical rule that adds an amount relation to the semantic content of possession verbs, as shown in (39). The hypothesis that possession verbs optionally include an amount relation is supported by the fact that they select the same prepronominal prefixes as count verbs when they combine with number names. In other words, the constraints in (35)–(38) apply to possession verbs as they do to count verbs, suggesting that, indeed, possession verbs include an amount relation in sentences such as (15).

(39) *Possession-Quantification lexical rule*

$$\begin{bmatrix} \text{SEM} \begin{bmatrix} \text{CONT}\,\boxed{2} \begin{bmatrix} possess\text{-}rel \\ \text{POSSESSOR}\ e \\ \text{POSSESSED}\ \boxed{1} \end{bmatrix} \end{bmatrix} \end{bmatrix} \mapsto \begin{bmatrix} \text{SEM} \begin{bmatrix} \text{CONT} \begin{bmatrix} amount\text{-}rel \\ \text{COUNTED} \quad \boxed{1} \\ \text{COUNT} \qquad e' \end{bmatrix} \wedge \boxed{2} \end{bmatrix} \end{bmatrix}$$

The relation between the count clause and the main clause.
Having described in some detail the internal structure of count clauses, we turn to the relation between the count clause and the main clause. We again use the example in (29) above for illustration, repeated here in (40).

(40) [Áhsʌ ni-ka-nláht-a-ke]_{count-cl}
     three PART-3z/N.SG.A-leaf-JN-amount.to[STV]

     ʌ-té-sk-u-ʔ·_{main-cl}
     FUT-CSL-2SG>1SG-give-PNC

     'The [tobacco] leaves that amount to three, you are to hand them to me.'
             (Olive Elm, Learning to Work in Tobacoo, recorded 1998)

Our analysis is that clauses headed by count verbs are internally-headed relative clauses, that the (agent) pronominal prefix of that verb references the counted argument of the count verb (when the counted argument is animate, since only animate arguments are referenced by pronominal prefixes), and that the index of the entire clause index is that of this (agent) argument. The example in (40) is, then, better glossed as 'The leaves that amount to three, you are to hand them to me'. Figure 1 below represents informally the structure of (40) and Figure 2 its semantic composition.

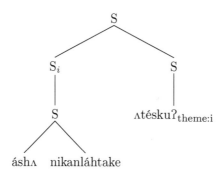

FIGURE 1 The combination of a count clause and a main clause.

The number name *áshʌ* 'three' combines with the verb *nikanláhtake* 'the leaves amounted to more than two' via the *pred-cx* construction. This combination then undergoes type-raising via the *ihrc-cx* which makes the index of the count argument *i* that of the entire clause.

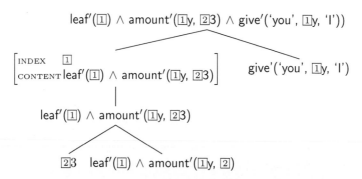

FIGURE 2 The semantic composition of sentence (40).

This index is then identified with an argument of the main verb via again the *pred-cx* construction (see Koenig & Michelson 2015b, 2019 for qualifications on this 'identification'), the theme argument in this case. Aside from type-shifting the index of clauses from situation indices to entity indices, semantic composition, as we stressed in the introduction, consists in conjoining the semantic content of daughters (the same is not necessarily true of clausal arguments; but as they are irrelevant for our purposes, we do not discuss them any further in this paper). We end this section by pointing out that to date we have not encountered an utterance that contains two count clauses. In other words, we have not seen Oneida utterances of the kind typically found in standard discussions of quantification in English such as (41).

(41)   Two workers invited three CEOs to the meeting.

Lest it be thought this absence is specific to quantification, we should note that in Michelson, Kennedy & Doxtator (2016), less than 0.5% of utterances contain two referring expressions external to verbs. The absence of two count clauses is thus hardly surprising.

3   Restrictions on Expressibility

The previous section briefly outlined our analysis of quantification over entities in Oneida and how the meaning of its component expressions is composed through the semantics of two constructions, the *pred-cx* and *ihrc-cx* constructions. But we did not provide much justification for our analysis. In this section, we justify our semantic analysis some more and discuss a restriction on expressibility that favors our analysis over more traditional analyses of quantity expressions as $< 1, 1 >$ quantifiers.

Since Barwise & Cooper (1981), quantification over entities is assumed to involve relations between sets or $< 1, 1 >$ quantifiers. The first set (the restriction) is expressed by the expression selected by the determiner, the second set (the nuclear scope) is expressed by the VP (we use English-appropriate terminology for ease of exposition). The assumption that quantifiers denote relations between sets allows for an adequate semantics of truly proportional quantifiers such as *most* (see Barwise & Cooper 1981), and it provides an appropriate semantics for negative quantifiers such as *no* (see Heim & Kratzer 1998); it also provides for a unified treatment of the meaning of determiners in English (see Keenan & Stavi 1986 among others). Do the arguments in favor of analyzing English determiners as denoting $< 1, 1 >$ quantifiers apply to Oneida count clauses?

No, because the main motivations for analyzing quantifiers as $< 1, 1 >$ quantifiers in languages like English do not exist in Oneida. There is no need to generalize over the range of meanings English determiners have, as there is only a small set of count verbs in Oneida and thus we do not have some of the recursive complexity English determiners/determiner phrases exhibit detailed by Keenan & Stavi (1986). There is no negative universal quantifier in Oneida (e.g. *No car*). Finally, as we shall see, there are no truly proportional quantifiers. Now, despite the absence of motivations for assuming Oneida quantification involves generalized quantifiers, could Oneida still be analyzed as involving generalized quantifiers? After all, one could argue that a generalized quantifier analysis is preferable, if possible at all, on cross-linguistic grounds. The answer is, again, *No*.

Treating Oneida quantification over entities the same way Barwise & Cooper treat English quantification over entities would amount to treating the count clause as a generalized quantifier and thus the main clause as equivalent to an English VP, i.e. as denoting a set of entities that serve as the nuclear scope of the quantifier. But as detailed in Koenig & Michelson (2012, 2014, 2015b), verbs in Oneida are functionally complete. They do not select external phrases and are fully saturated expressions. ʌtésku? 'you are to hand them to me' in (40) is a possible sentence of Oneida. (Discourse particles would typically be added in front of this verb, particularly when the verb occurs in a main clause, but those discourse particles are irrelevant to our point, as they do not affect the semantic type of the verb.) Count clauses, like any syntactic expression external to a verb, are 'adjoined' to functionally complete verbs which, on their own, are of type t, not $< e, t >$, an assumption we share with other Iroquoianists, and *mutatis mutandis*, Baker (1996). In other words, verbs and what we call here main clauses generally cannot serve as arguments of a putative generalized quantifier expressed by the count clause because that argument would be required to be of type $< e, t >$, while the verb and the main clause are of type t. The generalized quantifier hypothesis—which involves treating verbs in Oneida as denoting sets rather than propositions—is simply not available for Oneida. The unavailability of $< 1, 1 >$ quantifiers is one of the consequences of what we call the conjunctive mode of semantic composition that we are advocating for Oneida (leaving aside argument clauses, as mentioned earlier), where the meaning of nouns and verbs is simply conjoined when they syntactically combine rather than, as is typically the case in most languages, the result of applying one of the two expressions' meaning to the other expression's meaning via functional application.

Our analysis of the structure of Oneida basic clauses rules out analyzing Oneida quantification as $< 1, 1 >$ quantifiers, i.e. as relations between sets with the second corresponding to a VP meaning. The overall structure of Oneida clauses (the fact that verbs as heads of clauses are functionally complete, i.e. fully saturated) and the fact that quantification is expressed by verbs does not allow for quantifiers that take the denotation of VPs or the like as arguments. It does not rule out count clauses as < 1 > quantifiers though, i.e. that they denote properties of sets. There may be no quantifier that expresses relations between sets of entities in Oneida but there may be quantifiers that express properties of sets of entities. *Áhsʌ* in (40), according to this hypothesis, would be treated as a predicate over sets of leaves, whereas our analysis treats *áhsʌ* as a number name that serves as an argument of a predicate meaning 'amount to'.

There are two arguments for our analysis and against an analysis that would treat the quantity expression as a predicate. First, although some count verbs include in their meaning information about the number of entities involved (e.g. *-yashe-* 'be together' which, when used as a count verb, can only be predicated of sets of two animate entities), verbs like *-ke-* do not specify any quantity. The quantity is expressed by the prepronominal prefix or an external number. In order to analyze *-ke-* as a property of sets and as encoding a quantity, we would have to assume it denotes a general notion of quantity, something like 'has a number', and that the prepronominal prefix or external number expression would then combine with that abstract notion of quantity through something like the operator **Restrict'** described in Chung & Ladusaw (2003), i.e. via an operator that acts as a predicate meaning modifier. But there is no evidence for the use of **Restrict** in Oneida in general or, for that matter, for semantic selection (i.e. the putative selection of the count verb by *áhsʌ* 'three' in (40)). We would therefore have to posit a count-verb specific construction that combines the meaning of *áhsʌ* and the count verb via something like **Restrict'**. Our analysis has the advantage that it relies only on the general *pred-cx* construction we discussed above, a construction that every verb participates in.

The second argument in favor of our analysis of number expressions (and prepronominal prefixes, as embodied in the constraints in (36)–(38)) as specifying an argument of the count verb, i.e. as number names rather than properties of sets, is that is explains a restriction on the kind of quantifiers that can be expressed in Oneida. We state this restriction below.

Fact. *Oneida lacks expressions denoting proportions (at least for quantification over entities).*

The contrast between (42a) and (42b) illustrates the fact that when quantities are arguments, they cannot express proportions, since proportions must be predicates (i.e. take one or two, depending on one's analysis, sets as arguments).

(42) a. √Those cars numbered three.

b. #Those cars numbered most.

Now, as Jacques Jayez pointed out to us (p.c.), proportionally quantified noun phrases can occur as complements of verbs like *number*, *total*, *amount to*, as sentence (43) illustrates. (We slightly changed the wording to make it more idiomatic, but kept constant the semantic structure.)

(43) The knives never amounted to a quarter of the spoons in the drawer.

Critically, though, the proportional quantifier *a quarter of the spoons* in (43) describes a quantity. Proportional quantifiers in English can have a double life, it seems, either as denoting relations between sets or as functions that take sets as input and return a number that corresponds to the relevant proportion of the set. It is this second use of proportional quantifiers that sentence (43) illustrates: Proportions cannot be arguments, but quantities described through a functional use of proportional quantifiers can.

Given the contrast in (42) and the felicity of sentence (43), it is telling that Oneida does not include any expression that corresponds to English *most*, *two thirds of*, *four of* and the like, in other words, any partitive quantifier (including proportional quantifiers). The only expression that seems to correspond to proportionality over sets of entities is an expression that is translated into English as 'half'. But, interestingly, 'half' seems to be treated in Oneida as the name of a quantity, just like *tékeni* 'two' or *kayé* 'four', rather than as a proportion. 'Half' is expressed with the verb form *-ahsʌnʌ-* 'be in the middle of' plus coincident and dualic prepronominal prefixes. Uses of *-ahsʌnʌ-* in the spatial domain are provided in (44) and (45).

(44) Kwáh kwí· tsh-a?te-w-ahsʌná   tsi? ni·wá·
just   COIN-DL-3Z/N.SG.A-middle[STV] whatever size
Ukwehuwé·ne.
at the Native People's

'It (the school) was in the middle of the Settlement.'
        (Georgina Nicholas, An Oneida Childhood, recorded 1981)

(45) nʌ   uhte   tsh-aʔte-w-ahsʌnʌ́   niyo·lé·
then probably COIN-DL-3Z/N.SG.A-middle[STV] how far
niyukwe·nú̲.
we all have gone
'then I guess we had gone halfway (to the store, along the rail-
way tracks)'
(Barbara Schuyler, A Ghost on the Track, recorded 2008)

(44) exemplifies a predicative use of the verb -ahsʌnʌ- 'be in the middle'
and can be glossed as 'It was in the middle of whatever is the extent
of the reservation'. (45) exemplifies a more referential use of the same
verb and can be glossed as 'We had gone as far as the middle'. This
referential use of the verb is very frequent and has possibly become
lexicalized. It is this referential use that is at play in the metaphorical
quantity meaning exemplified in (46).

(46) Tsh-aʔte-w-ahsʌnʌ́   nikú   yahá-s-haw.
COIN-DL-3Z/N.SG.A-middle[STV] amount TRL-2SG.IMP-take

'Take half (of the bowl of candies, of a single [very large] candy
or treat).'

It is of course in principle possible that the absence of any Oneida
translation equivalent of English *most* is a lexical gap. But the absence
of any other proportional quantity expression makes this possibility
unlikely. There is further evidence that the absence of partitive quantifiers in Oneida is not just a lexical gap: There seems to be no way of
expressing partitive relations between sets in Oneida. What is missing
are not words that mean *most* and similar concepts, but a construction
that can be used to refer to or denote a subset of a larger set. The
absence of constructions that express partitive relations does not mean
that these kinds of relations cannot be conveyed. It means that partitive relations can only be conveyed through *inferences*. Consider the
excerpt in (47). The first sentence sets up a set of children; the next
sentence describes two children, and the following sentences describe
two and three children. The fact that these three sets are subsets of
the set of children introduced in the first sentence is not expressed in
Oneida. But it is easily inferred given the context.

(47) Kwáh lati-kwekú   te-hon-ate?khé·tslut-e?, (...)
just   3M.PL.A-all   DL-3M.DP.P-put.on.skates-STV
Te-hni-yáshe
DL-3M.DU.A-be.together[STV]
te-hni-?nyotálho-s. (...)
DL-3M.DU.A-hook.a.stick.over-HAB
Te-hni-yáshe   o-?swʌ́·t-a?
DL-3M.DU.A-be.together[STV] 3z/N.SG.P-black-NSF
lon-atya?tawí·t-u   khále? áhsʌ
3M.DP.P-put.on.a.shirt-STV and   three
ni-hat-í   o-wískl-a?
PART-3M.PL.A-total[STV] 3z/N.SG.P-white-NSF
ni-hu-hkwʌnyó·tʌ.
PART-3M.PL.A-have.on.an.outfit[STV]
'The children all have skates on. (...) Two are facing off. (...)
Two have on black shirts and three have on white uniforms.'
(Pedagogical text created by Mercy Doxtator)

We take the fact that Oneida does not include any expression that corresponds to partitive quantifiers as supporting our analysis of the meaning of (40) above as represented in (48a) rather than the putative meaning of quantity expressions and number words as properties of sets as expressed (48b). As the contrast in (42) shows, proportional quantifiers are predicted to be lacking in a language that treats quantities (numbers) as arguments of count predicates rather than predicates.

(48)   a. leaf′($\boxed{1}$)∧amount′($\boxed{1}$y, $\boxed{2}$3)∧give′('you', $\boxed{1}$y, 'I')
       b. leaf′($\boxed{1}$)∧three′($\boxed{1}$y)∧give′('you', $\boxed{1}$y, 'I')

The absence of proportional quantifiers in Oneida and the conjunctive mode of semantic composition we ascribe to Oneida constructions may seem limiting to readers. It is not. First, as (47) shows, partitive meaning can be inferred. Thus, something roughly equivalent to English *most* can be inferred from the use of words that mean a big group (of animate entities) or a big amount (of inanimate entities) such as the verb *nikʌtyohkwanʌ́* 'a large group' in (49). Relatively innocuous pragmatic inferences may give you proportional quantifiers after all. Proportionality can be conveyed even if it cannot be expressed literally.

(49) tho   kʌs   ni-kʌ-tyohkwanʌ́
      there usually PART-3z/N.SG.A-large.group[STV]
      kʌʔ nityukwayʌ́·saʔ tho   y-aʔ-t-yakw-átla-neʔ
      we young people   there TRL-FACT-DL-1EX.PL.A-meet-PNC
      thikʌ́ waʔ-akw-at-lʌn-ot-únyu-ʔ,
      that   FACT-1EX.PL.A-SRF-song-stand-DISTR-PNC

      'a large group of us young people would meet there [and] play
      music,'
                          (Olive Elm, Friday Nights, recorded 2005)

Second, although work such as Barwise & Cooper (1981) or Keenan
& Stavi (1986), treats all English determiners as $< 1, 1 >$ quantifiers,
as it allows a unified semantic analysis of all English determiners, only
proportional quantifiers like *most need to* be analyzed this way. Numer-
als need not (and, in analyses such as Landman 1996 and Krifka 1999,
do not), nor do *all, every, each*, as these expressions *can* be analyzed
via first-order quantifiers.

We end this section by coming back to our earlier claim that universal quantifiers are predicates in Oneida. Because of lack of space, we
focus here on *akwekú*, probably the most neutral expression of universal quantification in Oneida. *Akwekú* can be glossed as *be complete/be
whole*. Thus, sentence (50) is best literally glossed as 'Someone put it
in the dish and it was complete (not missing anything)'. (51a) indicates
how the (relevant part of the) meaning of (50) is composed and (51b)
provides the model-theoretic interpretation of the predicate complete′
that constitutes the meaning of *akwekú*.

(50) Thó·nʌʔ akwekú thikʌ́ tho   waʔ-é-ta-neʔ
      then   all   that   there FACT-3FI.A-put.in-PNC
      káksaku.
      in the dish

      'Then someone put it all in the dish.'
                          (Mercy Doxtator, After a Loss, recorded 2000)

(complete′(☐x)∧(put′(y,☐x,'there')))

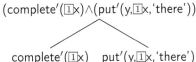

(51) a.   complete′(☐x)   put′(y,☐x,'there')

      b.   ⟦complete(x)⟧^{M,g} is true iff there is a contextually available
           set c assigned by g and the referent of x in M according to
           g is the maximum on the part–whole scale defined on c.

Sentence (52a), whose semantic representation is given in (52b), provides a more complex example of how conjunctive composition is compatible with universal quantification: There is a set of dresses, three in number, such there is no contextually appropriate larger set and that set of dresses is dirty.[6]

(52)   a.   Akwekú áhsʌ nikú   akw-atyá·tawiʔt
            all   three amount 1SG.POSS-dress
            yo-nista·kwálal-eʔ.
            3Z/N.SG.P-dirty-STV
            'All three of my dresses are dirty.'

        b.   amount$'(x, 3) \wedge$complete$'(x) \wedge$dress$'(x) \wedge$dirty$'(s,x)$

4 Conclusion

Over the last twenty years there has been much work on how quantification is expressed across languages (aside from Bach et al. 1995, which we cited above, see Matthewson 2008 and the two volumes of Keenan & Paperno 2012 and Paperno & Keenan 2017). Our paper suggests that there is more variation in how quantification is expressed crosslinguistically than sometimes assumed. Verbs heading count clauses can be the (almost) exclusive mean of expressing quantification in some languages. In addition we argued that there is also variation in how quantification over entities is conceptualized, i.e. as relations between sets or as statements of cardinality. The two conceptualizations are equivalent truth-conditionally, in that quantities can be expressed either way. Whether we represent the meaning of a phrase appropriately translated in English as *three leaves fell* as card$'(s, 3) \wedge$leaf$'(s) \wedge$fell$'(s)$, as three$'(s) \wedge$leaf$'(s) \wedge$fell$'(s)$, or as three$'(\lambda x.$leaf$'(x)$, $\lambda y.$fell$'(y))$ makes no difference truth conditionally, as long as we adjust the denotation of three$'$ or 3 accordingly. But, as we argue, if quantification consists exclusively of statements of cardinality, as in basic arithmetic, proportionality cannot be expressed. And this is exactly what happens in Oneida. The absence of generalized and proportional quantifiers is not unique to Oneida. Matthewson (2014) similarly claims that St'at'imcets lacks generalized quantifiers and that the lack of proportional quantifiers constitutes one piece of evidence that supports this claim. What

---

[6]Our translation leaves underspecified whether the main verb is predicated of the set as a whole or of each member, as in Landman's (1996) analysis of plurality. Although nothing critical hinges on this assumption, note that the following example contradicts Baker's (1996) analysis of *akwekú* in Mohawk as a distributor on a par with English postnominal *each*: *Akwekú wahatihala·táteʔ ká·slet* 'All of them lifted up/raised up the car'.

is interesting, though, is that the lack of generalized and proportional quantifiers in Oneida is not just a lexical gap. The former follows from the structure of Oneida clauses and the absence of syntactic or semantic selection that we have argued for elsewhere; the latter is part of a larger absence, that of any means for referring to subsets. As we have shown, though, Oneida's expressive lack might be semantically jarring, but it hardly hampers communication, as contextual inferences easily fill this gap.

9

The Meaning and Use of Romanian Subjunctive Interrogatives

GABRIELA BÎLBÎIE

1 Introduction

The Romanian subjunctive mood displays both Romance and Balkan features. On the one hand, Romanian shares with other Romance languages some specific subjunctive forms (i.e. a special verbal morphology in the third person) and the distribution of the subjunctive and indicative moods in complement clauses. On the other hand, Romanian displays Balkan properties through a specific subjunctive particle *să* (with an affixal behaviour; see Barbu 1999, Monachesi 2005, Bîlbîie & Mardale 2018) and through this subjunctive in interrogatives.

One of the recurring themes in the research on the subjunctive is the condition(s) motivating its distribution, in particular in contexts where it is

Constraint-Based Syntax and Semantics: Papers in Honor of Danièle Godard.
Anne Abeillé and Olivier Bonami (eds.).
Copyright © 2020, CSLI Publications.

in alternation with the indicative. We refer here to Godard (2012), who proposes (in line with Farkas 1992, 2003) that the subjunctive, as well as the indicative, is associated with its own motivation condition. Therefore, the indicative is semantically motivated when the propositional content belongs to the speaker's (or matrix subject's) beliefs. On the other hand, the subjunctive is semantically motivated when the interpretation involves a set of alternatives (i.e. the possibility of *p* along with that of non-*p*), and grammaticalized in other contexts in Romance languages (especially when both moods are semantically motivated, e.g. mixed predicates). Godard's theory aims to explain both root subjunctives (e.g. imperative contexts) and embedded subjunctives. However, she leaves the following question open: Why does the subjunctive not occur in French interrogatives, where it would be motivated?

In this paper, we concentrate on the use of subjunctives in Romanian interrogatives, a phenomenon which illustrates the uniqueness of Romanian among the Romance languages and its affinity with the Balkan languages.[1]

The subjunctive in root interrogatives is common in Romanian, in both yes/no questions, such as (1a) below, and *wh*-questions, such as (1b). In other Balkan languages, such as Bulgarian, in (2) below,[2] and Greek, in (3), the subjunctive particles (*da* and *na*, respectively) occur in root interrogatives too (see Pavlidou 1991,[3] Rouchota 1994), a phenomenon which seems to be related to the loss and/or attrition of the infinitive in these languages (Tomić 2004, 2006).

---

[1] In Portuguese, some yes/no questions display the subjunctive mood which is triggered by the presence of the modal adverb *talvez* 'maybe', as in (i) below (see Martins 2016).

(i)   Ele talvez   venha?
      he maybe   come.SUBJ.3SG
      'Might he come?' / 'Might it be that he will come?'

However, the subjunctive only appears in interrogatives if it is triggered by the same elements that would trigger it in declaratives (Martins p.c.). As we will see, the subjunctive uses in Romanian main interrogatives are quite different from this subjunctive use in Portuguese.

[2] Unless otherwise indicated, our Bulgarian and Greek examples come from our native-speaking consultants: Margarita Dimitrova and Snejana Gadjeva (for Bulgarian) and Dimitra Kolliakou (for Greek).

[3] According to Pavlidou (1991), subjunctives in Modern Greek occur much more frequently in main, nonmodal, verbs than in embedded contexts.

(1) a. **Să**   **fie**   ora   9?[4]   (Romanian)
         SUBJ   be.SUBJ.3SG   hour.DEF 9
         'Could/would it be 9 o'clock?'
     b. Unde   **să**   **merg**?
         where SUBJ   go.1SG
         'Where should I go?'

(2) a. **Da**   **kupi**   li knigata?   (Bulgarian)
         SUBJ   buy.PERF.PRES.3SG   Q   book.DEF
         'Should he buy the book?
     b. Kăde   **da**   **otida**?
         where SUBJ   go.PERF.PRES.1SG
         'Where should I go?'

(3) a. **Na**   **pao**   sinema?   (Greek)
         SUBJ   go.1SG   movies
         'Shall I go to the movies?   (Pavlidou 1991: 18)
     b. Pou   **na**   **pao**?
         where SUBJ   go.1SG
         'Where should I go?'

Other Romance languages do not allow the subjunctive in interrogatives, requiring instead other verbal moods: e.g. in French, the infinitive (4a) or the conditional (4b); in Portuguese, the future (5a) or the conditional (5b).[5]

(4) a. Où   **(pourrais**-je)   **aller**?   (French)
         where can.COND.PRES.1SG-I   go.INF
     b. Où   **irais**-je?
         where aller.COND.PRES.1SG-I
         'Where could/should I go?'

(5) a. Ela   **terá**   30 anos?   (Portuguese)
         she   have.FUT.3SG 30 years
         'Might she be 30 years old?'
     b. Ela   **teria**   30   anos   quando   a
         she   have.COND.3SG 30   years when   her.ACC
         conheci?
         met.1SG
         'Could/Would she be 30 years old when I first met her?'

---

[4] For the sake of clarity, the subjunctive verbal form (or its equivalent in other languages) is systematically highlighted in bold.

[5] We thank Ana Maria Martins for the Portuguese examples.

I will start by briefly arguing for the existence of an 'independent' (root) subjunctive in Romanian interrogatives (Section 2). I will then present a typology of subjunctive interrogatives (Section 3). Finally, I will propose an account of the subjunctive in interrogatives at the semantics–pragmatics interface (Section 4).

2 Against an Elliptical Approach

The subjunctive is traditionally viewed as a dependent mood (e.g. Jespersen 1924, Giannakidou 2009, Quer 2009), i.e. it is embedded under a matrix predicate. Under this assumption, there is no independent (root) subjunctive. Therefore, 'root' subjunctives should be reanalyzed as embedded clauses in disguise, i.e. the subjunctive is considered to be embedded under a covert modal verb (Null Modal Hypothesis). This position is adopted by Avram (2015) to explain 'mirative' subjunctive uses in Romanian. The same approach (in terms of null modals) is proposed by Grohmann (2000) for root infinitives in Germanic and Romance languages. Let us call it the elliptical approach.

However, such an elliptical approach is of interest in the case at stake only if: (i) one can reconstruct a modal matrix verb from any 'root' subjunctive in a regular fashion, and (ii) the syntactic, semantic and pragmatic properties of 'elliptical' occurrences are the same as that of full clauses. We briefly show below that these conditions are not always met.

A first problem for the elliptical approach is the underspecified modality. In her analysis in terms of null modals, Avram (2015) assigns a specific modality to each subjunctive construction. However, a closer examination of the data reveals that the modal value is not necessarily linked to a subjunctive construction type. In (6) below, several modal verbs[6] (with different modal values, drawn from Avram's taxonomy) can be identified in each example, e.g. an epistemic modal of possibility such as *a fi posibil* 'be possible', a subject-oriented modal of possibility *a putea* 'be able/can' or a deontic modal of necessity *a trebui* 'must'. In some cases, as in (6d), there are more candidates than modal verbs. This shows that a one-to-one mapping between a specific modality and a certain subjunctive interrogative type is not possible. If a syntactic reconstruction mechanism is involved in such cases, there are too many null operators as possible candidates for each case, and there is no regular mechanism which could guide the selection.

---

[6] For the sake of clarity, the modal verb which can be reconstructed is underlined in these examples.

(6) a. Cum (e posibil / se poate / poți) să nu te
how is possible REFL can.3SG can.2SG SUBJ NEG REFL
gândești la nimic?
think.2SG of nothing
'How {could it be possible to think / can one think} of nothing at all?'

b. Ce (era / trebuie / pot) să fac
what be.IMPERF.3SG must can.1SG SUBJ do.1SG
în asemenea situații?
in such situations
'What {could / should / can} I do in such a situation?'

c. Când (e posibil / trebuia / putea)
when is possible / should.IMPERF / can.IMPERF.3SG
să fi plecat?
SUBJ PERF left
'When {can / should / could} s/he have left?'

d. De unde (voiai / era / puteam)
of where want.IMPERF.2SG be.IMPERF.3SG could.IMPERF.1SG
să știu că tu ești vegetarian?
SUBJ know.1SG that you are vegetarian
'How could I know that you were vegetarian?'

A second problem for the elliptical approach strictly concerns syntactic reconstruction issues. In some cases (in particular, in conventionalized patterns), it is very difficult (or even impossible) to reconstruct any modal verb. For example, in so-called 'wh-imperatives' (where one uses an interrogative clause to make a suggestion), there is no modal verb which can be reconstructed (compare (7a) and (7b)), be it epistemic, deontic or subject-oriented, within Avram's taxonomy. In any case, if available, syntactic reconstruction of a modal verb would lose the specific pragmatic effects observed in these specific contexts.

(7) a. De ce să nu începem ziua de luni dansând și simțindu-ne bine?
(www.desenelecopilariei.com, 23 November 2009)
'Why not start Monday by dancing and having fun?'

b. De ce {#e posibil / #trebuie / #putem} să nu începem ziua de luni dansând și simțindu-ne bine?
'Why {can / must / may} we not start Monday by dancing and having fun?'

Moreover, the syntactic properties of 'root' subjunctive interrogatives are not (always) the same as those of full clauses, where a modal verb is syntactically reconstructed. In Romanian, interrogatives display some ordering constraints related to the position of the subject, i.e. they generally require postverbal subjects (Bîlbîie 2011; Vasilescu 2013: 539, 541). If one syntactically reconstructs the modal verb, one has to have the subject after the verb, as in (8a) below. We observe that, in the absence of the modal verb, the subject can only occur after the subjunctive form (compare (8b) and (8c)). If one had a covert modal at the syntactic level, the example in (8b) should be acceptable, which is not the case. The same contrast is observed in the attested example in (9a), where a topicalized subject precedes the subjunctive clause embedded by the complementizer *ca* 'that'. Such a topicalized subject cannot occur in the 'root' version (9b); the subject has to follow the subjunctive verb, as in (9c).

(8) a. Cum <u>ar   putea</u> [o mamă] **să-şi   uite**   copilul?
       how would.3SG can   a mother SUBJ-REFL forget.3 child.DEF
       'How could a woman forget her child?'

    b. ??Cum [o mamă] **să-şi   uite**   copilul?
       how   a mother SUBJ-REFL forget.3   child.DEF

    c. Cum **să-şi   uite**   [o mamă] copilul?
       how SUBJ-REFL forget.3   a mother child.DEF

(9) a. Cum <u>este posibil</u> ca [un om atât de deştept   ca
       how is   possible that a man so of intelligent as
       profesorul   Ţuţea] **să   creadă** în Dumnezeu?
       professor.DEF Ţuţea SUBJ believe.3 in God
                                          (*Lumina*, 29 November 2016,
       http://ziarullumina.ro/orgoliul-lui-Tutea117891.html)
       'How could such an intelligent man as professor Ţuţea believe in God?'

    b. *Cum (ca) [un om atât de deştept   ca   profesorul
       how that a man so   of intelligent as   professor.DEF
       Ţuţea] **să   creadă** în Dumnezeu?
       Ţuţea SUBJ believe.3 in God

    c. Cum **să   creadă** în   Dumnezeu [un om atât de
       how SUBJ believe.3 in   God   a man so of
       deştept   ca profesorul   Ţuţea]?
       intelligent as professor.DEF Ţuţea
       'How could such an intelligent man as professor Ţuţea believe in God?'

In addition to the problems presented above, we do not observe the same semantic and pragmatic effects in the 'elliptical' clauses compared to their reconstructed counterparts. Specifically, the subjunctive interrogative with a reconstructed (modal) verb is more restricted in its interpretation than the root subjunctive interrogative (without a modal). It is one of the goals of this paper to show the richness of the semantic and pragmatic effects involved in subjunctive interrogatives (in the absence of any overt modal).

Given these observations, we have to conclude that the elliptical approach (or Null Modal Hypothesis) cannot be formulated in a simple way and creates more problems than it solves. We assume that there is no ellipsis involved in root subjunctive interrogatives.[7] Thus, the traditional analysis of the subjunctive as a dependent mood should be reconsidered.

3 Towards a Typology of Subjunctive Interrogatives

In this section, we briefly draw a typology of the subjunctive interrogatives, based on two main discursive strategies.

In general, as Onea (2016: 50) assumes, questionhood can be best understood in terms of understanding answers to questions. In this respect, see also the quote from Dekker, Aloni & Butler (2007: 6): 'the meaning of questions really resides in its answerhood *conditions*'. Therefore, we use the Question/Answer minimal pair as a criterion to distinguish between two discursive strategies at work in subjunctive interrogatives. A first discursive strategy refers to cases where the subjunctive occurs in the first part of the pair (i.e. the question part) in initiative discourse moves, while the second discursive strategy refers to reactive uses, where the subjunctive occurs in the second part of the pair, i.e. an interrogative clause that reacts to an immediately preceding discourse move. The first strategy includes context-free uses of the subjunctive in interrogatives, in the sense that they can be uttered out-of-the-blue. The second strategy contains dialogical uses, in the sense that subjunctive interrogatives are context-dependent, the query responses being in these cases reactive utterances, and mostly rhetorical questions.

3.1 Out-of-the-blue Uses

In this subsection, we will briefly discuss two main subjunctive uses in interrogatives, namely 'deliberative' and 'dubitative' subjunctives.

3.1.1 Deliberative Subjunctives

A first class of out-of-the-blue uses of the subjunctive in interrogative clauses refers to 'deliberative' questions (or 'direction' questions, see Huddleston 2002: 877 footnote 9), in which the speaker requests advice with

---

[7] The arguments against reconstructing a matrix verb in root interrogatives can be extended to root subjunctives in imperative clauses.

respect to an intention or an obligation (see the label 'deliberative subjunctive' in Frâncu 2010). All major types of questions can be used: alternative questions (10a), polar questions (10b) or *wh*-questions (10c). As Pavlidou (1991) notes for Greek, a characteristic feature of deliberative subjunctive questions is the possibility that every polar or *wh*-question of this class has to be turned into an alternative question.

(10) a. **Să divorţez** sau {**să nu divorţez** / nu}?
   'Should I divorce or not?'
   b. **Să** mai **ieşim** din casă pe ploaia asta?
   'Should we go out in this rain?'
   c. Cu ce **să mă îmbrac**?
   'What should I wear?'

As deliberative questions generally express the speaker's dilemma, most typically it is the first person which is used. The predicates which are mostly used in subjunctive interrogatives of this type are action and intensional verbs. In terms of modal meaning, the subjunctive contributes in these contexts to a deontic modality (hence the label 'deontic subjunctive' in Zafiu 2011), understood in a very general sense, i.e. in consonance with certain laws, conventions, obligations or other such normative options, including also someone's desires or goals. These deontic uses (11A) are in close relation with the 'mandatory' subjunctive use in imperative clauses (11B), where the subjunctive is less direct than the imperative, displaying an attenuative mandatory force. Therefore, deliberative interrogative clauses in the subjunctive are questions whose answers have the force of directives (see also Huddleston 2002: 877).

(11) A: Când **să** **vin**?
   when SUBJ come.1SG
   'When should I come?'
   B: {**Să** **vii** / **vino**}   mâine.
   SUBJ come.2SG come.IMP.2SG tomorrow
   'Come tomorrow!'

Deliberative subjunctives are frequently used for title-making in instructions (e.g. headings for lists, notices, and the like). These are mostly *wh*-questions, like those in (12), and have a generic reading (see the use of the second person with a generic reading).

(12) a. Cum **să te laşi** de fumat?   (www.unica.ro, 15 September 2016)
'How to quit smoking?'

    b. Ce **să iei** seara ca să scapi de insomnie şi dureri de cap?

(www.bzc.ro, 9 August 2018)

'What should one take in the evening to no longer have insomnia and headaches?'

    d. Când **să mergi** la medicul oftalmolog?

(www.reginamaria.ro, 24 September 2015)

'When to see an ophthalmologist?'

    c. De ce **să alegi** produse eco?

(www.capital.ro, 17 November 2016)

'Why should one choose ecological products?'

It is worth noting that in these deliberative contexts one can use the indicative with the same meaning, seen in (13), while other Romance languages such as French make use of the infinitive, seen in (14).

(13) Cum **te laşi** de fumat? Strategia care te poate ajuta

(www.libertatea.ro, 29 March 2018)

'How to quit smoking? The strategy which can help you'

(14) Comment **arrêter** de fumer?

(https://www.dernierecigarette.com/comment-arreter-de-fumer.html)

'How to quit smoking?'

3.1.2 Dubitative Subjunctives

A second class of out-of-the-blue uses of the subjunctive in interrogative clauses includes 'dubitative' questions, in which the speaker expresses doubt or uncertainty with respect to hypotheses or suppositions based on present situations (as in (15a) and (16a)) or past situations (in (15b) and (16b)), either in polar questions like (15) or in *wh*-questions like (16). In many cases, an additional mirativity effect is observed (see the continuation of examples in (15a) and (16a)).

(15) a. **Să fie** ora 9? M-aş mira.
'Could it be 9 o'clock? I would be surprised.'

    b. **Să fi plecat** toţi fără să-mi spună?
'Could they all have left without telling me?'

(16) a. Oare cât **să fie** ceasul? Nu cred să fie mai mult de 10.
          'What time could it be? I don't believe it could be more than 10
          o'clock.'
      b. Cine **să fi fost** pe-aici? Văd urme.
          'Who could have been here? I see traces.'

Speaker doubt and uncertainty can be reinforced in these contexts by the
use of some modal epistemic adverbs, such as the interrogative particle *oare*
'I wonder' (a specialized interrogative adverb that marks uncertainty, see
Vasilescu & Vântu 2008; Zafiu 2008, 2013), as in (17a), or the adverb
cumva 'somehow' in (17b).

(17) a. <u>Oare</u> **să fie** el Mesia al României? Cine mai poate salva România?
                                    (www.ziare.com, 12 January 2011)
          'Could he be the Messiah of Romania, I wonder. Who could save
          Romania anymore?'
      b. Moartea Denisei naşte multe semne de întrebare. **Să fie** <u>cumva</u> vina
          medicilor?
                              (www.ziarulonline.com, 8 June 2017)
          'Denisa's death raises many questions. Could it be somehow the
          doctors' fault?'

This dubitative use of the subjunctive is therefore linked to an epistemic
modality (hence the label 'epistemic subjunctive' in Zafiu 2011), which
refers to the speaker's degree of certainty. This speaker's attitude of uncertainty explains the possibility of alternation between subjunctive ((18a) and
(19a) below) and presumptive ((18b) and (19b)) moods in all these dubitative contexts, with the same epistemic interpretation. The presumptive is a
Romanian-specific mood form primarily used to convey some form of uncertainty and, therefore, to express epistemic modality (Fălăuş 2014,
Giurgea 2018). In Romance languages such as French, this epistemic fla-
vour is given by the use of the conditional in these contexts (20).

(18) a. **Să fi plouat** afară?
          'Would it be the case that it rained (outside)?'
      b. **O fi plouat** afară?
          'Would it be the case that it rained (outside)?'

(19) a. **Să fie** ora 9?
          'Could it be 9 o'clock?'
      b. **O fi** ora 9?
          'Could it be 9 o'clock?'

(20) a. **Aurait**-il **plu**?
  'Would it be the case that it rained?'
  b. Est-ce qu'il **serait** déjà 9 heures?
  'Could it be 9 o'clock?'

Comparing the indicative and subjunctive mood alternations in (21), we observe that they do not convey the same meaning: when using the subjunctive in (21a), neither the speaker nor the addressee knows the answer, whereas with the indicative in (21b), the speaker hands the issue of the question over to the addressee in order to solve it. We come back to this contrast in Section 4.

(21) a. **Să fi plouat** afară?
  'Would it be the case that it rained (outside)?'
  b. **A plouat** afară?
  'Did it rain (outside)?'

Coming back to our two main uses of the subjunctive in out-of-the-blue interrogative clauses, we note that there are several properties which distinguish dubitative from deliberative cases. First, dubitative contexts favour the use of the third person, whereas deliberative contexts make use of the first person (as well as the second person with a generic reading). Second, dubitative contexts generally do not use the same kind of predicates as deliberative ones. If in the latter case, one mostly observes action and intensional verbs, in the former case the predicates which are mostly used in dubitative cases are state and nonintensional verbs. Lastly and most importantly, deliberative and dubitative subjunctives do not have the same behaviour with respect to embedding: unlike dubitative subjunctives such as (22a) and (23a) below, deliberative ones are felicitous under embedding – see (22b) and (23b).

(22) a. #Mă întreb dacă **să fie** ora 9.
  'I wonder if it can be 9 o'clock.'
  b. Mă întreb dacă **să plec** (sau nu).
  'I wonder if I have to leave (or not).'

(23) a. #M-a întrebat cât **să fie** un bilet până la Iaşi.
  '(S)he asked me how much a ticket would cost for Iaşi.'
  b. M-a întrebat ce **să facă**.
  '(S)he asked me what he should do.'

Based on the observations we have made on these two classes of out-of-the-blue uses, we assume that there is an implicit (deontic or epistemic) modality at work, carried by the subjunctive itself in subjunctive interrogatives (and not by a covert modal verb, recall Section 2 above): a deontic modality in deliberative contexts and an epistemic modality in dubitative contexts. In these cases, the subjunctive mood has the same contribution as a modal element.

3.2 Reactive Uses

As mentioned in the beginning of this section, the second discursive strategy generally implies subjunctive uses in a reactive discourse move. Utterances of this kind involve a reaction to a previously raised issue (i.e. they presuppose an immediately preceding conversational move, see Bruce & Farkas 2007); hence, these questions can never be initiating moves. As observed by Pavlidou (1991) in Greek, this kind of use covers a wide range of cases, which we classify here in three main subtypes: rhetorical questions (with and without repetition of the material in the preceding utterance), echo questions and 'wh-imperatives'.

3.2.1 Rhetorical Questions

Most of these reactive utterances are in fact rhetorical questions, to which the speaker does not expect an answer, since it is made explicit by the context (Caponigro & Sprouse 2007).

In most of our cases, subjunctive rhetorical questions can only receive a negative answer. In dialogical contexts, this rhetorical question is a refutation of the preceding utterance or a cancellation of the utterance presupposition. In (24) below, we illustrate such rhetorical uses with *wh*-questions; we observe that any *wh*-interrogative phrase can be used: *cine* 'who' (24a), *ce* 'what' (24b), *cum* 'how' (24c), *unde* 'where' (24d), *de ce* 'why' (24e). In all these contexts, there is an implicit negation (Sadock 1971). The bias for a negative answer triggered by these subjunctive rhetorical questions is sometimes explicitly supported by the context, as we can see in (25), where the subjunctive question is paraphrased by a negative clause.

(24) a. A: Ai văzut în ce hal vorbesc copiii ăştia?
A: 'Have you heard how these children speak?'
B: Cine **să-i educe**?
B: 'Who could educate them?'
b. A: Iei şi banii ăştia cu tine? / Ia cu tine şi banii ăştia.
A: 'Are you taking this money with you?' / 'Take this money with you.'
B: Ce **să fac** cu ei?
B: 'What can I do with it?'
c. A: Iţi ajung banii pentru toate cheltuielile?
A: 'Is this money enough for your expenses?'
B: Cum **să trăiesc** cu 700 de lei pe lună?
B: 'How could I live with 700 lei per month?'
d. A: Şi-a găsit Maria de lucru?
A: 'Has Maria found a job?'
B: Unde **să muncească**?
B: 'Where could she work?'
e. A: Ion vrea să-l ajuţi săptămâna viitoare; te duci?
A: 'Ion wants you to help him next week; can you help him?'
B: De ce **să muncesc** degeaba?
B: 'Why (would I) work for free?'

(25) a. Kim Jong Un a fumat o ţigară lângă racheta balistică, chiar înainte de lansare. Cine **să-i spună** că e interzis? ... Se pare că nimeni nu a îndrăznit să-i spună să nu mai fumeze în zonă...
(www.mediafax.ro, 9 July 2017)
'Kim Jong Un smoked a cigarette next to a ballistic missile, just before launching. Who could tell him that it is forbidden? ... It seems that nobody dared to tell him not to smoke in that area...'
b. Intrebat mai departe dacă mai participă la festivalul de la Cannes, actorul a spus că nu mai merge. ... "Probabil nu mă mai plac cei de la Cannes şi nici eu pe ei. Ce **să caut** eu acolo?", a susţinut Delon.
(www.ziare.com, 10 June 2017)
'Asked further whether he would still attend the Cannes Festival, the actor said that he would not attend it anymore. ... "Those from Cannes probably no longer love me, nor I them. What could I do there?", added Delon.'

By asking an ordinary, information-seeking question, one presupposes that it has a right answer and that the addressee is able to answer that question; in most cases, this is taken for granted and presented as uncontroversial background ('pragmatic presupposition', see Huddleston 2002: 897). However, by using a subjunctive in reactive contexts, the question is used without the presupposition that typically accompanies a question. Therefore, in these contexts, the subjunctive occurs with presupposition cancellation. This is illustrated in (26), where the subjunctive *wh*-question introduced by the interrogative phrase *de unde* 'from where' cancels the presupposition that speaker B could respond to the first question; the fact that the addressee is not able to answer it is explicited in (26b–c): in (26b), by the sequences *habar nu am* 'I have no idea', *nu ştiu* 'I don't know', and in (26c) by the proposal *întrebaţi-l pe domnul Rusu* 'ask Mr Rusu', following the subjunctive question.

(26) a. A: Cine e doamna de-acolo?   B: De unde **să ştiu** eu?
     A: 'Who is that lady?'   B: 'How could I know?'

   b. Întrebat sâmbătă la Parlament dacă, în opinia sa, PSD a ieşit mai întărit, ca partid majoritar în Parlament, după CEx, Kelemen Hunor a răspuns: "Habar nu am. De unde **să ştiu** eu? ... nu sunt psihologul pesediştilor. A ieşit mai întărit, nu a ieşit? Nu ştiu. E fix problema lor."

                            (www.mediafax.ro, 22 September 2018)
     'Asked last Saturday in Parliament whether, in his opinion, PSD became stronger after CEx, as the majority party in Parliament, Kelemen Hunor answered: "I have no idea. How could I know? ... I am not the PSD's psychologist. Has it become stronger or not? I don't know. It is just their affair."'

   c. Constantin Niţă, ministrul delegat pentru energie, a fost întrebat câţi bani a cheltuit România. "De unde **să ştiu** eu? Intrebaţi-l pe domnul Rusu!"

                           (www.economie.hotnews.ro, 21 May 2013)
     'Constantin Niţă, the Deputy Minister of Energy, was asked how much money Romania has spent. "How could I know? Ask Mister Rusu."'

As observed by Rohde (2006) and Caponigro & Sprouse (2007), the answer to a rhetorical question is biased because it is obvious for both the speaker and the addressee; it belongs to a set of common beliefs shared by them, i.e. the Common Ground (Stalnaker 1978). In many cases, the obviousness of a negative answer is made explicit by the content of the utterance itself, as in (27) below. More generally, these rhetorical uses come with additional pragmatic effects, such as surprise, protest, indignation, irony, compassion, etc.

(27) a. Ce **să caute** un intelectual la ţară?   (*Cotidianul*, 19 April 1999)
'What could an intellectual do in the countryside?'

b. Cum **să fie** creatura creator? (www.doxologia.ro, 1 January 2018)
'How could the creature be creator?'

c. Sunt bătrână, ce **să fac** eu cu banii? (www.cancan.ro, 4 June 2014)
'I am an old lady. What could I do with money?'

d. Becali nu rezistă nici două luni la închisoare, de unde **să stea** trei ani?   (www.sport.ro, 20 May 2013)
'Becali does not even endure two months in a prison, how could he stay there three years?'

The bias for a negative answer occurs not only in *wh*-questions but also in polar questions with what is called 'mirativity subjunctive'[8] (Avram 2015), marking speaker's surprise with respect to the preceding context, as seen in (28) below. As Peterson (2013) indicates, mirativity is related to new information that is not easily assimilated by the speaker. The speaker's surprise and incredulity can be made explicit by an initial interrogative pronoun used as a discursive particle (*cine* 'who' (28a), *ce* 'what' (28b), *cum* 'how' (28c)), as well as by an overt negative coda (e.g. *niciodată* 'never', *imposibil* 'it's impossible' (28b); *nu pot să cred* 'I don't believe that', *nu mă aşteptam* 'I didn't expect it at all' (28c)). This mirative component is best observed in (28c): the subjunctive interrogative clause cannot be followed by a coda which contradicts its mirative meaning such as *nu mă surprinde deloc* 'it doesn't surprise me at all'. Prosodically, mirative subjunctive questions have a special intonation contour (progressive raising contour, plus prosodic stress). The fact that both *wh*-questions and polar questions can be used with the same pragmatic effects is best observed in the attested example in (28d), which combines mirative polar questions and *wh*-questions.

---

[8] Alternative labels are e.g. 'Mad Magazine sentences' in Akmajian (1984) and 'Incredulity Response Construction' in Lambrecht (1990).

(28) a. (Cine?) Iohannis **să facă** asta? 0% şanse.
   '(Who?) Iohannis do this? 0% chance.'
   b. (Ce?) Dragnea **să-şi ceară scuze**?
   {Niciodată. / Imposibil. / Visezi.}
   '(What?) Dragnea ask for an apology?
   {Never. / It's impossible. / You are dreaming!}'
   c. (Cum?) **Să nu dai** tu niciun semn de viaţă atâta timp?
   {Nu pot să cred. / Nu mă aşteptam. / #Nu mă surprinde deloc.}
   '(What?) You not making any sign of life for such a long time?
   {I can't believe it. / I didn't expect it at all. / It doesn't surprise me
   at all.}'
   d. Cum? Eu **să citesc**? Da' de ce **să îmi bat** creierii degeaba, când am
   atâtea programe TV care îmi ocupă timpul, îmi ramolesc gândirea
   şi mă relaxează? Cum? Eu **să dau** 20 de lei pe o carte? Te-ai tâm-
   pit? De ce **să arunc** banii pe o carte când pot să îmi iau pizza, bere
   şi seminţe de ei? Să îmi pun eu burta la cale, asta contează!
   (www.mariussescu.ro, 18 October 2010)
   'What? Me read? Why should I get worked up for nothing, when I
   have so many TV programs which occupy my time, put my
   thought on standby and relax me! What? Me spend 20 lei on a
   book? Have you lost your head? Why should I waste money on a
   book when I can buy a pizza, a beer and seeds instead? To be
   filled, that is what counts!'

3.2.2 Rhetorical Questions with Repetition of the Same Material

In the beginning of this section, we noted that reactive questions involve a
reaction (e.g. refutation, presupposition cancellation, surprise) to the preceding utterance. A specific linguistic device which is used in many rhetorical
questions with the subjunctive is the repetition of the lexical material from
the preceding utterance (in particular, the verbal lexeme of the previous
utterance – usually in the indicative – is repeated in a interrogative clause
with subjunctive morphology). This may apply to polar interrogatives (in
mirative contexts, see reaction B_1 in (29a) below), but also to *wh*-
interrogatives (see reaction B_2 in (29a)). Furthermore, in most cases, these
rhetorical questions mark a bias for a negative answer, but they can also
allow positive answers, as we can see in (29b) where reaction B_1 can only
receive a negative answer, whereas reaction B_2 is only compatible with a
positive one.

(29) a. A: Te superi dacă te întreb ceva?
     A: 'Will you get angry if I ask you something?'
     B_1: Eu **să mă supăr**? B_2: Cum **să mă supăr**?
     B_1: 'Me get angry?' B_2: 'How could I get angry?'
  b. A: Nu mă mai cunoşti?
     A: 'Do you not recognize me anymore?'
     B_1: De unde păcatele mele **să te cunosc**? (= Nu te cunosc.)
     B_1: 'How in God's name could I recognize you?'
     B_2: Cum dracu' **să nu te cunosc**?
     B_2: 'How the hell could I not recognize you?'

More generally, this repetition mechanism is involved in many *wh*-interrogatives to mark the obviousness of the answer, i.e. the fact that the answer to the first question is known to both the speaker and the addressee. Any interrogative phrase can be used with this strategy, as illustrated in (30) below: *cine* 'who' (30a), *ce* 'what' (30b), *cum* 'how' (30c), *unde* 'where', etc. By repeating the same lexical material in a subjunctive rhetorical question, speaker B treats the question asked by speaker A as 'non-receivable', since s/he knows that the other should be able to know the answer as well. This is made explicit in (30a), where the subjunctive rhetorical question is followed by a reproach made against speaker A (*parcă dumneata n-auzişi* 'as if you have not heard'). The fact that the answer is very obvious in these contexts explains why speaker B very often chooses to reduplicate his answer by such subjunctive rhetorical questions, which can either precede (30b) or follow it (30c–d).

(30) a. A: <u>Cine mai muri</u> iarna asta? întrebă una.
     B: Păi <u>cine **să mai moară**</u>, parcă dumneata n-auzişi? Se duse şi
        Vasiloaia...

                              (Eugen Barbu, *Morcovii*)
     A: 'Who died last winter? asked one of them.'
     B: 'Well, who could die, as if you have not heard? It is Vasiloaia
       who died...'
  b. A: <u>Ce faceţi</u>, surorile mele?
     B: Bine, <u>ce **să facem**</u>?

                              (Eugen Barbu, *Morcovii*)
     A: 'What are you doing, my sisters?'
     B: 'Well, what could we do?'

c. A: <u>Cum e</u> să fii adolescent la volan?
   B: Păi, <u>**cum să fie**</u>? Super bine şi plin de adrenalină.
                           (www.gandul.info, 29 March 2007)
   A: 'How is it to be a teenager driver?'
   B: 'Well, how could it be? Very well and full of adrenaline.'

d. A: <u>Unde s-a greşit?</u>
   B: <u>Unde **să se greşească**</u>, nicăieri!
                          (www.libertatea.ro, 16 November 2001)
   A: 'Where has a mistake been made?'
   B: 'Where could a mistake have been made, nowhere!'

After presenting all the uses of the subjunctive in rhetorical questions, a general observation concerning the modality involved in these contexts is the fact that the subjunctive mood is linked here to an epistemic interpretation.

As for the potential alternation with other moods, we have to mention that, unlike the previous types (i.e. the deliberative and dubitative cases), there is no possible alternation with the indicative or the presumptive mood. The infinitive is also prohibited in these contexts, unlike in other Romance languages, such as French (or Germanic languages), which prefer the infinitive in these 'mirative' contexts (31a), though it may be in alternation with the subjunctive in French[9] (31b).

(31) a. Moi, **faire** une chose pareille!
      'Me, do such a thing?'
   b. Moi, **que je fasse** une chose pareille!
                    (Riegel, Pellat & Rioul 1994: 323)
      'Me, do such a thing?'

3.2.3 Echo Questions

Echo questions refer to reactive cases involving clarification requests, i.e. query responses that concern the content or form of the preceding utterance that was not adequately heard or understood (Purver, Ginzburg & Healey 2001, Schlangen 2004). Thus, they are unlike the previous reactive cases which involve rhetorical questions (i.e. where the speaker does not expect an answer from the interlocutor). As the name indicates, echo questions are based on a reprise mechanism, which can be either a literal reprise (in polar interrogatives, as in (32a) below) or *wh*-substituted reprise (in *wh*-interrogatives, as in (32b)). The verb of the preceding utterance (which usu-

---

[9] Ţenchea (2001) mentions a correlation between the mood alternation and the person in these mirative contexts: the subjunctive would be more frequent with the first person, while the infinitive is most frequent with the other persons.

ally is an imperative clause) is repeated under a subjunctive form in the echo question. As these clarification requests typically echo a directive speech act from the preceding utterance, they keep its deontic modality. They cannot be confused with other subjunctive interrogatives, since they have a special (rising) intonation contour. In these specific contexts, no alternation with other mood is available. Interestingly, these echo questions occur in other Romance languages too, as illustrated in (33) for French polar interrogatives.

(32) a. A: Du-te acasă! B: **Să mă duc** acasă?
A: 'Go home!' B: 'Me go home?'

b. A: Du-te la dracu'! B: Unde **să mă duc** eu, Marcelică?
A: La dracu'! B: Aha.
(Toma Caragiu, *Momente de Aur*)

A: 'Go to hell!' B: 'Where to go, Marcelică?'
A: 'Go to hell.' B: 'Aha.'

(33) a. A: Va dans ta chambre! B: **Que j'aille** dans ma chambre?
A: ' Go in your room!' B: 'Me go in my room?'

b. LE MEDECIN: Abdiquez, Sire, cela vaut mieux.
Doctor: 'Abdicate, Sir. That would be best.'
LE ROI: **Que j'abdique**?
King: 'Abdicate? Me?'
MARGUERITE: Oui. Abdique moralement, administrativement.
Marguerite: Yes. Abdicate morally and governmentally.'
LE MEDECIN: Et physiquement. (Eugène Ionesco, *Le roi se meurt*)
Doctor: 'And physically!'

3.2.4 *'Wh-*imperatives'

Apart from the rhetorical and echo questions, there is a conventionalized[10] *wh-*interrogative construction which, like the other reactive uses, cannot be an initiating move. This specific pattern refers to so-called *'wh-*imperatives', seen in (34) below, where one makes an indirect proposal (a suggestion) by using the prepositional phrase *de ce* 'why' generally with a negated verbal form (e.g. the particle *nu* 'not').[11] These *wh-*imperatives are not queries, but rather assertions, as shown by B's responses with factive adjectives such as *super* or *perfect*, which require the content to be part of

---

[10] Other (lexicalized) cases are discussed in Bîlbîie & Mardale (2018), in particular *wh-*interrogatives with *ce* 'what' followed by the verbs *a spune, a zice* 'to say', *a vedea* 'to see' and *a face* 'to do', to express various pragmatic effects (irony, refutation, delay answering, surprise, etc.).

[11] Many *wh-*imperatives of this type use the first person plural, the speaker including him/herself in the addressee's sphere.

the set of facts in the Common Ground (Fernández & Ginzburg 2002). These specific interrogative clauses may alternate subjunctive and conditional moods, as illustrated in (35a) and (36). The fact that both moods can be used with the same pragmatic effect is best observed in the example in (36), where both conditional and subjunctive moods are used in free alternation: the conditional *wh*-interrogative clause *noi de ce n-am face-o* ('why not do it') is followed by a coordination of two subjunctive *wh*-interrogative clauses: *de ce să nu luăm bunele practici și să le implementăm* ('why not take good practice of Europe and implement it'). The '*wh*-imperative' label is justified by the possibility to use an imperative clause (35b) instead of a *wh*-interrogative clause (35a), the modality involved in these contexts being a deontic one.

(34) a. A: De ce **să nu începem** cu desertul?   B: Super.
     A: 'Why not start with the dessert?'   B: 'Super.'
   b. A: De ce **să nu facem** cum a zis el?   B: Perfect.
     A: 'Why not do as he says?'   B: 'Perfect.'

(35) a. Dacă poți   să faci   un bine, de ce {**să**
     if   can.2SG SUBJ do.2SG a   good   why   SUBJ
     nu-l   **faci** / **nu** l-**ai**   **face**}?
     NEG-ACC.3SG do.2SG   NEG ACC.3SG-AUX.2SG do.INF
     'If you can do a good deed, why {not do it / you would not do it}?'
   b. Dacă poți să faci un bine, **fă**-l!
     'If you can do a good deed, do it!'

(36) Dacă în Germania, Franța, Spania, Marea Britanie, Slovacia, Slovenia s-au luat măsuri de plafonare a dobânzilor, noi de ce **n-am face**-o? De ce **să nu luăm** bunele practici din Europa și **să** le **implementăm** și noi?

                                                   (www.dcnews.ro, 9 December 2017)
     'If interest rates have been capped in Germany, France, Spain, the UK, Slovakia, Slovenia, why not do it? Why not take the good practices of Europe and implement them?'

As is the case with deliberative questions and rhetorical questions, other Romance languages such as French make use of the infinitive in these *wh*-imperative contexts, as illustrated in (37).

(37) a. Pourquoi pas **commencer** le golf, c'est la rentrée!
      'Why not start with golf, it's the start of the new school year!'
   b. Si vous vous passionez du sport, pourquoi pas **faire** une randonnée en haute montagne?
      'If you are passionate about sport, why not go for a hike in the high mountains?'

Table 1 summarizes subjunctive interrogative clause types discussed in this section. We observe that the various types of subjunctive interrogative clauses carry an implicit modality, either a deontic or an epistemic interpretation.[12] As for the alternation between the subjunctive and other moods in Romanian, even though in some contexts the subjunctive may occur in (relatively) free distribution with other moods, there are interrogative clauses where the subjunctive mood is the only option. From a Romance perspective, we can easily observe the singular behaviour of Romanian among other Romance languages, the subjunctive mood being extremely rare in the interrogative clauses of the other Romance languages such as French.

Table 1 Typology of Romanian subjunctive interrogative clauses.

Context	Type	Modality	Mood alternation	Romance (French) mood
Out-of-the-blue	Deliberative-q	deontic	indicative	infinitive
Out-of-the-blue	Dubitative-q	epistemic	presumptive	conditional
Reactive	Rhetorical-q (± repetition)	epistemic	—	infinitive
Reactive	Echo-q	deontic	—	subjunctive
Reactive	*Wh*-imperatives	deontic	conditional	infinitive

4 Towards an Explanation at the Semantics–Pragmatics Interface

Against this rich typology of Romanian subjunctive interrogatives, the following big question arises: How can one explain the different interpretations of subjunctive interrogatives? In other words, what are the general properties of subjunctive interrogatives which apply to the various uses pre-

---

[12] Our data seem to challenge the assumption made in the literature (Becker 2010, Zafiu 2013) that deontic modality would be the main value of the Romanian subjunctive. There are various subjunctive contexts carrying an epistemic interpretation.

sented in the previous section? To answer this question, we focus on the interaction between the subjunctive mood and the interrogative clause. However, this is by no means an easy task, as mentioned in Portner (2016: 14): 'Nobody knows much about subjunctive interrogatives'.

First of all, despite the rich typology of subjunctive interrogatives in Romanian, all subtypes (polar or *wh*-interrogatives) are syntactically interrogative clauses, as shown in (38) below by their compatibility with the interrogative particle *oare*, which can be found only in interrogatives (not in declaratives, exclamatives or imperatives; for more details, see Farkas 2018 and Giurgea 2018).

(38) a. Cum **să te laşi** <u>oare</u> de fumat?　　　　(deliberative)
　　　'How to quit smoking?'
　　b. **Să fie** <u>oare</u> ora 9?　　　　　　　　　(dubitative)
　　　'Could it be 9 o'clock?'
　　c. Ce **să caute** <u>oare</u> un intelectual la ţară?　　(rhetorical)
　　　'What could an intellectual do in the countryside?'
　　d. A: Du-te acasă!　　B: **Să mă duc** acasă <u>oare</u>?　(echo)
　　　A: 'Go home!'　　B: 'Me go home?'
　　e. De ce **să nu începem** <u>oare</u> cu desertul?　　(*wh*-imperative)
　　　'Why not start with the dessert?'

Furthermore, a crucial property of subjunctive interrogatives is their infelicity in regular information-seeking contexts, in which the addressee is assumed to answer the question; interestingly, the same property characterizes *oare*-interrogatives in general, discussed by Bruce & Farkas (2007), Farkas & Bruce (2010) and Farkas (2018). We can readily see in (39) below that the subjunctive is generally not used in neutral contexts, with pure information-seeking questions, in (39a–b), or quiz questions, in (39c), where only the indicative is allowed (the '#' diacritic marks the unacceptable subjunctive). The same observation is made by Pavlidou (1991: 37) for Greek: 'in using subjunctive interrogatives one does not neutrally seek information about the world as is the case with "real" questions'. This shows that there is something special about these subjunctive uses at both the semantic and the pragmatic level.

(39) a. *Context: A police officer asking a driver to legitimate him/herself.*
Cum {#**să** vă **cheme**/ vă **cheamă**}?
how SUBJ ACC.2SG call.SUBJ.3 ACC.2SG call.IND.3
'What is your name?'

b. *Context: A traveler asking information at the ticket office.*
Cât {#**să coste** / **costă**} un bilet până la Iaşi?
how.much SUBJ cost.SUBJ.3 cost.IND.3 a ticket until to Iaşi
'How much does a ticket to Iaşi cost?'

c. *Context: A teacher asking her students a quiz question.*
Cât {#**să facă** / **fac**} doi plus doi?
how.much SUBJ equal.SUBJ.3 equal.IND.3PL two plus two
'How much is two plus two?'

4.1 Semantic Aspects

We follow Ginzburg & Sag (2000) and Beyssade & Marandin (2006) in assuming that the semantic content of interrogative clauses is a question, i.e. a propositional abstract obtained by abstraction of 0 parameters (in the case of polar interrogatives) or 1, or several parameters (in the case of *wh*-interrogatives). We have thus a correspondence between a syntactic type (i.e. an interrogative clause) and a type of semantic content (i.e. a question).

While one does not know much about the interaction between subjunctives and interrogatives (see Portner's remark above), we may easily observe a semantic property that subjunctives and interrogatives share. Both invoke the notion of alternatives.

Consider the interrogatives first. In alternative semantics, it is generally assumed that the denotation of an interrogative clause is the set of propositions (= alternatives) that serve as its possible complete answers (Hamblin 1973, Karttunen 1977, Groenendijk & Stokhof 1984, etc.). With polar interrogatives, there is an alternative between *p* and non-*p* (positive vs. negative polarity). With alternative questions, the speaker offers the list of possible answers from which the addressee is supposed to choose the correct one. With *wh*-interrogatives, the *wh*-phrase has a focus-semantic value (Hamblin 1973, Rooth 1992) corresponding to relevant alternatives in its domain; these alternative propositions correspond to possible answers to the question. In other semantic frameworks, such as inquisitive semantics, an interrogative clause is treated as a set of possibilities too.

Consider now the subjunctive mood. As Farkas (1985, 1992), Villalta (2007, 2008), Godard (2012) and others have shown, the subjunctive mood is motivated in contexts where the interpretation requires that one takes into account alternative situations (or in Villalta's terms the set of contextually relevant alternatives). The interrogative domain creates such an environment. The interrogative domain is generally a phenomenon of interlocution (mainly dialogue), where the speaker is explicit (s/he doubts, doesn't believe, hesitates, etc.). Therefore, in the case studied here, the interpretation of an interrogative clause corresponds to the condition imposed by the subjunctive mood, explaining thus the affinity between them in Romanian.

Much work has been dedicated to the subjunctive mood (e.g. Farkas 1985, 1992, 2003; Villalta 2007, 2008; Giannakidou 2009, 2016; Godard 2012). Despite the differences we observe across the various approaches to subjunctives, a semantic feature commonly invoked in relation to the subjunctive contexts is evaluativity. In subjunctive contexts, the interpretation requires taking into account both possibilities p and non-p (Farkas 1992, Giorgi & Pianesi 1997, Godard 2012). In comparison-based approaches, the subjunctive mood marks a modal semantics involving comparison/evaluation between possible worlds (Portner 2016). This partitioning of modal domains into p and non-p worlds recalls the notion of nonveridicality, considered by Giannakidou (2016) as an underlying property of all subjunctive contexts. According to her, the evaluative subjunctive creates a nonveridical modal space, i.e. a weakened commitment to p. We follow Gazdar (1981) and Beyssade & Marandin (2006) in extending the notion of commitment, traditionnally restricted to commitment to propositions p (Hamblin 1971). When the speaker utters a question, s/he makes a move by which s/he becomes committed to an issue (Beyssade & Marandin 2006). In the case of subjunctive interrogatives, we will say that, at least in some cases, the nonveridical modal space is a weakened commitment to the issue raised by the question. We can now explain the subjunctive/indicative alternation in interrogative clauses (see the examples in (39) above) by saying that indicative contexts imply a full commitment to the issue raised by the question, whereas subjunctive ones involve a weakened commitment to that issue.

All subjunctive uses discussed in this paper have an evaluative component, encoded in the subjunctive mood itself. This leads us to make an amendment to the Farkas's (1992, 2003) proposal (which concerned the embedding predicates and the indicative/subjunctive alternation in embedded complement clauses). The context change potential (defined by the semantic feature [–*assertion*] or [–*realis*] in the case of subjunctive contexts) is not necessarily linked to the semantics of some matrix predicates triggering the subjunctive in embedded clauses. The contribution of interrogatives to this evaluative component of subjunctives lies in the fact that they open the possibility space of the subjunctive, i.e. they require to take into account several possibilities, not only p and non-p. As proposed by Bruce & Farkas (2007) for non-canonical *oare*-interrogatives, we can say that our subjunctive interrogatives widen the set of alternatives, leaving the addressee more choice.

Finally, in the light of the data presented in the previous section, one has to conclude that all uses of the subjunctive in interrogative clauses involve an implicit modality, i.e. syntactically there is no covert modal involved (see the discussion in Section 2 above), but semantically there is an implicit – deontic or epistemic – modality contributed by the subjunctive itself.

4.2 Pragmatic Aspects

In the previous section, we observed that all subjunctive interrogative subtypes in Romanian are syntactically interrogative clauses which are semantically associated with a question (i.e. propositional abstract).

As for the traditional association between clause types and illocutionary forces, we crucially adopt here the divide proposed by Beyssade & Marandin (2006) between speaker's commitment and speaker's call-on-addressee in a dialogical perspective. The first import refers to a relation between the speaker and a content type (i.e. the speaker's attitude, such as belief, ignorance, desire, etc.), while the second one refers to sorts of obligation exerted on the addressee (i.e. the speaker calls for the addressee to do something with the content of her utterance). Whereas clause types are associated with speaker's commitment in a one-to-one manner (being a source of information relative to the speaker's commitment), there is no one-to-one correspondence between clause types and speaker's call-on-addressee (i.e. clause types do not determine a specific call-on-addressee). Therefore, speaker's commitment and speaker's call-on-addressee need not be identical.

In the case of subjunctive interrogative clauses, the speaker commits him/herself to an issue (i.e. the speaker is interested in knowing the answer, though there is a weaker commitment than in regular questions); therefore, the speaker's commitment seems to be the same for all our subtypes of interrogatives. However, the various subtypes of our subjunctive interrogative clauses do not all convey the same type of call-on-addressee. This is made explicit in Table 2 below, where there are two subtypes of interrogative clauses which do not have a questioning call-on-addressee as expected: rhetorical questions have an assertoric use (i.e. the speaker asks the addressee to take up her utterance as an assertion), and *wh*-imperatives have a directive use (i.e. the speaker asks the addressee to take up her utterance as a suggestion).

Table 2 The relation between syntax, semantics and pragmatics.

Type	Clause type	Semantic content	Speaker's commitment	Call-on-addressee
Deliberative-q	Interrogative	question	issue	query
Dubitative-q	Interrogative	question	issue	query
Rhetorical-q	Interrogative	question	issue	assertion
Echo-q	Interrogative	question	issue	query
Wh-imperatives	Interrogative	question	issue	outcome

The most intriguing cases are nevertheless those corresponding to a questioning call-on-addressee; recall the fact that our subjunctive interrogatives are infelicitous in regular information-seeking contexts, in which the addressee is assumed to answer the question. As mentioned in the beginning of the present section, the same observation is made for *oare*-interrogatives by Farkas & Bruce (2010) and Farkas (2018), who conclude that *oare*-interrogatives are not regular interrogatives, since they allow for no addressee response. Their suggestion is that *oare*-interrogatives are non-canonical questions, 'non-intrusive questions' (Farkas 2018), in that the speaker signals that s/he does not wish to put the addressee on the spot for providing the answer. Non-intrusive questions weaken the effect of the addressee compliance assumption of canonical questions, i.e. the speaker does not assume anymore that the addressee will necessarily resolve the question. Furthermore, we add here the proposal made by Giurgea (2018), who analyzes *oare*-interrogatives as 'tentative questions', because of the weakening of the addressee competence assumption, i.e. the addressee is not necessarily in a position to know the answer for sure.

Our intuition is that something similar is at work at least in some of our cases. There is something special about the speaker's call-on-addressee in these subjunctive interrogatives.

Let us now move to the indicative/subjunctive alternation illustrated in Section 3.1 above by the examples in (21), repeated for convenience in (40) below. We noted that the interrogative using the indicative mood in (40b) behaves as a regular information-seeking question (i.e. requiring an explicit response from the addressee). On the other hand, the interrogative displaying the subjunctive mood in (40a) does not have the behaviour of an ordinary question, i.e. it does not necessarily require a response from the addressee, since in this particular case neither the speaker nor the addressee knows the answer.

(40) a. **Să fi plouat** afară?
'Would it be the case that it rained (outside)?'
b. A **plouat** afară?
'Did it rain (outside)?'

All these observations indicate that there is something special about the illocutionary force of an interrogative clause using the subjunctive mood. As they are less directly addressed than indicative interrogatives (they are 'softened' questions), subjunctive interrogatives crucially involve a weak call-on-addressee (i.e. no obligation exerted on the addressee).

There are two pieces of evidence that a weak call-on-addressee is at work in these contexts. The first test comes from the use of the interrogative particle *oare*. This particle cannot be used with pure information-seeking questions. When it occurs, it signals the optionality of the answer (i.e. it removes the obligation from the addressee to answer that question), see Bruce & Farkas (2007). Thus, in an interrogative clause using the indicative mood, the presence or absence of this particle triggers pragmatic differences. If the particle *oare* is absent, as in (41a) below, we have an explicit call-on-addressee, as in regular questions. If, on the other hand, the particle is present, as in (41b), there is a weak call-on-addressee. Coming back to subjunctive interrogatives, we observe in (41c) that they are perfectly compatible with the particle *oare*, which reinforces the dubitative-epistemic meaning.

(41) a. Cine **a venit**?
'Who came?'
b. Cine <u>oare</u> **a venit**?
'Who could have come?'
c. Cine (<u>oare</u>) **să fi venit**?
'Who could have come?'

The similarity between *oare*-interrogatives and our deliberative questions can be easily observed in (42): in both *oare*-interrogatives – one with indicative, as in (42a), and the other a subjunctive interrogative, as in (42b) – the addressee competence and compliance assumptions are absent; the speaker does not assume that the addressee knows the answer, and the addressee is not necessarily required to settle the issue (the speaker invites the addressee to think together to find the answer).

(42) *Context: A mathematician to a colleague with whom s/he is working.*
  a. <u>Oare</u> ecuaţia asta **are** o soluţie?   (Farkas 2018)
     'Does this equation have a solution, I wonder?'
  b. (Oare) **Să aibă** o soluţie ecuaţia asta?
     'Would it be the case that this equation has a solution?'

The second piece of evidence concerns illocutionary modifiers, such as the English *honestly*, which make explicit the call-on-addressee and force the addressee to answer. If one compares the indicative and the subjunctive interrogatives in this respect, the contrast between them becomes clear immediately. Therefore, we observe that such an illocutionary modifier is infelicitous in subjunctive environments (43a), while it is acceptable in indicative contexts (43b). This once again demonstrates the specific role of the subjunctive in these interrogative clauses.

(43) a. #<u>Spune-mi sincer</u>, cine **să fi venit**?
        'Be honest/honestly, who could have come?'
  b. <u>Spune-mi sincer</u>, cine **a venit**?
     'Be honest/honestly, who could have come?'

The same discursive behaviour is observed in Greek subjunctive interrogatives on an even larger scale. Pavlidou (1991) and Rouchota (1994) consider that in Greek even a deliberative question does not necessarily require an answer from the addressee. The differences we observe in Romanian between deliberative and dubitative cases (see Section 3.1.2, e.g. with respect to embedding) suggest that there is a gradience in the call-on-addressee strength: the call-on-addressee is weaker in some cases (e.g. dubitative interrogatives) than in others (e.g. deliberative interrogatives). This can be observed in (44), where the illocutionary modifier *ce zici* 'what do you think/what do you say' is felicitous with a deliberative subjunctive in (44a), but infelicitous in the dubitative context (44b).

(44) a. <u>Ce zici</u>, **să mă căsătoresc** cu fata asta?
        'What do you think, should I marry this girl?'
  b. <u>Ce zici</u>, {e / #**să fie**} ora 9?
     'What do you think, is it 9 o'clock?'

This weakened call-on-addressee is made clearer in the reactive uses. Recall that most cases of reactive uses are in fact rhetorical questions, which by definition do not require an explicit answer from the addressee. We agree with Caponigro & Sprouse (2007) who consider that rhetorical questions behave syntactically and semantically like regular questions but differ from them at the pragmatic level, i.e. the addressee is not expected to answer, since the information requested is already provided in the background. In formal terms, rhetorical questions are interrogatives conveying a biased question whose answer is Common Ground (i.e. predictable or known by both the speaker and the addressee) and whose dialogue impact requires the activation of such a content (Marandin 2008). The bias in a rhetorical question can be made explicit by a fragment such as *parcă n-ai şti* 'you know it very well', as in (45).

(45) A: Ce face Ion? B: Ce **să facă**? <u>Parcă n-ai şti</u>, pierde timpul!
      A: 'How is Ion?' B: 'How could he be? As if you didn't know, he is wasting his time.'

In conclusion, we can say that subjunctive interrogatives are 'softened' questions, in the sense that the speaker's call-on-addressee is weaker than in canonical questions. Our intuition is that, in these subjunctive interrogatives, the speaker and the addressee are at the same level of ignorance as to what the possible answers are. The gradience we observed in the call-on-addressee strength (in particular, between dubitative and deliberative subjunctives) should be analyzed in more detail in further research.

5   Conclusion

The Romanian data show the rich semantic and pragmatic potential of the subjunctive mood in the interrogative domain in Romanian, compared to other Romance languages (represented mostly by French), where the discursive effects presented above are covered by other moods (indicative, conditional, infinitive). We could say that the main aim of the subjunctive interrogatives is not to request information (as in regular information-seeking questions), but rather to express a variety of illocutionary meanings related to the speaker's attitude.

If one takes into account the bipartite structure of the illocutionary force, the specific contribution of (at least some of) the subjunctive interrogative contexts in Romanian could be summarized as follows: a weakened speaker's commitment along with a weak call-on-addressee. The first property seems to be shared by all subjunctive contexts (see Giannakidou 2016), whereas the second property seems to be representative of subjunctives in interrogative clauses.

Overall, our study documents the heterogeneous behaviour of the subjunctive mood crosslinguistically and even within the same language, lending support to the assumption made by Wiltschko (2016), namely that the subjunctive is not a natural class in terms of one modality, or one type of subjunctive across languages; moreover, it is not a universally uniform category.

A natural continuation of this study would be to go deeper into the semantic and pragmatic formalization of the effects mentioned in this paper and also to complement our data with experimental and other corpus data, to build a quantitative perspective on this phenomenon and to test our theoretical proposals.

Acknowledgements

This work was supported by strand 2 of the LabEx Empirical Foundations of Linguistics. We would like to thank Anne Abeillé, Donka Farkas, Ion Giurgea, Danièle Godard, Jean-Marie Marandin, and Mara Panaitescu for their valuable comments and advice. The various types of subjunctive interrogatives presented here are also discussed in Bîlbîie & Mardale (2018).

10

Deconstructing Subjects: Presentational Sentences in Swedish

Elisabet Engdahl, Annie Zaenen and Joan Maling

1 Introduction

In his seminal paper, Keenan (1976: 307) notes that 'subjects of certain sentences, and more generally of certain sentence types, will be more subject-like than the subjects of others ... Thus the subjecthood of an NP (in a sentence) is a matter of degree'. In this paper we take Keenan's statement as the starting point for a comparison of canonical subjects, as in (1), and so called pivots in presentational constructions in modern Swedish, as in (2).[1]

(1) Katten kom in i köket.
    cat.DEF came into in kitchen.DEF
    'The cat came into the kitchen.'

(2) Det kom in **en katt** i köket.
    EXPL came in a cat in kitchen.DEF
    'A cat came into the kitchen.'

We assume that whether a sentence is realized with a canonical subject or a pivot is the result of a negotiation between different grammar components which impose their violable and non-violable constraints on the outcome and we will model our findings in terms of constraints on the alignment. For the purpose of this paper, the lexical layer and

---

[1] In the examples, pivots are shown in bold. Other terms for pivots are 'logical subject' and 'associate (of the expletive)'.

Constraint-Based Syntax and Semantics: Papers in Honor of Danièle Godard.
Anne Abeillé and Olivier Bonami (eds.).

the information structure layer are the most important. The result of their negotiation is the surface realization of the sentence, which has a structured syntactic component also relevant for the phenomena that we are discussing. We assume that each layer has its own hierarchy and that the least marked realization is the result of harmonic alignment (Aissen 1999) in which all the elements of each layer are mapped onto the surface structure in their hierarchical order.

We start by giving an overview in Section 2 of the syntactic properties of canonical subjects and pivots, paying special attention to the differences between actives and passives. We then discuss lexical properties of pivots in Section 3, and relevant information-structural notions in Section 4, before outlining a mapping account in Section 5. Section 6 concludes with some remarks on the role of grammatical functions.

2 Syntax

Keenan (1976: 324) subdivides the subject properties into three groups:

- coding properties: position, case marking, verb agreement
- behavior and control properties: deletion, movement, case changing, control of cross reference, etc.
- semantic properties: agency, autonomous existence, selectional restriction, etc.

The third group of properties is closely related to the lexical and the information-structural properties of the subject and will be discussed in Sections 3 and 4. The first two pertain to what we consider to be syntax proper. We first look at the coding properties and then at the behavioral ones.

Swedish is a so-called verb second language; in declarative main clauses, the finite verb follows the first constituent. For the purpose of this article, we assume the following minimal phrase structure rules for declarative main clauses (cf. Börjars, Engdahl & Andréasson 2003, Engdahl, Andréasson & Börjars 2004):

(3) S —> XP V_{+FIN} (NP) ADV* (VP)
     VP —> (V_{-FIN}) (Prt) (NP) (NP) PP*

In this paper we will use a flat topological structure, shown in (4), where we distinguish a Vorfeld, a Mittelfeld and a Verbalfeld.[2] We number the NP arguments for ease of reference.

(4)

Vorfeld	Mittelfeld		Verbalfeld				
XP	V [+FIN]	NP1 ADV*	V [-FIN]	Prt	NP2	NP3	PP*

We refer to the material before the tensed verb as the Vorfeld. It is a single constituent, an XP, that can carry any grammatical function but is often the subject.[3] In the Mittelfeld we find the finite verb, the subject if it is not in the Vorfeld, sentential adverbs and modal particles.[4] The Verbalfeld starts with the non-finite verb or a verbal particle, followed by objects, prepositional objects and adjuncts.

2.1 Position and Case

Since Swedish is a verb second language, the subject appears either in the Vorfeld, right before the finite verb as in (5), or in the Mittelfeld after the finite verb when some other constituent precedes the verb, as shown in (6).

(5) Vi   har varit i köket.
     we.NOM have been in kitchen.DEF
     'We have been in the kitchen.'

(6) Här har vi   varit.
     here have we.NOM been
     'We have been here.'

In the following, we will refer to the subjects in (5) and (6) as 'canonical subjects' (i.e. subjects preceding and following the finite verb). Canonical subjects have nominative case, although this is only visible on personal pronouns; lexical NPs do not show case marking in modern Swedish.

---

[2]This type of topological schema is often used in descriptive grammars for German and Scandinavian, see Diderichsen (1946) and Teleman, Hellberg & Andersson (1999), but also in constraint-based frameworks, see Kathol (2004), Müller (2013). The schema may be adjusted to a more hierarchical structure, as e.g. in Sells (2001), but this won't be necessary for the discussion in this article.

[3]In Swedish, only unstressed modal particles are excluded from the first position.

  (i) *Ju har vi   varit här.
     PRT have we.NOM been here

[4]The order between the subject and sentential adverbs in the Mittelfeld is not fixed but is influenced by scope and information-structural factors like topichood. See Engdahl et al. (2004) for an Optimality Theory account. Similar ordering variations are found in the German Mittelfeld, see Frey (2006).

In presentational sentences, an expletive *det* appears in either of the canonical subject positions and the pivot appears in the Verbalfeld. In (7) and (8), the pivot appears after a non-finite verb, and in (9) and (10), it appears after a verb particle.

(7) Det   har varit **en katt** i köket.
     EXPL has a   cat been in kitchen.DEF
     'There has been a cat in the kitchen.'

(8) Här har det   varit **en katt**.
     here has EXPL been a   cat
     'There has been a cat here.'

(9) Det kom in **en katt** i köket.
     EXPL came in a   cat   in kitchen.DEF
     'A cat came into the kitchen.'

(10) Sen kom det   in **en katt** i köket.
     then came EXPL in a   cat   in kitchen.DEF
     'Then a cat came into the kitchen.'

In declarative sentences with just a single finite verb and no verb particle, the pivot follows the finite verb. It can still be distinguished from a canonical subject in the Mittelfeld by the requirement that it be indefinite (see Section 4). Consequently we assume that *en katt* is in the Verbalfeld in (11), just as in (9).

(11) Det   sitter **en katt**/*katten i   köket.
     EXPL sits   a   cat/ cat.DEF in kitchen.DEF
     'There is a cat sitting in the kitchen.'

Canonical subjects of passive sentences appear in the same positions and are also marked with nominative case.

(12) Vi   bjöds   in till festen.
     we.NOM invited.PASS in to party.DEF
     'We were invited to the party.'

(13) Sen bjöds   vi   in till festen.
     then invited.PASS we.NOM in to party.DEF
     'Then we were invited to the party.'

Subjects of passive sentences are also possible pivots, as shown in (14).

(14) Det   bjöds   in **en musiker** till festen.
     EXPL invited.PASS in a   musician to party.DEF
     'A musician was invited to the party.'

In Swedish it is difficult to determine the case of the pivot since only pronouns are case-marked and they are normally not possible as pivots. There is however one context where pronouns can be used, see Teleman et al. (1999, 3: 387). In sentences with existential predicates, a demonstrative pronoun followed by a relative clause can be used to introduce a non-specific group of referents. As shown in (15), the case of the pronoun has to be nominative, just as for canonical subjects.

(15) Det   finns **de/*dem**   som tycker annorlunda.
      EXPL exist those.NOM/ACC who think differently
      'There are those who think differently.'

We see then that, as far as can be determined, Swedish pivots have the same case properties as canonical subjects but differ in position.

We now turn to what Keenan calls behavioral properties. They can be different from language to language. We have identified the following relevant subject properties for Swedish: control of reflexives, subject ellipsis and control of infinitival adjunct clauses, a phenomenon that has not been studied extensively in Swedish grammar. We conclude that the pivots of active sentences in Swedish clearly behave like canonical subjects, but that this is not the case with passives.[5] We discuss this difference between actives and passives here in more detail.

2.2   Control of Reflexives

In Swedish, a personal or possessive pronoun that is locally bound by a canonical subject has to be reflexive. This holds regardless of whether the clause is active (16) or passive (17).

(16) Några studenter hade kommit ut   från sina/*deras
      some students had come   out from REFL/NON-REFL
      kontor.
      offices
      'Some students had come out from their offices.'

(17) Några studenter hade körts   ut från sina/*deras
      some students had kick.PASS out from REFL/NON-REFL
      kontor.
      offices
      'Some students had been kicked out of their offices.'

---

[5]Two additional properties are raising to subject and equi, but they are not very revealing when it comes to looking at properties of pivots since in Swedish, it is the expletive that raises. The case in Icelandic is more interesting, see Zaenen et al. (2017).

If the antecedent is an object, the non-reflexive form is preferred by most speakers:

(18) Vi hade kört   ut några studenter från deras/?sina
     we had kicked out some students from NON-REFL/REFL
     kontor.
     offices
     'We had kicked out some students from their offices.'

The reflexivization control facts for pivots in active sentences are the same as for subjects in canonical positions, but passive pivots behave differently, as illustrated in the following examples:

(19) Det   hade kommit ut **några studenter** från
     EXPL had   come   out some students   from
     sina/*deras   kontor.
     REFL/NON-REFL offices
     'Some students had come out from their offices.'

(20) Det   hade körts   ut **några studenter** från
     EXPL had   kick.PASS out some students   from
     sina/?deras   kontor.
     REFL/NON-REFL offices
     'There had been some students kicked out of their offices.'

The situation is not exactly the same as for objects in the active version of this sentence, where the preferences go the other way (18), nor as for a canonical subject instead of a pivot, where a reflexive is obligatory, see (17).

2.3 Subject Ellipsis

In a coordinated structure, the subject of the second conjunct may be omitted, here marked by Ø, under identity with the canonical subject of the first clause, regardless whether this is initial or follows the finite verb. The second clause can be active or passive, see (23).[6]

(21) Vi mötte en flicka och Ø hälsade på henne.
     we met   a girl   and   greeted on her
     'We met a girl and said hello to her.'

---

[6]For perspicuity we here use the periphrastic passive in which the perfect participle shows agreement with the subject. See Engdahl (2006) and Laanemets (2012) on how the morphological s-passive and the periphrastic passive are used.

(22) Sen mötte vi en flicka och Ø hälsade på henne.
then met we a girl and greeted on her
'Then we met a girl and said hello to her.'

(23) Sen mötte vi en flicka och Ø blev bjudna hem till
then met we a girl and became invited.PL home to
henne.
her
'Then we met a girl and were invited to her house.'

This is not possible under identity with an object:

(24) *Vi mötte en flicka och Ø hälsade på oss.
we met a girl and greeted on us
Intended: 'We met a girl and she said hello to us.'

(25) *Vi mötte en flicka och Ø blev igenkänd.
we met a girl and was recognized.SG
Intended: 'We met a girl and she was recognized by us.'

Subjects can also be omitted under identity with a pivot, especially in so called 'pseudo-coordination' where the first VP is a posture verb (Börjars & Vincent 2005, Engdahl 2006). Note that the auxiliary is also omitted in the second conjunct.

(26) Hela dagen har det suttit **en katt** i fönstret och
all day has EXPL sat a cat in window.DEF and
(*har) spanat på småfåglarna.
has looked at small-birds.DEF
'All day a cat has been sitting in the window, watching the small birds.'

Pivots in passive sentences don't allow subject ellipsis when the second conjunct is active. Since posture verbs normally are not used in the passive, we here use the same passive verb as in (14).

(27) *Det har bjudits in **några musiker** till festen och
EXPL have invited.PASS in some musicians to party.DEF and
blivit glada.
become glad.PL
Intended: 'Some musicians has been invited to the party and they became glad.'

Some speakers, however, find that subject ellipsis is possible if the second conjunct is also passive, as in (28).

(28) Det har sålts **många bilar** och exporterats till
EXPL have sold.PASS many cars and exported.PASS to
Polen.
Poland
'There have been many cars sold and exported to Poland.'

2.4 Control of Infinitival Adjuncts

A test that we did not consider in Zaenen, Engdahl & Maling (2017)
is control into infinitival adjuncts. The problem with the test is that
in many languages arguments that are clearly not surface subjects can
be controllers in such situations (see e.g. Hoekstra 1984 for Dutch),
but it is fairly clear that objects cannot be controllers. Here, too, we
find a contrast between active and passive pivots. In Swedish canonical
subjects of dynamic verbs can be controllers of active adjuncts (29) and
for many speakers this also holds for the presentational version in (30).

(29) En man satte sig på bänken utan att se sig för.
a man sat REFL on bench.DEF without to look REFL for
'A man sat down on the bench without looking.'

(30) Det satte sig **en man** på bänken utan att se
EXPL sat REFL a man on bench.DEF without to look
sig för.
REFL for
'A man sat down on the bench without looking.'

Note that passive versions of these sentences are not acceptable when
the adjunct is active, see (31) and (32).

(31) *En man placerades på bänken utan att se sig för.
a man place.PASS on bench.DEF without to look REFL for

(32) *Det placerades **en man** på bänken utan att se
EXPL place.PASS a man on bench.DEF without to look
sig för.
REFL for

However, if the adjunct is passive, a canonical subject of a passive clause
can control the unexpressed subject of the adjunct. The unexpressed
agents in the two clauses have to have the same reference.

(33) Några brev hade postats igår   utan   att ha
     some letters had post.PASS yesterday without to have
     frankerats.
     stamped.PASS
     'Some letters had been mailed yesterday without having had
     stamps put on.'

But the presentational version of this example, shown in (34), is unacceptable to several speakers. This suggests that the pivot in a passive clause lacks the ability to control a passive adjunct.

(34) *Det hade postats **några brev** igår   utan   att
      EXPL had post.PASS some letters yesterday without to
      ha   frankerats.
      have stamped.PASS

Other speakers assign one question mark to (34) and find (35), with an animate controller, grammatical.[7]

(35) Vilken skandalmatch! I andra halvlek bars   det
     what scandal-match in second half   carried.PASS EXPL
     ut **en spelare** utan   att vara skadad.
     out a player   without to be injured
     'What a scandalous match! In the second period, a player was carried out without being injured.'

It seems that some hitherto unnoticed parallelism constraints are at work here which need further investigation.

With respect to the behavioral properties, pivots of active sentences behave by and large like canonical subjects; they bind reflexive pronouns, allow subject deletion in a coordinated structure regardless of the voice of the second clause and control subjects in infinitival adjunct clauses. Passive pivots do not require reflexives and only allow subject deletion when the second clause is also passive. For most speakers passive pivots do not control adjunct clauses, and for the speakers for whom animate passive pivots can control passive adjuncts, a similar parallelism requirement shows up: only passive adjuncts can be controlled, see (35).

---

[7]This example is based on an Icelandic example from Einar Freyr Sigurðsson.

3 Lexical Layer

It is generally assumed that the the arguments of predicates are organized according to principles that are at least in part universal. Most accounts of lexical (conceptual) structure assume a total or partial ordering, but they differ in the details of this ordering. This is most likely due to the fact we do not have any evidence for this ordering that is independent from language. The most explicit attempts to provide such an independent motivation are found in the cognitive grammar discussions of event structure (see e.g. Croft 2012). We will follow them in assuming that event structure underlies the argument structure of predicates. For the Swedish data we are considering here, we assume that the following two principles are relevant: (i) an instigator/cause comes before an effect, (ii) an inclination to see human experience and, human participation in general, as being more central than that of non humans.

To see if and how these principles are reflected in Swedish presentational constructions, we adopt a classification according to thematic roles, expanding on the analysis in Maling (1988). We assume, with Platzack (2009, 2010), that Swedish verbs can take at most three direct arguments, realized as NPs (see (3) above). There are few thematic constraints on canonical subjects in Swedish. Pivots, however, exhibit an array of thematic constraints that seem to be sensitive to the valency of the verbs. We first present Swedish data for intransitives, transitives and ditransitives, and then discuss what they show us about the organization of the lexical level.

3.1 Lexical Constraints

3.1.1 Intransitives

So far the examples with pivots we have discussed involve predicates of existence like *vara* 'be' and *finnas* 'exist' and posture verbs like *sitta* 'sit'. In these cases, the thematic role generally assumed is that of Theme. Other common predicates are verbs that denote (dis)appearance in a situation, as in (36) and in (37), repeated here from (9).

(36) Det har försvunnit **ett viktigt   papper**.
      EXPL has disappeared an important paper
      'An important paper has disappeared.'

(37) Det kom in **en katt** i köket.
      EXPL came in a   cat   in kitchen.DEF
      'A cat came into the kitchen.'

But we also find presentational sentences with verbs that normally take Agent subjects:

(38) Det   har   arbetat **två hundra människor** här.
      EXPL have worked two hundred people   here
      'Two hundred people have worked here.'

(39) Det   har ringt   **någon**   till dig.
      EXPL has phoned someone to you
      'Someone has phoned you.'

However, Experiencers and Instruments are not acceptable as pivots:

(40) *Det   hade frusit **några barn**   i   natt.
      EXPL had   frozen some   children in night
      Intended: 'Some children had felt cold last night.'

(41) *Det   hade skurit **en kniv** igenom   väggen.
      EXPL had cut   a   knife through wall.DEF
      Intended: 'A knife had cut through the wall.'

With respect to Stimuli, the situation is not completely clear. Sentences with verbs like *blink, beep*, etc. are fine, as illustrated in (42), but they are not usually classified as having a Stimulus as subject.

(42) Det   tutade **ett tåg**   bakom kröken.
      EXPL beeped a   train behind bend.DEF
      'A train beeped behind the bend.'

With classical Stimulus verbs such as *stink* the construction is impossible.[8]

(43) *Det   stank **en rutten fisk** på stranden.
      EXPL stank a   rotten fish on beach.DEF
      Intended 'There was a rotten fish stinking on the beach.'

---

[8]In general verbs like *smell, taste*, etc. take a different impersonal construction in Swedish, see Viberg (2008).

(i) Det   stank fisk på stranden.
     EXPL stank fish on beach.DEF
     'It stank of fish on the beach.'

3.1.2 Monotransitives

With active monotransitives, presentational sentences are impossible with Agent pivots regardless of whether the pivot precedes or follows the other argument.

(44) *Det   har stulit   **någon student** cykeln.
     EXPL has stolen some   student   bike.DEF
     Intended: 'Some student has stolen the bike.'

(45) *Det   har stulit   cykeln   **någon student**.
     EXPL has stolen bike.DEF some   student
     Intended: 'Some student has stolen the bike.'

(46) *Det   har hjälpt   **en student** den gamle mannen.
     EXPL has helped a   student   the old   man.DEF
     Intended: 'A student has helped the old man.'

(47) *Det   har   försökt **många** att bestiga berget.
     EXPL have tried   many   to climb   mountain.DEF
     Intended: 'Many people have tried to climb the mountain.'

But if the pivot is a Theme, it may be preceded by an Experiencer or a Goal, as pointed out in Platzack (1983) and Maling (1988):[9]

Theme–Experiencer:

(48) Det   hade hänt   honom **något   konstigt**.
     EXPL had   happened him   something strange
     'Something strange had happened to him .'

(49) Det   kunde vänta mig **en verklig överraskning** när   jag
     EXPL could   await me   a   real   surprise   when I
     kom   hem.
     came home
     'A real surprise could be waiting for me when I came home.'

Theme–Goal:

(50) Det   hade nått   Tomas **ett brev** hemifrån.
     EXPL had   reached Thomas a   letter from-home
     'A letter from home had reached Thomas.'

---

[9]We have changed the examples slightly so that the pivot is clearly in the Verbalfeld.

(51) Det   har slagit mig **något**   **intressant**.
EXPL has struck me something interesting
'Something interesting has struck me.'

When the pivot is a Stimulus, however, the result is ungrammatical.

Stimulus–Experiencer:

(52) *Det   hade skrämt   barnen   **en film**.
EXPL had   frightened children.DEF a   film
Intended: 'A film had frightened the children.'

The distinction between Theme and Stimulus we propose here relies on the dynamic/causal character of the Stimulus against the inert character of a Theme. A test that brings out the contrast is the use of degree modification with the predicate. Compare:

(53) Filmen   skrämde   barnen   mycket.
film.DEF frightened children.DEF a-lot
'The film frightened the children a lot, i.e. caused the children to be very frightened.'

(54) *En överraskning väntade mig mycket.
a   surprise   awaited me a-lot

Experiencer or Goal pivots are also impossible.

Experiencer–Theme/Stimulus:

(55) *Det   hade sett **några studenter** röken.
EXPL had seen some   students   smoke.DEF
Intended: 'Some students had seen the smoke.'

(56) *Det   hade fruktat **många** en ny   tsunami.
EXPL had feared   many   a new tsunami
Intended: 'Many people had feared a new tsunami.'

Goal–Theme:

(57) *Det   hade mottagit **en student** priset.
EXPL had received a   student prize.DEF
Intended: 'A student had received the prize.'

We now turn to passive versions of monotransitives. The presentational construction is possible when the pivot is a Theme or a Patient and the suppressed subject is an Agent, as already illustrated above in (14), repeated here for convenience:

(58) Det bjöds   in **en musiker** till festen.
     EXPL invited.PASS in a   musician to party.DEF
     'A musician was invited to the party.'

The passive construction is also possible when the role of the suppressed active subject is an Experiencer and the passive pivot is a Theme:

(59) Det hade setts   **rök**   i skogen.
     EXPL had   see.PASS smoke in forest.DEF
     'Smoke had been seen in the forest.'

But when the pivot is a Stimulus the result is ungrammatical:

(60) *Under lång tid   har det   fruktats **en ny tsunami**.
     under long time has EXPL fear.PASS a   new tsunami
     Intended: 'For a long time there has been a fear of a new tsunami.'

In (59), the pivot is a Theme (not causally linked to the eventuality), whereas in (60), it is a Stimulus (causally linked to the eventuality).

Clear Goal pivots in passives where the Agent is a Theme, as in (61), are ungrammatical,

(61) *Det hade nåtts   **en journalist** av nyheten.
     EXPL had reach.PASS a   journalist by news.DEF
     Intended: 'The news had reached a journalist.'

but the following, where the suppressed subject is an Agent, is grammatical:

(62) Det skulle hjälpas   **en man** över gatan.
     EXPL should help.PASS a   man over street.DEF
     'There was a man who needed to be helped over the street.'

In Icelandic, the corresponding verb *hjálpa* 'help' takes a dative argument which is assumed to be a Goal. In Swedish, *hjälpa* seems to have been reanalysed as taking a Patient argument. Given that the difference between Theme/Patient and Goal is one of affectedness (see e.g. Platzack 2005, Croft 2012), such a reanalysis for *hjälpa* is not surprising.

3.1.3 Ditransitives

Recall that Swedish verbs can take at most three arguments realized as NPs. The PS rules in (3) provide only two positions for direct NP arguments in the Verbalfeld. Active ditransitive presentationals are thus impossible, but passive versions might exist, given that we have just seen that presentational versions of passive monotransitives with suppressed Agents are grammatical, see (58) above. Although only a few ditransitive verbs are used in the passive in Swedish, there are some that are acceptable for most speakers. As shown in Haddican & Holmberg (2019), these verbs tend to be morphologically complex, like *tilldela* 'award'. With those verbs, both the Goal and the Theme argument can be canonical subjects:

Goal subject:

(63) Studenten   hade tilldelats   priset.
      student.DEF had   awarded.PASS prize.DEF
      'The student had been awarded the prize.'

Theme subject:

(64) Priset   hade tilldelats   studenten.
      prize.DEF had   awarded.PASS student.DEF
      'The prize had been awarded to the student.'

But only one presentational version is acceptable, namely the one where the indefinite pivot is the Theme:

(65) Det   hade tilldelats   studenten **ett pris**.
      EXPL had   awarded.PASS him   a   prize
      'There had been awarded a prize to the student.'

(66) *Det   hade tilldelats   **en student** priset.
      EXPL had   awarded.PASS a   student   prize.DEF
      Intended: 'There had been awarded a student the prize.'

This conforms to the pattern we noted above in Section 3.1.2, that only Theme pivots are possible when there is another NP argument in the Verbalfeld.

3.2 Swedish Thematic Hierarchy

Assuming the cognitive principles stated in the beginning of this section, we see that event structure is reflected in the lexical structure in a rather direct way in Swedish. Several orderings such as Agent<Theme/Patient, Agent<Goal, Instrument<Theme, Stimulus< Experiencer, Theme<Experiencer) are motivated by the assumption that the instigator/cause comes before the effect. The inclination to see human experience, and in general human participants, as being more central than non-human ones favors the Experiencer<Stimulus and Experiencer<Theme ordering. With respect to structures with three argument, it is again not immediately clear what event structure notions should yield. Most of the predicates in this class have an Agent, a Theme and a Goal/Beneficiary/Recipient. One way to construe the event is to see it progressing from the Agent to the Theme to the Goal/Beneficiary/Recipient. But again one can argue that the tendency to concentrate on human participants might overrule this causal order, giving us Agent<Goal/Beneficiary/Recipient<Theme which is the order found in Swedish.

Given the data we are considering, we only have evidence for the partial order shown in (67), where we refer to the first equivalence class as having the high role (**HR**), the second as having the intermediate one (**IR**) and the third as having the low role (**LR**).

(67) **HR**(Agent,Cause) < **IR**(Experiencer, Goal, Instrument, Stimulus) < **LR**(Theme, Patient)

On this view, canonical monotransitive predicates have a high and a low participant. Experiencer verbs have an intermediate and a low participant. Ditransitive verbs have a high, an intermediate and a low participant.[10]

---

[10]This comes very close to the argument structure proposed by Platzack (2010: 75f.) who assumes that there are three 'role families', each associated with a different position in the hierarchical structure. Platzack adopts the *Uniformity of Theta Assignment Hypothesis* of Baker (1997) and links the agentive role family (Agent, Cause, Instrument) to the specifier of vP, the Goal role family (including Experiencer, Recipient, Benefactive and Patient) to the specifier of the root and the Theme role family (including Content, Result and Path) to the complement of the root. In our data we have no evidence for a Cause distinguished from the Agent (there are no intransitive verbs with a causer as their sole argument). There are two important differences between Platzack's hierarchy and our ordering in (67). We assume that Instrument is in the intermediate equivalence class and Patient is in the lowest class. If one adopts the analysis we propose in Section 5, Platzack's ordering predicts, contrary to what we have found, that a sentence like (41) should be grammatical and (62) should be ungrammatical.

4   Information Structure

Whereas the lexical layer postulates an organization based on the way humans perceive the unfolding of events independently of a particular discourse, the information structure layer proposes an organization that is based on the place the description of an eventuality has within the transmission of information from the speaker/writer to the hearer/reader. Ultimately, this prominence hierarchy should follow from the fact that discourse normally progresses from what is given to what is new.

4.1   Terminology

The terms *given* and *new* are often used when talking about information structure, but we want to make an important further distinction. Following Gundel & Fretheim (2004: 176ff.), we distinguish between *referential* givenness–newness and *relational* givenness–newness. We use the referential pair given–new when talking about the accessibility (Ariel 1988), cognitive status or givenness (Gundel, Hedberg & Zacharski 1993) of a referent in the discourse as being hearer-old/new (Prince 1981, 1992). This distinction primarily affects the choice of linguistic expressions: given referents tend to be referred to by pronouns and definite NPs whereas new referents tend to be referred to by indefinite NPs.

The relational given–new distinction has to do with a partitioning of the content of the utterance into a given part (what the sentence is about) and the new information (to the hearer) that is predicated of this. For this distinction we use the traditional terms *topic* and *focus*, despite the confounding uses of these terms in the literature (see discussion in Vallduví & Engdahl 1996). Referential givenness and relational topichood are often aligned in that given referents that are known to both speaker and hearer provide good topics. But a highly given referent, like the addressee, may still be relationally new, i.e. focus, in an exchange like the following. The context question is given in English.

(68)   a.   Who are you looking for?

   b.   Jag söker DIG.
     I   seek   you
     'I'm looking for YOU.'

Similarly, in uttering (69), the speaker may very well intend the stressed and focussed *HON* to refer to the discourse referent Eva, mentioned in the matrix clause, and hence referentially given.

(69) Eva sa   att HON vann.
      Eva said that she   won
      'Eva said that SHE won.'

In Swedish topics are generally realized in the Vorfeld or the Mittelfeld, as illustrated in (70) and (71). (71) also shows that the Vorfeld may be filled by a locative or temporal scene setting topic, what (Erteschik-Shir 2019) calls a *stage* topic, which should be distinguished from what Reinhart (1981) calls *aboutness* topics.

(70) [Eva_ABOUT-TOP] gick till köket.
      Eva   went to kitchen.DEF
      'Eva went to the kitchen.'

(71) [Sen_STAGE-TOP] gick [Eva_ABOUT-TOP] till köket.
      then   went Eva   to kitchen.DEF
      'Then Eva went to the kitchen.'

Both examples can be paraphrased as 'X said about Eva that she went to the kitchen', using Reinhart's rewriting test for aboutness topics. Stage topics have in common with aboutness topics that they need to have a determined reference for the hearer as well as the speaker when they are encountered.

If there is no referential aboutness topic in the utterance, an expletive has to be inserted, either in the Vorfeld or the Mittelfeld:

(72) Det   hade regnat hela sommaren.
      EXPL had   rained all summer.DEF
      'It had rained all summer.'

(73) Hela sommaren   hade det   regnat.
      all summer.DEF had EXPL rained
      'All summer it had rained.'

As mentioned above, topics tend to be referentially given; consequently such topics are often pronominal, definite, or specific, whereas non-specific indefinites rarely function as topics, see Mikkelsen (2002) and Erteschik-Shir (2007) for discussion. Bare plurals in the Vorfeld tend to get a generic interpretation, referring to the kind rather than to instances of the kind, just as in English (see Carlson 1977).

(74) Katter jamar.
      cats   meow
      'Cats meow.'

The Vorfeld is however not reserved for topics. A narrow focus may appear there, marked with stress, as shown in (75). A stressed constituent in the Vorveld may also give rise to so called all-focus, or thetic, readings as in (76).

(75)   a. Who won?

        b. DU vann.
          you won
          'YOU won.'

(76)   [$_{FOCUS}$ SOLen skiner].
          sun.DEF shines
          'The SUN is out.'

Apart from such examples, where a focus in canonical subject position is signaled with special intonation, the focus tends to follow the topic.[11]

How much of the utterance is focus depends on what issues have been activated in the context. In (77) the whole VP in the Verbalfeld is focus whereas in (78) only the object is focus.[12]

(77)   a. What are you going to do?

        b. Jag ska [$_{FOCUS}$ köpa MJÖLK].
          I   will   buy milk
          'I'm going to buy milk.'

(78)   a. What are you going to buy?

        b. Jag ska köpa [$_{FOCUS}$ MJÖLK].
          I   will buy   milk
          'I'm going to buy milk.'

4.2 Information Structure of Presentational Constructions

With this background, we can turn to the information structure of presentational constructions. A succinct way to capture this is to say that a pivot has to be simultaneously referentially new and relationally new. This means that it is used to introduce a referent that is new or unknown as part of the relational focus of the utterance.[13] The

---

[11]However, this should not be considered a linguistic universal. Lambrecht (1994) shows that not all languages exhibit this ordering.

[12]Verbal material which is neither topic or focus is sometimes referred to as *background* or *tail* (Vallduví & Engdahl 1996).

[13]This observation is of course not new. Lødrup (1999) uses the term 'presentational focus construction'.

requirement that the pivot has to be referentially new is commonly known as the Definiteness effect (Milsark 1974). This explains why singular, plural and quantificational indefinite pivots are fine, as shown above and in (79), but not partitives which presuppose a specific set of referents, as in (80).

(79) Det lekte **några barn** på ängen.
EXPL played some children on field.DEF
'Some children played in the field.'

(80) *Det lekte **fem av barnen** på ängen.
EXPL played five of children.DEF on field.DEF
Intended: 'Five of the children played in the field.'

Presentational sentences are often characterized as all-focus or topicless sentences (see e.g. Lambrecht 1994). We agree with Erteschik-Shir (2019) that it is better to see them as sentences in which there is an, often unexpressed, temporal or locative stage topic, which may also be overt, as shown in (81).

(81) På eftermiddagen lekte det **några barn** på ängen.
on afternoon.DEF played EXPL some children on field.DEF
'In the afternoon some children played in the field'

Whether a locative argument counts as part of the focus or background depends on whether it has already been activated in the context, as shown in (77) and (78). Given the lead-in question in (82) the locative *där* is not part of the focus.

(82) a. What was going on in the field?

b. Det lekte **några barn** där.
EXPL played some children there
'Some children were playing there.'

Presentational constructions are preferred when the pivot is referentially new and introduced as (part of) focus. Recall, however, that there are structural and thematic restrictions on pivots; agentive transitive verbs cannot be used in presentational constructions, as shown in (44)–(46) and intransitive verbs with Experiencers are also impossible as shown in (40). Before addressing the interaction of the constraints on the different layers in Section 5, we look at some additional restrictions on pivots.

4.3 Agentivity Constraints

We turn now to the relation between the pivot and the rest of the scene that is presented. We have seen that in some contexts agentive pivots are possible in Swedish, see (38) and (39), repeated here as (83) and (84).

(83) Det har arbetat **två hundra människor** här.
EXPL have worked two hundred people   here
'Two hundred people have worked here.'

(84) Det har ringt **någon** till dig.
EXPL has phoned someone to you
'Someone has phoned you.'

However, as noted by Anward (1981) and Teleman et al. (1999), these pivots differ from canonical subjects in ways which shed additional light on the way presentational constructions are used in Swedish. Whereas agentive subjects in canonical position can be modified by Agent oriented adverbs like *motvilligt* 'reluctantly', these are infelicitous in the corresponding presentational versions.

(85) Två hundra människor har motvilligt arbetat här.
two hundred people   have reluctantly worked here
'Two hundred people have reluctantly worked here.'

(86) *Det har motvilligt arbetat **två hundra människor** här.
EXPL have reluctantly worked two hundred people   here

Similarly manner adverbs are fine with canonical subjects but sound strange in presentational constructions (see Teleman et al. 1999, 3: 400).

(87) Många islänningar sjöng entusiastiskt   på matchen.
many Icelanders sang enthusiastically at match.DEF
'Many Icelanders sang enthusiastically at the match.'

(88)?*Det sjöng **många islänningar** entusiastiskt   på
EXPL sang many Icelanders enthusiastically at
matchen.
match.DEF

The infelicity of these agent oriented adverbs suggests that it is not the referent of the Agent argument, with its disposition or properties, that is focused. Rather it is the whole event, or the whole described situation, that is brought out as relationally new. So (83) can be used to say something about what people have typically done at some particular place, viz. *arbetat* 'worked', but not to convey their attitude to work.

In this respect the Agent pivots behave more like inert Themes, as shown by inability to add degree modifiers, see the contrast between (53) and (54). Adding *mycket* 'a lot' to (83) sounds very strange.

(89) *Det har arbetat **många människor** mycket här.
     EXPL have worked many   people   a-lot   here
     Intended: 'Many people have worked a lot here.'

This test is not only applicable to agentive pivots but works for presentational sentences in general. Consider (90):

(90) *Det har suttit **en katt** mycket i fönstret   .
     EXPL has sat   a   cat   a-lot   in window.DEF
     Intended: 'A cat has been sitting in the window a lot.'

Somehow adding the intensifying adverb *mycket* does not go well with focusing the whole scene.

5 A Mapping Account

We assume that acceptable sentences are the result of a negotiation between different grammar components which impose their violable and non-violable constraints on the outcome. The result of their negotiation is the surface realization of the sentence. We will model our analysis in terms of preference orders and linking rules. Based on the data and the general theoretical considerations discussed above, it seems that, in Swedish, the unmarked lexical order is as in (67), repeated here as (91), where **HR** stands for High Role, **IR** for Intermediate Role, and **LR** for Low Role.

(91) **HR**(Agent,Cause) < **IR**(Experiencer, Goal, Instrument, Stimulus) < **LR**(Theme, Patient)

As already mentioned, the unmarked information structure order is as in (92), which should be understood as saying that a constituent that functions as a topic precedes material that is relationally new, i.e. focus.[14]

(92) topic < focus

Moreover we assume the topological structure in (93), repeated from (4).

---

[14]The relation to the hierarchical constituent structure clearly needs to be made more precise, as pointed out by a reviewer, but in the interest of space we don't spell this out here.

(93)

Vorfeld	Mittelfeld			Verbalfeld				
XP	V [+FIN]	NP1	ADV*	V [-FIN]	Prt	NP2	NP3	PP*

When both the lexical and the information structure constraints are respected, we get a line-up in which the highest lexical role is mapped to a topic in the Vorfeld or Mittelfeld and the lowest lexical role to a focus in the Verbalfeld. This is what we find in unmarked transitive and ditransitive sentences. According to this alignment, the highest lexical argument of the verb maps outside the VP, onto a canonical subject position. The Theme/Patient argument maps onto the lowest VP internal argument position which is the one that carries the sentence stress in so-called neutral contexts.

All languages have ways to depart from this basic structure to signal communicative needs that are different from the simple assignment of a quality to an entity. One of these means is the presentational construction, which is used when the highest lexical argument is a non-specific indefinite and hence does not qualify as a topic. Instead it is mapped onto the lowest syntactic position. However, as we have seen, not all non-specific indefinites make acceptable pivots in Swedish, so this mapping is subject to further constraints.

Starting with the syntax, the Vorfeld is the least constrained position in Swedish. Here we find all thematic roles and all grammatical functions. The Vorfeld is the unmarked position for a referentially given topic; a focus may appear there but only if it is prosodically marked, see (75) and (76). The NP1-position in the Mittelfeld is also open to all thematic roles and this is where we find aboutness topics if the Vorfeld is occupied by e.g. a stage topic, see (71) and (81). One restriction is that only subjects are mapped onto NP1.[15]

In the Verbalfeld we find more constraints, in particular that only NP3 can be a pivot (see the ungrammaticality of (66)). It seems likely that this has to do with the way focus projection works inside the Verbalfeld in Swedish. If NP3, the last NP argument in the Verbalfeld, carries focal stress, the whole VP can be focus (so called wide focus), see (94), but if NP2 is stressed as in (95), the only interpretation is with narrow focus on *studenten*.

(94) a. What did you do?

   b. Vi [tilldelade studenten   ett PRIS.]
      we awarded   student.DEF a   prize

      'We awarded the student a prize.'

---

[15]In German, also objects can be mapped onto NP1, if they are topics, see Frey (2006).

(95) a. Who did you give the prize?
      b. Vi tilldelade [stuDENten] ett pris.
          we awarded   student.DEF a   prize
          'We awarded the student a prize.'

Since presentational constructions often involve wide focus on the whole
Verbalfeld, we believe that the requirement that pivots appear last ultimately has to do with the unmarked prosodic alignment in Swedish.
Thematically, NP3 is not constrained but since the order of the **IR** and
the **LR** element in the Verbalfeld is fixed in Swedish, we will assume
a constraint that the arguments in the Verbalfeld are always in harmonic alignment with the conceptual/lexical structure. This will have
as a result that an **HR** cannot follow an **IR** or an **LR** element in the
Verbalfeld.

NP2 in the Verbalfeld is moreover dedicated to the **IR** (Experiencer,
Goal, Instrument and Stimulus); when they are realized in the VP, they
have to be mapped onto NP2 and only they can be mapped onto NP2.

One important consequence of these restrictions is that presentational sentences with agentive transitive verbs are not possible, as
shown in (44)–(47). Such verbs have an **HR** and an **LR**, both of which
can be mapped onto NP3, but, crucially, the second argument cannot
be mapped onto NP2. Similarly with ditransitive predicates, the thematic restriction on NP2 ensures that only the line-up with a Goal
mapped onto NP2 and a Theme mapped onto NP3 is possible, as in
(65).

The proposed constraints on the mapping from thematic roles to argument positions hold in general in Swedish and are not
specific to presentational constructions. But together they constrain the
grammatical output so that the highest lexical argument can only be
realized as a pivot if it is either an **LR** or an **HR**, and in the latter
case, only when there is no **IR** present.

6   The Role of Grammatical Functions

In our discussion of the mapping between the lexical and the information structure layer, we have so far not referred to grammatical functions. They do not seem to be necessary in order to define the mapping
itself. Remember, however, that we drew attention to a difference between pivots in active and passive sentences in Section 2; active pivots
exhibit (most of) the behavioral characteristics of canonical subjects in
that they they control reflexivization, allow subject deletion in coordinated structures and control of infinitival adjunct clauses. Pivots in
passive sentences show less consistent subject properties and further-

more seem to require voice parallelism; a coordinated VP or controlled adjunct also has to be passive. We conclude by discussing the consequences of this difference for our approach.

We assume that passive is a lexical operation that 'demotes' but does not delete the agent/causer argument. We will call the highest argument of a basic lexical form, the **highest lexical** argument, and the one that is the result of possible lexical operations such as passivization, the **highest functional** argument. If we want to maintain the SUBJECT label for the NP with the behavioral characteristics discussed in Section 2, we have to revise the assumptions that are generally made about the mapping from the lexical layer to grammatical functions in e.g. LFG. The subject function cannot be defined based on lexical properties alone; in order to exhibit subject properties, an NP has to be either the most prominent on the lexical scale or the most prominent on the informational scale. When the highest functional argument is a topic, it has subject properties such as nominative case and control of reflexives even when it is not the highest lexical argument, as in the case of a passive subject. But when this argument is a pivot, i.e. not a topic and hence not the highest on the informational ordering in (92), then it does no longer behave as a subject in terms of requiring obligatory reflexivization, permitting subject deletion and adjunct control. An active pivot, however, remains the highest lexical argument, so it counts as a subject, even when it is not a topic. Under this view, grammatical functions are not only determined by the lexical properties of their predicate but also by the information structure of the sentence in which they occur. A similar conclusion is reached in Dalrymple & Nikolaeva (2011) on the basis of totally different data. A problem that remains unsolved by this proposal is how to characterize the passive pivot in terms of grammatical functions. As we have seen, it is object-like but it does not behave exactly the same way as an object. All in all, the facts discussed in this paper seem to suggest that the behavior of syntactic arguments is more fluid than a grammatical function approach suggests and more in line with the observations in Keenan (1976).

Acknowledgements

This paper was in part inspired by Bonami, Godard & Marandin (1999). Initially it was our hope to compare Scandinavian subject inversion phenomena with the French ones but the differences are so substantial that this would not have been a reasonable contribution to this volume. We acknowledge comments from participants at the seminar in honor of Danièle Godard, 27 March 2017, from a reviewer and from the editors.

11

Incrementality and HPSG: Why not?

Jonathan Ginzburg, Robin Cooper, Julian Hough
and David Schlangen

1 Introduction

Incremental processing at least as fine grained as word-by-word has long
been accepted as a basic feature of human processing of speech (see e.g.
Schlesewsky & Bornkessel 2004) and as an important feature for design
of spoken dialogue systems (see e.g. Schlangen & Skantze 2011, Hough
et al. 2015). The ability to deal with incrementality has for many years
been a selling point of Categorial Grammar in both its versions CCG
(Ades & Steedman 1982; Steedman 1996) and TLG (Morrill 2000), and
in LTAG (Demberg et al. 2013). It has also served as the motivation for
new formalisms, e.g. Dynamic Dependency Grammar (Milward 1994)
and, more recently, Dynamic Syntax (Kempson et al. 2001). Over the
years there has been some work on incremental versions of HPSG (e.g.
Güngördü 1997) and recently (Haugereid & Morey 2012). Nonetheless,
on the whole, incrementality in HPSG has been viewed as a performance issue – see e.g. Sag & Wasow (2015: 53):

> The locality of the constraints maximizes the information available in
> partial structures and supports a variety of processing regimes (top-
> down, bottom-up, left-corner, probabilistic, etc.). Hence, this property
> of our sign-based model of grammar is useful in modeling the *incre-*
> *mentality of processing* [our italics].

Constraint-Based Syntax and Semantics: Papers in Honor of Danièle Godard.
Anne Abeillé and Olivier Bonami (eds.).
Copyright © 2020, CSLI Publications.

Over the last few years, several works have appeared detailing the view that grammars should be viewed as systems that classify an utterance as it occurs in conversation (see e.g. Ginzburg 2012, Ginzburg & Poesio 2016, Kempson et al. 2016, Cooper 2019). Thus, Ginzburg & Poesio (2016) argue that phenomena such as disfluencies, non sentential utterances, quotation, and co-speech gestures are as rule-governed as binding, control, and dislocation – traditional sentence-level phenomena captured in formal grammars. Given the existence of formal accounts for all these conversational phenomena within frameworks such as KoS (Ginzburg 2012), PTT (Poesio & Rieser 2010), SDRT (Asher & Lascarides 2003), Dynamic Syntax (Kempson et al. 2016), and other related frameworks,[1] this suggests the need for a new view wherein grammar is a means for directly characterizing speech events, abolishing the performance/competence distinction (though recasting this in a way that allows maintaining a distinction between the task of describing the linguistic phenomena from the task of describing how they get processed).[2]

Indeed, with respect to incrementality, once one examines ongoing conversational data even in a fairly cursory fashion, as we exemplify below, one discovers the pervasive nature of phenomena whose analysis requires incremental semantic composition.

Consequently, we believe that such data push any grammar formalism that aspires to handle conversation, and this includes without doubt HPSG, to adapt and offer means of handling incremental semantic composition. However, this does not, as we will suggest, *force* one to radically redesign one's formalism, as long as one allows for a sufficiently tight coupling between grammar and conversational context.

We start therefore, in Section 2, with a cursory examination of phenomena from conversation that requires incremental semantic composition from which we draw basic specifications for incremental semantics. In Section 3 we present the necessary background concerning KOS and

---

[1] Neither KoS nor PTT are acronyms, though the former is a name of a Dodacanese island and suggestive of *conversationally oriented semantics*, whereas the latter's origin relates to its founder's surnames; SDRT *is* an acronym for Segmented Discourse Representation Theory.

[2] J.P. Koenig asks whether we really want to abolish the performance/competence distinction. A detailed range of answers is given by Ginzburg & Poesio (2016). Minimally, we wish to abolish its use as an excuse not to deal with phenomena that are intrinsically conversational such as quotation and disfluencies. This requires grammars that can classify as grammatical utterances like 'And then Billie went "I breaked the cup"' or 'I spunk I mean spanked him'. A related perspective we are sympathetic to is that articulated by (Lau et al. 2017), which abolishes competence as a binary notion in favour of a probabilistic notion.

TTR, a type theory with records, the frameworks we employ for representing dialogue, grammar, and semantics. In Section 4, we sketch an account of dialogical incremental processing, which we apply to some of the data from Section 2 in Section 5.

2   Incremental Composition: Data and Initial Specification

Example (1) exemplifies the fact that at any point in the speech stream of A's utterance B can interject with an acknowledgement whose force amounts to B understanding the initial segment of the utterance (Clark 1996). (1) requires us to be able to write a lexical entry for 'aha' and 'yeah' (and their counterparts cross linguistically, e.g. French: 'ouais', 'mmh', . . .) whose context is/includes 'an incomplete utterance'.

(1)   A: Move the train . . .
        B: Aha
        A: . . . from Avon . . .
        B: Right
        A: . . . to Danville.   (Trains corpus)

(2a, b, c) exemplify a contrast between three reactions to an 'abandoned' utterance: in (2a) B asks A to elaborate, whereas in (2b) she asks him to complete her unfinished utterance; in (2c) B indicates that A's content is evident and he need not spell it out. (2a, b, c) requires us to associate a content with A's incomplete utterance which can either trigger an elaboration query (1a), a query about utterance completion (1b), or an acknowledgement of understanding (1c).

(2) a. A(i): John . . . Oh never mind. B(ii): What about John/What happened to John? A: He's a lovely chap but a bit disconnected.

     b. A(i): John . . . Oh never mind. B(ii): John what? A: burnt himself while cooking last night.

     c. A: Bill is . . . B: Yeah don't say it, we know.

(3) is an attested example of an abandoned utterance in mid-word. (3) requires us to integrate within-utterance and (in this case, visual) dialogue context processing.

(3)   [Context: J is in the kitchen searching for the always disappearing scissors. As he walks towards the cutlery drawer he begins to make his utterance, before discovering the scissors once the drawer is opened.] J: Who took the sci-. . .

(4) exemplifies two types of expressions – filled pauses and exclamative interjections – that can in principle, be inserted at any point

in the speech stream of A's utterance; the interjection 'Oh God' here reacts to the utterance situation conveyed incrementally. (4) requires us to enable the coherence of a question about what word/phrase will follow, essentially at any point in the speech stream; It also requires us to enable the coherence of an utterance expressing negative evaluation of the current incomplete utterance.

(4) Audrey: Well it's like th- it's like the erm (pause) oh God! I've forgotten what it's bloody called now?

(British National Corpus)

(5a–e) illustrate that an incomplete clause can serve as an antecedent for a sluice, thereby going against the commonly held assumption that sluicing is an instance of 'S-ellipsis'. (5) requires us to enable either incomplete argument frames or Q(uantified)NPs immediately after their utterance to trigger sluices.

(5) a. The translation is by – who else? – Doris Silverstein.

(The TLS, Feb 2016)

b. He saw — can you guess who? — The Dude.

c. Queen Rhonda is dead. Long live ... who?

(New York Times, Nov 2015)

d. A: A really annoying incident. Someone ...
   B: Who?
   A: Not clear.
   B: OK
   A: has taken the kitchen scissors.

e. (From a live blog:) On 2nd & 4, Brady finds, who else?, Damon Amendola who stretches out to make a touchdown catch that gives the Patriots the lead.

3 Background

3.1 KoS

For our dialogical framework we use KoS (Ginzburg 1994, 2012; Larsson 2002; Purver 2006). KoS provides a cognitive architecture in which there is no single common ground, but distinct yet coupled Dialogue GameBoards, one per conversationalist. The structure of the dialogue gameboard (DGB) is given in Table 1. The *Spkr* and *Addr* fields allow one to track turn ownership; *Facts* represents conversationally shared assumptions; *VisualSit* represents the dialogue participant's view of the visual situation and attended entities; *Pending*, the nature of which we explicate in more detail below, represents moves that are in the process of being grounded and *Moves* represents moves that have been grounded; *QUD* tracks the questions currently under discussion, though not simply questions *qua* semantic objects, but pairs of entities which we call *InfoStrucs*: a question and an antecedent sub-utterance.[3] This latter entity provides a partial specification of the focal (sub-)utterance, and hence it is dubbed the *focus establishing constituent* (FEC). This is similar to the *parallel element* in higher order unification-based approaches to ellipsis resolution (e.g. Gardent & Kohlh se 1997) and to Vallduví (2016), who relates the focus establishing constituent with a notion needed to capture *contrast*.

Table 1 Dialogue gameboard.

component	type	Keeps track of
Spkr	Individual	*Turn*
Addr	Individual	*ownership*
utt-time	Time	
Facts	Set(propositions)	*Shared assumptions*
VisualSit	Situation	*Visual scene*
Moves	List(Locutionary propositions)	*Grounded utterances*
QUD	Partially ordered set(⟨question, FEC⟩)	*Live issues*
Pending	List(Locutionary propositions)	*Ungrounded utterances*

3.2 Type Theory with Records (TTR)

The logical underpinnings of KoS is Type Theory with Records (TTR), a type theory with records (Cooper 2012; Cooper & Ginzburg 2015). Key notions of TTR are the notion of a *judgement* and the notion of a *record*.

- The typing judgement: $a : T$ classifying an object a as being of type T.
- Records: A record is a set of fields assigning objects to labels and is represented graphically as in (6a). A concrete instance is exemplified in (6b). Records are used here to model events and states, including utterances, and dialogue gameboards.

---

[3]Extensive motivation for this view of QUD can be found in Fernández (2006) and Ginzburg (2012), based primarily on semantic and syntactic parallelism in non-sentential utterances such as short answers, sluicing, and various other non-sentential utterances.

(6) a. $\begin{bmatrix} l_1 = val_1 \\ l_2 = val_2 \\ \ldots \\ l_n = val_n \end{bmatrix}$

b. $\begin{bmatrix} \text{x} & = & 22 \\ \text{e-time} & = & \text{2AM, Sept 17, 2018} \\ \text{e-loc} & = & \text{Paris} \\ c_{temp-at-in} & = & \text{o1} \end{bmatrix}$

- Record Types: A record type is like a record except that each field contains a type rather than an object, as in (7a). The fields in record types are partially ordered by a notion of *dependence* since a type in a field may depend on another field. Record types are used to model utterance types (HPSG *signs*), as in (7b), components of semantic entities such as propositions and questions, and to express rules of conversational interaction.

(7) a. $\begin{bmatrix} l_1 : T_1 \\ l_2 : T_2 \\ \ldots \\ l_n : T_n \end{bmatrix}$

b. $\begin{bmatrix} \text{PHON : is georges here} \\ \text{CAT} = \text{V[+fin]} : Syncat \\ \text{CONSTITS} = \left\{ \text{is, georges, here, is georges here} \right\} : \text{set}(Sign) \\ \text{DGB-PARAMS :} \begin{bmatrix} \text{spkr} : Ind \\ \text{addr} : Ind \\ \text{utt-time} : Time \\ \text{c1 : address(spkr,addr,utt-time)} \\ \text{s} : Sit \\ \text{l} : Loc \\ \text{g} : Ind \\ \text{c3: named(g, "georges")} \end{bmatrix} \\ \text{CONT} = \text{ask(spkr,addr, ?} \begin{bmatrix} \text{sit = s} \\ \text{sit-type = In(l,g)} \end{bmatrix}) : IllocProp \end{bmatrix}$

In (7b) the types 'address(spkr,addr,utt-time)' (on the path 'DGB-PARAMS.c1') and 'named(g,*georges*)' (on the path 'DGB-PARAMS.c3') are dependent types since they depend on the fields labelled 'spkr', 'addr', and 'utt-time' and on the field labelled 'g' respectively. In the fields labelled 'CAT', 'CONSTITS' and 'CONT' we make use of the notation $[x{=}k : T]$ which is based on the notion of *a manifest field* (Coquand, Pollack & Takeyama 2003). This is a shorthand for $x : T_k$ where T_k is the singleton subtype of T whose only witness is k. For instance, 'CAT $=$ V[+fin] : syncat' means CAT : syncat$_{V[+fin]}$, so in such a case CAT is restricted to the subtype of the type *syncat* whose sole witness is V[+fin].

TTR is a framework that draws its inspirations from two quite distinct sources. One source is Constructive Type Theory (Ranta 1994) for the repertory of type constructors, and in particular records and record types (Betarte & Tasistro 1998), and the notion of witnessing conditions. The second source is situation semantics (Barwise 1989) which TTR follows in viewing *semantics as ontology construction*. This is what underlies the emphasis on specifying structures in a model theoretic way, introducing structured objects for explicating properties, propositions, questions, etc. It also takes from situation semantics an emphasis on *partiality* as a key feature of information processing. This aspect is exemplified in a key notion in TTR –the witnessing relation between records and record types: the basic relationship between the two is that a record r is of record type T if each value in r assigned to a given label l_i satisfies the typing constraints imposed by T on l_i:

(8)   *Record Witnessing*
       The record:
       $$\begin{bmatrix} l_1 & = & a_1 \\ l_2 & = & a_2 \\ \dots \\ l_n & = & a_n \end{bmatrix}$$
       is of type:
       $$\begin{bmatrix} l_1 & : & T_1 \\ l_2 & : & T_2(l_1) \\ \dots \\ l_n & : & T_n(l_1, l_2, \dots, l_{n-1}) \end{bmatrix}$$
       iff $a_1 : T_1, a_2 : T_2(a_1), \dots, a_n : T_n(a_1, a_2, \dots, a_{n-1})$

This allows for cases where there are fields in the record with labels not mentioned in the record type. This is important when e.g. records are used to model contexts and record types model rules about context change –we do not want to have to predict in advance all information that could be in a context when writing such rules.

To exemplify record type witnessing, (9a) is a type for (6b), assuming the conditions in (9b) hold.

(9) a.
$$\begin{bmatrix} x & : & Ind \\ \text{e-time} & : & Time \\ \text{e-loc} & : & Loc \\ c_{temp-at-in} & : & \text{temp\_at\_in(e-time,e-location,x)} \end{bmatrix}$$

b. 22 : *Ind*; 2AM, Sept 17, 2018 : *Time*; Paris : *Loc*;
o1 : temp_at_in(2AM, Sept 17, 2018, Paris, 22)

To take a more linguistic example, a conversational state r given in (10a) will be a record of type DGBType as given in (10b) (corresponding to the specification of the gameboard we had in Table 1 above and this requires that the conditions in (10c) hold.

(10) a. $r =$
$$\begin{bmatrix} \text{spkr} = A \\ \text{addr} = B \\ \text{utt-time} = t \\ \text{c-utt} = u \\ \text{FACTS} = cg \\ \text{Moves} = \langle m_1,\dots,m_k \rangle \\ \text{QUD} = Q \\ \text{Pending} = \langle p_1,\dots,p_k \rangle \end{bmatrix}$$

b. DGBType $=$
$$\begin{bmatrix} \text{spkr} : Ind \\ \text{addr} : Ind \\ \text{utt-time} : Time \\ \text{c-utt} : \text{addressing(spkr,addr,utt-time)} \\ \text{FACTS} : \text{Set}(Proposition) \\ \text{VisualSit} : \text{Sit} \\ \text{Moves} : \text{list}(LocutionaryProposition) \\ \text{QUD} : \text{poset}(InfStruc) \\ \text{Pending} = \text{list}(LocutionaryProposition) \end{bmatrix}$$

c. A: *Ind*, B: *Ind*, t: *Time*, u: addressing(A,B,t);
cg: Set(*Proposition*); v : Sit; $\langle m_1,\dots,m_k \rangle$: list(*LocutionaryProposition*);
Q : poset(*InfStruc*); $\langle p_1,\dots,p_k \rangle$: list(*LocutionaryProposition*)

For what follows, we require use of an analogue to priority unification for record types, namely *asymmetric merge* (Cooper 2012; Hough 2015) defined as: given two record types $R1$ and $R2$, $R1 \boxed{\wedge} R2$ will yield a record type which is the union of all fields with labels not shared by $R1$ and $R2$ and the asymmetric merge of the remaining fields with the same labels, whereby R2's type values take priority over R1's fields, yielding a resulting record type with R2's fields only in those cases.

(11)   *Asymmetric Merge*

$$\begin{bmatrix} a{:}T_1 \\ b{:}T_2 \\ c{:}T_3 \end{bmatrix} \boxed{\dot\wedge} \begin{bmatrix} b{:}T_2 \\ c{:}T_4 \end{bmatrix} = \begin{bmatrix} a{:}T_1 \\ b{:}T_2 \\ c{:}T_4 \end{bmatrix}$$

Conversational Rules

Context change is specified in terms of *conversational rules*, rules that specify the *effects* applicable to a DGB that satisfies certain *preconditions*. This allows both illocutionary effects to be modelled (preconditions for and effects of greeting, querying, assertion, parting, etc.), interleaved with *locutionary effects*. We mention here two rules, one of which we will use subsequently. The first Q(uestion)SPEC(ificity) is a fundamental conversational rule, KoS's version of Gricean Relevance –it characterizes the contextual background of reactive queries and assertions. QSPEC says that if q is QUD-maximal,[4] then subsequent to this either conversational participant may make a move constrained to be q-specific (i.e. either a partial answer or sub-question of q). The second rule, Assertion QUD-incrementation, encodes the assumption that in the aftermath of an assertion p, QUD gets updated with the question $p?$, the intuition being that in interaction an assertion p requires the issue $p?$ to be considered, leading either to acceptance or discussion. This rule plays a role in our explication of incremental sluicing in Section 5.3 below.

---

[4]QUD is partially ordered, hence a member q_0 of QUD such that for any other element of QUD q_1 $q_0 \geq q_1$ holds, is said to be QUD-maximal.

(12) a. $QSPEC =$

$$
\begin{bmatrix}
\text{pre} \; = \begin{bmatrix}
\text{spkr} & : & Ind \\
\text{addr} & : & Ind \\
\text{qud} & : & \text{poset}(Question) \\
\text{q} & : & Question \\
\text{c} & : & \text{max(q,qud)}
\end{bmatrix} \\
\text{effects}=\lambda r: \begin{bmatrix}
\text{spkr}:Ind \\
\text{addr}:Ind \\
\text{qud}:\text{poset}(Question) \\
\text{q}:Question \\
\text{c}:\text{max(q,qud)}
\end{bmatrix} \begin{bmatrix}
\text{spkr}:(Ind_{\text{pre.spkr}} \vee Ind_{\text{pre.addr}}) \\
\text{addr}:((Ind_{\text{pre.spkr}} \vee Ind_{\text{pre.addr}}) \wedge \neg Ind_{\text{spkr}}) \\
\text{p}:AbsSemObj \\
\text{R}:(AbsSemObj \rightarrow (Ind \rightarrow (Ind \rightarrow IllocProp))) \\
\text{LatestMove}=\text{R(p)(addr)(spkr)}:IllocProp \\
\text{c1}:\text{Qspecific(p,pre.q)}
\end{bmatrix}
\end{bmatrix}
$$

b. *Assertion QUD-incrementation =*

$$
\begin{bmatrix}
\text{pre} \; = \begin{bmatrix}
\text{spkr}:Ind \\
\text{addr}:Ind \\
\text{qud}:\text{poset}(Question) \\
\text{p}:Prop \\
\text{LatestMove}=\text{Assert(p)(addr)(spkr)}:IllocProp
\end{bmatrix} \\
\text{effects}=\lambda r: \begin{bmatrix}
\text{spkr}:Ind \\
\text{addr}:Ind \\
\text{qud}:\text{poset}(Question) \\
\text{p}:Prop \\
\text{LatestMove}=\text{Assert(p)(addr)(spkr)}:IllocProp \\
[\text{c:qud} := \text{pre.qud} \cup \{p?\} \wedge \text{max(p?,qud)}]
\end{bmatrix}
\end{bmatrix}
$$

Update procedure: Using asymmetric merge, we employ the following update process for a dialogue context C and for some rule R, a record of type (13).

(13)
$$
\begin{bmatrix}
\text{pre} & : & RecType \\
\text{effects} & : & (\text{pre} \rightarrow RecType)
\end{bmatrix}
$$

Thus, for example, when updating from one context C_i to the next C_{i+1} with the rule QSPEC:

(14)   If $C_i : T_{C_i}$ and T_{C_i} is a subtype of QSPEC.pre,
then QSPEC licenses the creation of
$C_{i+1} : T_{C_i} \boxed{\wedge} \text{QSPEC.effects}(C_i)$

The updates operate on various levels of information which can be arbitrarily fine-grained (even phonetic). This gives us the requisite apparatus for the incrementality discussed in Section 2.

3.3 Grounding/Clarification Interaction Conditions

Much recent work in dialogue has emphasized two essential branches that can ensue in the aftermath of an utterance:

- **Grounding**: The utterance is understood, its content is added to common ground, uptake occurs.
- **Clarification Interaction**: Some aspect of the utterance causes a problem; this triggers a clarification question to repair the problem.

KoS's treatment of repair involves two aspects. One is straightforward, drawing on an early insight of Conversation Analysis, namely that repair can involve 'putting aside' an utterance for a while, a while during which the utterance is repaired. That in itself can be effected without further ado by adding further structure to the DGB, specifically the field introduced above called *Pending*. 'Putting the utterance aside' raises the issue of *what is it that we are 'putting aside'*. In other words, how do we represent the utterance? The requisite information needs to be such that it enables the original speaker to interpret and recognize the coherence of the range of possible clarification queries that the original addressee might make. Ginzburg (2012) offers detailed arguments on this issue, including considerations of the phonological/syntactic parallelism exhibited between clarification requests and their antecedents and the existence of clarification requests whose function is to request repetition of (parts of) an utterance. Taken together with the obvious need for *Pending* to include values for the contextual parameters specified by the utterance type, Ginzburg concludes that *Pending* should combine tokens of the utterance, its parts, and the constituents of the content with the utterance type associated with the utterance.

An entity that fits this specification is the *locutionary proposition* defined by the utterance. A locutionary proposition is a proposition whose situational component is an utterance situation, typed as in (15a) and will have the form of record (15b):

(15) a. $LocProp =_{def}$ $\begin{bmatrix} \text{sit} : Sign \\ \text{sit-type} : RecType \end{bmatrix}$

  b. $\begin{bmatrix} \text{sit} = u \\ \text{sit-type} = T_u \end{bmatrix}$

Here T_u is a grammatical type for classifying u that emerges during the process of parsing u. It can be identified with a *sign* in the sense of

HPSG (Pollard & Sag 1994). This is operationalized as follows: given a presupposition that u is the most recent speech event and that T_u is a grammatical type that classifies u, a record p_u of the form (15b), gets added to *Pending*. The two branches lead to the following alternative updates:

- Grounding, utterance u understood: Update MOVES with p_u, and respond appropriately (with the second half of an adjacency pair, etc.)
- Clarification Interaction:
  1. p_u remains for future processing in PENDING;
  2. CQ(u), a clarification question calculated from p_u, updates QUD and CQ(u) becomes a discourse topic.

3.4 Quantified Noun Phrases

The last piece of background combines all the ingredients we have seen hitherto. A basic requirement for any account of incremental semantics is the ability to deal with quantification since on standard accounts such contents, in contrast to referential ones, are dependent on other contents to be fully resolved; this is also a key ingredient in any account of incremental sluicing (examples (5) above). Here we will rely on a recent proposal, due to Lücking & Ginzburg (2019), which treats quantified NPs as akin to referential ones, eschewing higher order denotations. A starting point of such an account is a distinction into *dgb-params* and *q-params* as far as labelling nominal meaning. The labels corresponding to the *dgb-params* elements are intended to be instantiated in context, whereas the asserted proposition has the force of existentially quantifying over the *q-params* element(s).[5] A schematic meaning for (16a) is in (16b) and its instantiation in context is in (16c). In (16b) *q-params* is a sub-record type of the content. In what follows, a notational simplification we adopt – an abuse to be precise – is to factor out *q-params* from the descriptive content, as in (16d).

---

[5]For a more detailed discussion of a similar example, see Ginzburg (2012: 331–333)

(16) a. A thief stole my ipod.

b.
$$
\begin{bmatrix}
\text{dgb-params} : \begin{bmatrix}
\text{spkr} & : & Ind \\
\text{addr} & : & Ind \\
\text{z} & : & Ind \\
\text{c1} & : & \text{poss(spkr,z)} \land \text{ipod(z)} \\
\text{s0} & : & Sit
\end{bmatrix} \\
\text{cont} = \text{Assert(spkr,addr,} \\
\begin{bmatrix}
\text{sit} = \text{s0} \\
\text{sit-type} = \begin{bmatrix}
\text{q-params} : \begin{bmatrix} \text{x} & : & Ind \\ \text{r2} & : & \text{thief(x)} \end{bmatrix} \\
\text{nucl} : \text{steal(q-params.x,} \\
\text{dgb-params.z)}
\end{bmatrix}
\end{bmatrix}) : IllocProp
\end{bmatrix}
$$

c.
$$
\begin{bmatrix}
\text{dgb-params} = \begin{bmatrix}
\text{spkr} & = & A \\
\text{addr} & = & B \\
\text{z} & = & j1 \\
\text{c1} & = & p1 \\
\text{s0} & = & sit0
\end{bmatrix} \\
\text{cont} = \text{Assert(spkr,addr,} \\
\begin{bmatrix}
\text{sit} = \text{s0} \\
\text{sit-type} = \begin{bmatrix}
\text{q-params} : \begin{bmatrix} \text{x} & : & Ind \\ \text{r2} & : & \text{thief(x)} \end{bmatrix} \\
\text{nucl} : \text{steal(q-params.x,j1)}
\end{bmatrix}
\end{bmatrix})
\end{bmatrix}
$$

d.
$$
\begin{bmatrix}
\text{dgb-params} : \begin{bmatrix}
\text{spkr} & : & Ind \\
\text{addr} & : & Ind \\
\text{z} & : & Ind \\
\text{c1} & : & \text{poss(spkr,z)} \land \text{ipod(z)} \\
\text{s0} & : & Sit
\end{bmatrix} \\
\text{q-params} : \begin{bmatrix} \text{x} & : & Ind \\ \text{r2} & : & \text{thief(x)} \end{bmatrix} \\
\text{cont} = \text{Assert(spkr,addr,} \\
\begin{bmatrix}
\text{sit} = \text{s0} \\
\text{sit-type} = \\
\begin{bmatrix} \text{nucl} : \text{steal(q-params.x,dgb-params.z)} \end{bmatrix}
\end{bmatrix}) : IllocProp
\end{bmatrix}
$$

More specifically, Lücking & Ginzburg (2019) introduce additional structure within *q-params*. On this account, a singular indefinite such as 'a music lover' would have as its content the type in (17). In (17) the maxset introduces a set, which is constituted out of individuals sharing a property as required by the field c1 (the arrow type distributes this property over the elements of the maxset); the reference set, obtained as the singleton set of the referenced individual (in the field labelled 'refind'), and the comp(lement)set (provided in the field labelled 'compset') partition the maxset.[6]

$$
(17) \quad
\begin{bmatrix}
\text{dgb-params:} RecType \\
\text{q-params:}
\begin{bmatrix}
\text{maxset:} \mathrm{Set}(Ind) \\
\text{c1:} \overrightarrow{\text{music\_lover}}(\text{maxset}) \\
\text{refind:} Ind \\
\text{c}_{\mathrm{ppty}}\text{:music\_lover(refind)} \\
\text{compset:} \mathrm{Set}(Ind) \\
\text{c2:partition(\{\{refind\},compset\},maxset)}
\end{bmatrix}
\end{bmatrix}
$$

As discussed by Lücking & Ginzburg (2019), the various sets introduced in QNP meanings can, in principle, be elaborated in discussion and give rise to anaphora. Here we exemplify compset/refset eliciting enumerations:

(18) a. A: Most students came to the party.
  B: Most students?
  A: Yes, all but Tristan and Isolde. [$\rightarrow$ compset enumeration]

  b. A: Few students came to the party.
  B: Few students?
  A: Yes, just Tristan and Isolde. [$\rightarrow$ refset enumeration]

4 An Incremental Perspective on Grounding and Clarification

4.1 Incrementalizing Dialogue Processing

The account in Section 3.3 was extended to self-repair by Ginzburg, Fernández & Schlangen (2014): the basic idea is to incrementalize the perspective from the turn level to the word level:[7] as the utterance unfolds incrementally there potentially arise questions about what has

---

[6]If X and Y are sets, then 'partition(X,Y)' is a type. Z : partition(X,Y) iff $Z = X$ and X is a partition of Y.

[7]In fact, this is a convenient simplifying assumption. As the attested (3) illustrates, self-monitoring occurs with higher frequency, as Susan Brennan (p.c.) has reminded us; does it respect syllable or morpheme boundaries? This remains, to the best of our knowledge, an open question. Thanks also to J.P. Koenig for alerting us to this point.

happened so far (e.g. *what did the speaker mean with sub-utterance u1?*) or what is still to come (e.g. *what word does the speaker mean to utter after sub-utterance u2?*). These can be accommodated into the context if either uncertainty about the correctness of a sub-utterance arises or the speaker has planning or realizational problems. Overt examples for such accommodation are provided by self-addressed questions (*she saw the ... what's the word?, je suis comment dire?*), as explained below.

The account of Ginzburg et al. (2014) exemplified some incremental contents and explained a significant conceptual change that would need to be assumed – that *Pending* would have incremental utterance representations. It did not, however, begin to spell out concretely the nature of such representations, which are crucial in a third option a speaker has apart from grounding and (self-)clarifying, namely *prediction* (see examples (2) and (3) above).

We can summarize this picture of processing as in (19), the monitoring and update/clarification cycle is modified to happen *at the end of each word utterance event*, and in case of the need for repair, a repair question gets accommodated into QUD.

(19) a. Ground: Continue (Levelt 1983).

b. Predict: Stop, since content is predictable.

c. (Self-)Clarify: Generate a clarification request given lack of expected utterance.

In the rest of this section we sketch an account of incremental utterance representations, including in particular incremental semantic contents.

4.2 Update Rules for Specifying Syntax

An essential presupposition of our approach (already in its non-incremental version, see above) is a view of syntax as speech event classification by an agent. For a very detailed exposition of such a view see Cooper (2019), a précis of which can be found in Cooper (2013). Starting at the word level – if $\text{Lex}(T_w, C)$ is a sign type[8] which is one of the lexical resources available to an agent A and A judges an event e to be of type T_w, then A is licensed to update their DGB with the type $\text{Lex}(T_w, C)$. Intuitively, this means that if the agent hears an utterance of the word 'composer', then they can conclude that they have heard a sign which has the category noun. This is the beginning of *parsing*, which Cooper shows how to assimilate to a kind of update akin to that involved in non-linguistic event perception. The licensing condition corresponding to lexical resources like (19) is given in (20). We will return below to

---

[8]For example, Lex('Beethoven', NP) representing something like

how this relates to gameboard update. (20) says that an agent with lexical resource Lex(T, C) who judges a speech event, u, to be of type T is licensed to judge that there is a sign of type Lex(T, C) whose 's-event.e'-field contains u.

(20)   If Lex(T, C) is a resource available to agent A, then for any u, $u :_A T$ licenses $:_A$ Lex(T, C) $\boxed{\wedge}$ $\left[\text{s-event:}\left[\text{e}=u:T\right]\right]$

Strings of utterances of words can be classified as utterances of phrases. That is, speech events are hierarchically organized into types of speech events in a way akin to the complex event structures needed to model non-linguistic activities. Agents have resources which allow them to reclassify a string of signs of certain types ("the daughters") into a single sign of another type ("the mother"). For instance, a string of type Det⌢N (that is, a concatenation of an event of type Det and an event of type N) can lead us to the conclusion that we have observed a sign of type NP whose daughters are of the types Det and N respectively.

The resource that licences this is a rule which is modelled as the function in (21a), which we represent as (21b).

(21)   a. $\lambda u : Det^\frown N$. NP $\boxed{\wedge}$ $\left[\text{syn:}\left[\text{daughters}=u:Det^\frown N\right]\right]$
        b. RuleDaughters(NP, $Det^\frown N$)

'RuleDaughters' is to be the function in (22). Thus 'RuleDaughters', if provided with a subtype of $Sign^+$ and a subtype of $Sign$ as arguments, will return a function which maps a string of signs of the first type to the second type with the restriction that the daughters field is filled by the string of signs:

(22) $\lambda T_1 : Type$.
        $\lambda T_2 : Type$.
        $\lambda u : T_1$. T_2 $\boxed{\wedge}$ $\left[\text{syn:}\left[\text{daughters}=u:T_1\right]\right]$

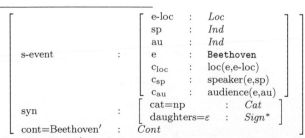

where 'Beethoven'' is whatever your theory gives you as the content of the proper noun 'Beethoven'.

4.3 Semantic Composition Using Asymmetric Merge

As we mentioned earlier, we use asymmetric merge to integrate utterances into the DGB. We postulate as the denotation associated with the root of the tree the type *illocutionary proposition*, which is hence compatible with declarative, interrogative and imperative utterances. This gets refined as each word gets introduced using asymmetric merge, which enables us to effect a combinatory operation that synthesises function application and unification.

We exemplify how this works in explicating the evolution of the speaker's information state in example (3), repeated here as (23).

(23)   [Context: J is in the kitchen searching for the always disappearing scissors. As he walks towards the cutlery drawer he begins to make his utterance, before discovering the scissors once the drawer is opened.] J: Who took the sci-...

(24) $\text{InfState}_0 : T_0$ where T_0 is

$$\left[\text{private:} \begin{bmatrix} \text{agenda} = \langle \text{ask(speaker,} q_0) \rangle : \langle \textit{Type} \rangle \\ \text{vis-sit:} \textit{NoScissors} \end{bmatrix} \right]$$

Here we use *NoScissors* to represent a type of types, $\mathcal{T}$, such that for any type, T, $T : \mathcal{T}$ iff there is no relabelling, T', of the type (25) such that $T \sqsubseteq T'$.

(25) $\begin{bmatrix} \text{x} & : & \textit{Ind} \\ \text{e} & : & \text{scissors(x)} \end{bmatrix}$

That is, the speaker judges the visual situation to be one which does not show any evidence of scissors. For discussion of the relabelling of types see Cooper (2019).

We assume that an utterance, u, of an interrogative NP such as *who* results in the update of the type of the current information state, T_0, in (26).

(26) $\text{InfState}_1 : T_0 \boxed{\wedge}$

$$\left[\text{DGB.Pending} = \begin{bmatrix} \text{sit} =u : \textit{Sit} \\ \text{sit type} = \begin{bmatrix} \text{phon : who} \\ \text{cont} = \begin{bmatrix} w : (\textit{Ppty} \rightarrow \textit{WhQ}) \end{bmatrix} : \textit{RecType} \end{bmatrix} : \textit{RecType} \end{bmatrix} : \textit{RecType} \right]$$

Here *Ppty* is the type given in (27).

(27) $([\text{x}:\textit{Ind}] \rightarrow \textit{RecType})$

The content associated with the utterance involves *projection* in a sense we explicate shortly. Here it is projected to be a question of type *Wh-Question* (*WhQ*).

(28) $\quad (\begin{bmatrix} \text{x:}Ind \\ \text{c:person(x)} \end{bmatrix} \rightarrow Rec\,Type)$

The function, w, in (26) which might be seen as serving as the incremental content (see Milward & Cooper 1994) of *who* is given in (29), though we could also regard it as a straightforward static content in a compositional semantics.[9]

(29) $\quad w = \lambda P{:}Ppty \;.\; \lambda r{:}\begin{bmatrix} \text{x:}Ind \\ \text{c:person(x)} \end{bmatrix} \;.\; [\text{e:}P(r)]$

We posit the content of the verb *took* to be (30a) (ignoring tense) of type (30b). We represent this content as 'take''.

(30)   a. $\text{take}' = \lambda r_1{:}[\text{x:}Ind] \;.\; \lambda r_2{:}[\text{x:}Ind] \;.\; [\text{e:take}(r_2.x,\, r_1.x)]$
     b. $([\text{x:}Ind] \rightarrow Ppty)$

Thus the incremental content of *who took* can be computed in line with Milward & Cooper (1994) as (31a) which can be expressed with reference to InfState$_1$ as (31b).

(31)   a. $\lambda r{:}[\text{x:}Ind] \;.\; w(\text{take}'(r))$
     b. $\lambda r{:}[\text{x:}Ind] \;.\; \text{InfoState}_1.\text{DGB.Pending.sit-type.cont}(\text{take}'(r))$

We abbreviate (31b) as *wt*. We can compute a type for InfState$_2$ as in (32).

(32)   InfState$_2 : T_1 \;\boxed{\wedge}$

$$\begin{bmatrix} \text{DGB.Pending} = \begin{bmatrix} \text{sit} = u_2{:}Sit \\ \text{sit-type} = \begin{bmatrix} \text{phon : who took} \\ \text{cont} = wt : ([\text{x:}Ind] \rightarrow WhPQ) \end{bmatrix}{:}Rec\,Type \end{bmatrix}{:}Rec\,Type \end{bmatrix}$$

We use T_2 to represent the type computed in (32). J opens the drawer and sees the scissors there. This updates the type of the visual situation so that it now requires the presence of scissors. This, in turn, implies that no one took the scissors, and hence, given the existence of a resolving answer to the question, the original motivation for asking it is eliminated. We can now compute a type for the next information state in which the agenda is empty.

---

[9]Milward & Cooper (1994) offer an explicit procedure that converts such lambda terms to existentially quantified propositions. Their fragment considered only declarative utterances. In the current work we could adapt their procedure to yield existentially quantified *illocutionary* propositions by converting functions to record types, in this case, for example:

$$\begin{bmatrix} \text{P} & : & Ppty \\ \text{r} & : & \begin{bmatrix} \text{x} & : & Ind \\ \text{c} & : & \text{person(x)} \end{bmatrix} \\ \text{e} & : & \text{P(r)} \end{bmatrix}$$

What we have sketched here is an approach to incrementality like that in Milward & Cooper (1994) which is similar to that which can be taken in a categorial grammar framework such as CCG (Demberg 2012). Another approach to incrementality is to use something similar to charts in chart parsing, which we sketch in the next section. We believe that, ultimately, the two approaches need to be combined to provide a complete treatment of incremental semantics.

4.4 Pending and Charts

Information included in the 'Pending'-field of the dialogue gameboard includes a type that represents the agent's view of the ongoing parse as the utterance unfolds. We call this type a *chart-type* because we appeal to a notion of chart parsing for this purpose, though as will become clear our approach is compatible with various other approaches for such representations, for instance Hough's graph-based representation (Hough 2015) which synthesizes a graph-based Dynamic Syntax view of parsing (Sato 2011) with the Incremental Unit (IU) framework of Schlangen & Skantze (2011) for incremental processing.

The type of Pending remains *LocProp*, as in (33). The issue that remains is how to explicate T_{chart} in order to understand how incremental content arises.

(33) $$\begin{bmatrix} \text{sit} = s \\ \text{sit-type} = T_{chart} \end{bmatrix}$$

We present here the briefest sketch of chart parsing as it is used in computational linguistics; for a recent textbook introduction to chart parsing see Jurafsky & Martin (2009: Chapter 13), whereas for its implementation in TTR see Cooper (2019). The idea of a chart is that it should store all the hypotheses made during the processing of an utterance which in turn allow us to compute new hypotheses to be added to the chart. Charts can be updated incrementally for each word and they can represent several live possibilities in a single data structure. We will say that a chart is a record and we will use our resources to compute a chart type on the basis of utterance events.

4.5 Charts: A Simplified Example

Suppose that we have so far heard an utterance of the word *Jill*. At this point we will say that the type of the chart is (34)

(34) $$\begin{bmatrix} e_1 & : & \texttt{Jill} \\ e & : & [e_1:\text{start}(e_1)] ^\frown [e_1:\text{end}(e_1)] \end{bmatrix}$$

The main event of the chart type (represented by the e-field) breaks the phonological event of type `Jill` down into a string of two events, the start and the end of the Jill-event.[10] Thus (34) records that we have observed an event of the phonological type who and an event consisting of the start of that event followed by the end of that event. Given that we have the resource $\text{Lex}_{\text{NP}_{\text{prop-name}}}(\text{Jill})$ available which yields the sign type for an utterance of Jill, we can update (34) to (35):

$$(35) \quad \begin{bmatrix} e_1 & : & \text{Jill} \\ e_2 & : & \text{Lex}_{\text{NP}_{\text{prop-name}}}(\text{Jill}) \boxed{\wedge} \left[\text{s-event}: \left[e=e_1:Phon\right]\right] \\ e & : & \begin{bmatrix} e_1:\text{start}(e_1) \\ e_2:\text{start}(e_2) \end{bmatrix} \frown \begin{bmatrix} e_1:\text{end}(e_1) \\ e_2:\text{end}(e_2) \end{bmatrix} \end{bmatrix}$$

That is, we add the information to the chart that there is an event (labelled 'e_2') of the type which is the sign type corresponding to Jill and that the event which is the speech event referred to in that sign type is the utterance event, labelled by 'e_1'. Furthermore the duration of the event labelled 'e_2' is the same as that labelled 'e_1'.

The type $\text{Lex}_{\text{NP}_{\text{prop-name}}}(\text{Jill})$ is a subtype of *NP*. Thus the event labelled 'e_2' could be the first item in a string that would be appropriate for the function which we have abbreviated as (36a), which has the type (36b).

(36) a. $S \longrightarrow NP\ VP\ |\ VP'(NP')$

  b. $(NP^\frown VP \rightarrow Type)$

Cooper (2019) argues for an analogy between non-linguistic event prediction and the prediction that occurs in parsing.[11] So on observing a noun-phrase event one can predict that it might be followed by a verb phrase event thus creating a sentence event. We add a hypothesis event to our chart which takes place at the end of the noun-phrase event as in (37).[12]

---

[10]These starting and ending events correspond to what are standardly called *vertices* in the chart parsing literature.

[11]Indeed he suggests that this might extend to non-linguistic event prediction among non-humans, e.g. the prediction by a dog playing Fetch that it should run after a stick which is held up.

[12]In terms of the traditional chart parsing terminology this corresponds to an *active edge* involving a *dotted rule*. The fact that the addition of this type to the chart type is triggered by finding something of an appropriate type to be the leftmost element in a string that would be an appropriate argument to the rule corresponds to what is called a *left-corner* parsing strategy.

(37)

$$\begin{bmatrix} e_1{:}\texttt{Jill} \\ e_2{:}\mathrm{Lex}_{\mathrm{NP}_{\mathrm{prop-name}}}(\texttt{Jill}) \boxed{\wedge} \begin{bmatrix} \text{s-event:} [e{=}e_1{:}Phon] \end{bmatrix} \\ e_3{:} \begin{bmatrix} \mathrm{rule}{=}S \longrightarrow NP\ VP \mid NP'(VP'){:}(NP{^\frown} VP \to Type) \\ \mathrm{fnd}{=}e_2{:}Sign \\ \mathrm{req}{=}VP{:}Type \\ e{:}\mathrm{required}(\mathrm{req},\mathrm{rule}) \end{bmatrix} \\ e\ {:} \begin{bmatrix} e_1{:}\mathrm{start}(e_1) \\ e_2{:}\mathrm{start}(e_2) \end{bmatrix} {^\frown} \begin{bmatrix} e_1{:}\mathrm{end}(e_1) \\ e_2{:}\mathrm{end}(e_2) \\ e_3{:}\mathrm{start}(e_3){^\frown}\mathrm{end}(e_3) \end{bmatrix} \end{bmatrix}$$

In the e_3-field the 'rule'-field is for a syntactic rule, that is, a function from a string of signs of a given type to a type. The 'fnd'-field is for a sign or string of signs so far found which match an initial segment of a string of the type required by the rule. The 'req'-field is the type of the remaining string required to satisfy the rule as expressed in the 'e'-field. This hypothesis event both starts and ends at the end of the event of the noun-phrase event e_2.

5 Incremental Dialogue Processing: Principles and Examples

With a basic means of representing utterances in progress, we can now formulate certain principles which will use to explicate several of the phenomena discussed in Section 2.

5.1 Utterance Projection

The first principle we introduce corresponds to the 'stop option' in our utterance protocol (19b) – it says that if one projects that an utterance will continue in a certain way, then one can actually use this prediction to update one's DGB. This is of course a dangerous principle to apply in an unconstrained fashion, and would ideally be formulated using probabilities about the projection, for instance using the framework of Cooper et al. (2015), though we do not do so here. (38) is an update rule which moves a locutionary proposition from Pending to LatestMove.

(38) *Utterance Projection*

$$\begin{bmatrix} \mathrm{pre} & = \begin{bmatrix} \mathrm{pending} & : & LocProp \end{bmatrix} \\ \mathrm{effects}{=}\lambda r{:} \begin{bmatrix} \mathrm{pending.proj}{:}LocProp \end{bmatrix} . \\ \qquad\qquad \begin{bmatrix} \mathrm{LatestMove}{=}r.\mathrm{pending.proj}{:}LocProp \end{bmatrix} \end{bmatrix}$$

5.2 Forward-looking Disfluencies

Forward-looking disfluencies are disfluencies where the moment of interruption is followed not by an alteration, but just by a completion of the utterance which is delayed by a filled or unfilled pause (hesitation) or a repetition of a previously uttered part of the utterance (repetitions). As we mentioned with respect to example (4) and in our discussion in Section 4.1, we need a means of enabling at any point in the speech stream the emergence of a question about what is still to come in the current utterance. Forward Looking Disfluencies involve the update rule in (39): given a context where an initial segment of utterance by A has taken place, the next speaker – underspecified between the current one and the addressee – may address the issue of what A intended to say next by providing a co-propositional utterance:

(39)   *Forward Looking Utterance Rule*

$$
\begin{bmatrix}
\text{pre} = \begin{bmatrix} \text{spkr} & : & Ind \\ \text{addr} & : & Ind \\ \text{pending} & : & LocProp \end{bmatrix} \\[2em]
\text{effects} = \lambda r : \begin{bmatrix} \text{spkr}{:}Ind \\ \text{addr}{:}Ind \\ \text{pending}{:}LocProp \end{bmatrix} . \begin{bmatrix} \text{spkr}{:}(Ind_{r.\text{spkr}} \vee Ind_{r.\text{addr}}) \\ \text{addr}{:}((Ind_{r.\text{spkr}} \vee Ind_{r.\text{addr}}) \wedge \neg Ind_{\text{spkr}}) \\ \text{qud}{:}poset(Question) \\ \text{q} = \lambda x{:}Ind \ . \ \text{MeanNextUtt}(r.\text{spkr}, r.\text{pending}, x){:}Question \\ \text{c}{:}\max(\text{q},\text{qud}) \\ \text{LatestMove}{:}LocProp \\ \text{c2}{:}\text{copropositional}(\text{LatestMove},\text{q}) \end{bmatrix}
\end{bmatrix}
$$

A consequence of (39) is that it offers the potential to explain cases like (40). In the aftermath of a filled pause an issue along the lines of the one we have *posited* as the *effect* of the conversational rule (39) actually gets uttered:

(40) a. Carol 133 Well it's (pause) it's (pause) er (pause) what's his name? Bernard Matthews' turkey roast.

(British National Corpus, block: KBJ)

  b. They're pretty ... um, how can I describe the Finns? They're quite an unusual crowd actually.

(http://www.guardian.co.uk/sport/2010/sep/10/
small-talk-steve-backley-interview)

On our account such utterances are licensed because these questions are co-propositional with the issue 'what did A mean to say after u0?'. This suggests that a different range of such questions will occur depending on the identity of (the syntactic/semantic type of) u0. This expectation is met, as discussed by Tian, Murayama & Ginzburg (2016), who also discuss cross-linguistic variation with self addressed questions in English, Chinese, and Japanese.

5.3 Sluicing, Incrementally

Finally we return to incremental sluicing examples, as in (5), one example of which is repeated here as (41):

(41)   A: A really annoying incident. Someone...
        B: Who?
        A: Not clear.
        B: OK
        A: has taken the kitchen scissors.

We very briefly sketch an analysis of this case. Ginzburg & Sag (2000) offered a detailed account of (direct, non-reprise) sluicing. However, due to the type feature structure-based semantic formalism they were using, which lacked genuine variable binding, it could not capture the semantic dependency between quantified antecedent and *wh*-phrase; moreover, it implied that *direct sluicing* strongly resembles *short answers* as a construction, a prediction challenged by acquisition data in Ginzburg & Kolliakou (2009). Ginzburg (2012) offers an account of direct sluicing in KoS-TTR, which improves on the one offered by Ginzburg & Sag (2000) in these respects *inter alia*. On this view, summarized semi-formally in (42a), a direct sluice denotes a question (i.e. a function from records into propositions) whose domain is the type denoted by the *wh*-phrase and whose range is that given by MaxQUD's proposition where the *wh*-phrase's variable is substituted for that associated with the antecedent quantified NP. (42b, c) offer an example

(42)   a. sluice-int-cl.cont =
           (whP.rest)MaxQUD.prop[antecedent.x $\mapsto$ whP.x]
        b. A: A student left. B: Who?
        c. Who? $\mapsto \lambda r: \begin{bmatrix} \text{x:}Ind \\ c_1\text{:person(x)} \end{bmatrix} \cdot \begin{bmatrix} \text{x}=r\text{.x} & : & Ind \\ c_2 & : & \text{student(x)} \\ c_3 & : & \text{leave(x)} \end{bmatrix}$

Assume, following Lücking & Ginzburg (2019), as discussed in Section 3.4, that a QNP such as 'someone' has a content of the form (43).

$$(43) \quad \begin{bmatrix} \text{dgb-params:} RecType \\ \text{q-params:} \begin{bmatrix} \text{maxset:Set}(Ind) \\ \text{c1:}\overrightarrow{\text{person}}(\text{maxset}) \\ \text{refind:} Ind \\ \text{c}_{\text{ppty}}\text{:person(refind)} \\ \text{compset:Set}(Ind) \\ \text{c2:partition(\{\{refind\},compset\},maxset)} \end{bmatrix} \end{bmatrix}$$

The sluice in (41) is triggered by utterance prediction that for some property P LatestMove is *A asserts that someone P'ed*. This gives rise to an update of QUD, via Assertion QUD-incrementation with (44a) as maximal element of QUD and the antecedent for a sluice, as in (44b), which is predicted to mean (44c) – paraphrasable as (44d) – after it is uttered:

$$(44) \quad a. \ ? \begin{bmatrix} \text{q-params:} \begin{bmatrix} \text{maxset:Set}(Ind) \\ \text{c1:}\overrightarrow{\text{person}}(\text{maxset}) \\ \text{refind:} Ind \\ \text{c}_{\text{ppty}}\text{:person(refind)} \\ \text{compset:Set}(Ind) \\ \text{c2:partition(\{\{refind\},compset\},maxset)} \end{bmatrix} \\ P:Ppty \\ \text{nucl:} P(refind) \end{bmatrix}$$

b. A: Someone... B: Who?

c. Who? $\mapsto \lambda r: \begin{bmatrix} \text{x:} Ind \\ \text{c}_1\text{:person(x)} \end{bmatrix}$.

$$\begin{bmatrix} \text{refind} = r.\text{x:} Ind \\ \text{c}_{\text{ppty}}\text{:person(refind)} \\ \text{compset:Set}(Ind) \\ \text{c2:partition(\{\{refind\},compset\},maxset)} \\ P:Ppty \\ \text{nucl:} P(refind) \end{bmatrix}$$

d. 'Who is that person (that has some as yet uninstantiated property)?'

6 Conclusions and Further Work

That people process linguistic input incrementally is a widely shared view. But does this mean that the 'competence grammar' must be formulated in a way that enables incremental (minimally word by word and even mid-word) semantic composition to be effected? Various frameworks have responded affirmatively to this question, but HPSG has over the years indomitably resisted such a conclusion, preferring to assume that incrementality is merely an aspect of performance. In this paper we have reiterated the view that grammars should be viewed as systems that classify an utterance as it occurs in conversation, a view that has recently been articulated in some detail (Ginzburg 2012; Ginzburg & Poesio 2016; Kempson et al. 2016). Once one examines ongoing conversational data even in a fairly cursory fashion, one discovers the pervasive nature of phenomena whose analysis incontrovertibly requires incremental semantic composition. In the paper we sketch how this can be done in a way that allows one to utilize existing 'non-incremental' grammars such as HPSG as long as they interface in a radical way with the conversational context. This approach has parallels to Dynamic Syntax (Kempson et al. 2001), and particularly recent dialogue-friendly versions (Purver, Eshghi & Hough 2011, Kempson et al. 2016), where the central idea is online, incremental construction of meaning representations. However, the incremental account presented here not only allows the representation of utterances, but the internal state of a dialogue agent, including background beliefs and the events in the situated context, to be updated online for entire interactions.

In a more detailed presentation we will present a small grammar/context fragment. In future work we hope to investigate experimentally the processing of data of the kind presented here.

Acknowledgements

This work is dedicated with friendship to Danièle Godard. Portions of this work were presented at Sinn und Bedeutung 2016, held in September 2016 in Edinburgh and at the workshop to honour Danièle, held at the Hôtel de Lauzon in March 2017.

This work is supported by a public grant overseen by the French National Research Agency (ANR) as part of the program Investissements d'Avenir (reference: ANR-10-LABX-0083). It contributes to the IdExz Université de Paris – ANR-18-IDEX-0001. This research was also supported by a senior fellowship to the first author by the Institut Universitaire de France and by VR project 2014-39 for the establishment of the Centre for Linguistic Theory and Studies in Probability (CLASP) at the University of Gothenburg. We thank J.P. Koenig for his very useful comments on an earlier version of the paper and Andy Lücking for discussion.

References

Abbott, Clifford. 1984. Two Feminine Genders in Oneida. *Anthropological Linguistics* 26:125–137.

Abeillé, Anne & Danièle Godard. 1996. La complémentation des auxiliaires en français. *Langages* 122:32–61.

Abeillé, Anne & Danièle Godard. 1999. A Lexical Approach to Quantifier Floating in French. In Gert Webelhuth, Jean-Pierre Koenig & Andreas Kathol (eds.), *Lexical and Constructional Aspects of Linguistic Explanation*, 81–96. Stanford, CA: CSLI Publications.

Abeillé, Anne & Danièle Godard. 2002. The Syntactic Structure of French Auxiliaries. *Language* 78:404–452.

Abeillé, Anne, Danièle Godard, Philip [H.] Miller & Ivan A. Sag. 1997. French Bounded Dependencies. In Sergio Balari & Luca Dini (eds.), *Romance in HPSG*, 1–54. Stanford, CA: CSLI Publications.

Abeillé, Anne, Danièle Godard & Frédéric Sabio. 2008. Two Types of NP Preposing in French. In Stefan Müller (ed.), *Proceedings of the 15th International Conference on Head-driven Phrase Structure Grammar*, 306–324. Stanford, CA: CSLI Publications.

Ades, Antony & Mark Steedman. 1982. On the Order of Words. *Linguistics and Philosophy* 6:517–558.

Aissen, Judith. 1999. Markedness and Subject Choice in Optimality Theory. *Natural Language & Linguistic Theory* 17(4):673–711.

Ajmer, Karin & Anne Marie Simon-Vandenbergen. 2003. The Discourse Particle *well* and its Equivalents in Swedish and Dutch. *Linguistics* 41(6):1123–1161.

Alotaibi, Mansour. 2015. Wh-*questions in Modern Standard Arabic: Minimalist and HPSG Approaches*. Ph.D. dissertation, University of Essex.

Akmajian, Adrian. 1984. Sentence Types and the Form–Function Fit. *Natural Language & Linguistic Theory* 2(1):1–23.

Anward, Jan. 1981. *Functions of Passive and Impersonal Constructions: A Case Study from Swedish*. Ph.D. dissertation, Uppsala University.

Aoun, Joseph Elabbas Benmamoun & Lina Choueiri. 2010. *The Syntax of Arabic*. Cambridge: Cambridge University Press.

Ariel, Mira. 1988. Referring and Accessibility. *Journal of Linguistics* 24:67–87.

Arnold, Doug & Robert D. Borsley. 2014. On the Analysis of English Exhaustive Conditionals. In Sefan Müller (ed.), *Proceedings of the 21st International Conference on Head-driven Phrase Structure Grammar*, 27–47. Stanford, CA: CSLI Publications.

Asher, Nicholas & Alex Lascarides. 2003. *Logics of Conversation*. Cambridge: Cambridge University Press.

Audibert-Gibier, Monique. 1992. Étude de l'accord du participe passé sur des corpus de français parlé. *Langage et société* 61:7–30.

Avram, Larisa. 2015. A Mirativity Subjunctive in Romanian. In Nicolae Mocanu (ed.), *Inspre și dinspre Cluj. Contribuții lingvistice. Omagiu profesorului G.G. Neamțu la 70 de ani*, 62–74. Cluj: Editura Scriptor – Argonaut.

Bach, Emon, Eloise Jelinek, Angelika Kratzer & Barbara Partee (eds.). 1995. *Quantification in Natural Languages*. Dordrecht: Springer.

Baker, Mark. 1996. *The Polysynthesis Parameter*. Oxford: Oxford University Press.

Baker, Mark. 1997. Thematic Roles and Syntactic Structure. In Liliane Haegeman (ed.), *Elements of Grammar: Handbook in Generative Syntax*, 73–127. Dordrecht: Kluwer.

Barbu, Ana-Maria. 1999. Complexul verbal. *Studii și cercetări lingvistice* 1:39–84.

Barwise, Jon. 1989. *The Situation in Logic* (CSLI Lecture Notes). Stanford, CA: CSLI Publications.

Barwise, John & Robin Cooper. 1981. Generalized Quantifiers and Natural Language. *Linguistics and Philosophy* 4:159–219.

Beaver, David I. & Brady Z. Clark. 2008. *Sense and Sensitivity: How Focus Determines Meaning*. Chichester: Wiley-Blackwell.

Beaver, David I., Craige Roberts, Mandy Simons & Judith Tonhauser. 2017. Questions under Discussion: Where Information Structure Meets Projective Content. *Annual Review of Linguistics* 3:265–284.

Becker, Martin. 2010. Mood in Rumanian. In Björn Rothstein & Rolf Thieroff (eds.), *Mood in the Languages of Europe*, 251–270. Amsterdam & Philadelphia, PA: John Benjamins.

Bender, Emily M. 2001. *Syntactic Variation and Linguistic Competence: The Case of AAVE Copula Absence*. Ph.D. dissertation, Stanford University.

Bennett, Michael. 1978. Demonstratives and Indexicals in Montague Grammar. *Synthese* 39(1):1–80. *Logic and Linguistics*, Part II, 1–80.

Betarte, Gustavo & Alvaro Tasistro. 1998. Extension of Martin-Löf's Type Theory with Record Types and Subtyping. In Giovanni Sambin & Jan M. Smith (eds.), *Twenty-five Years of Constructive Type Theory* (Oxford Logic Guides 36), 21–39. Oxford: Oxford University Press.

Beyssade, Claire & Jean-Marie Marandin. 2006. The Speech Act Assignment Problem Revisited: Disentangling Speaker's Commitment from Speaker's Call on Addressee. *Empirical Studies in Syntax and Semantics* 6:37–68.

Bîlbîie, Gabriela. 2011. *Grammaire des constructions elliptiques. Une étude comparative des phrases sans verbe en roumain et en français*. Ph.D. dissertation, Université Paris Diderot – Paris 7.

Bîlbîie, Gabriela & Alexandru Mardale. 2018. The Romanian Subjunctive in a Balkan Perspective. In Iliyana Krapova & Brian Joseph (eds.), *Balkan Syntax and (Universal) Principles of Grammar* (Trends in Linguistics: Studies and Monographs 285), 278–314. Berlin: Mouton de Gruyter.

Bittner, Maria & Naja Trondhjem. 2008. Quantification as Reference: Evidence from Q-verbs. In Lisa Matthewson (ed.), *Quantification: A Cross-linguistic Perspective*, 7–66. Bingley: Emerald.

Blanche-Benveniste, Claire. 2006. L'accord des participes passés en français parlé contemporain. In Céline Guillot, Serge Heiden & Sophie Prévost (eds.), *À la quête du sens: Études littéraires, historiques et linguistiques en hommage à Christiane Marchello-Nizia*, 33–47. Lyon: ENS Éditions.

Bonami, Olivier 2015. Periphrasis as Collocation. *Morphology* 25:63–110.

Bonami, Olivier, Robert D. Borsley & Maggie O. Tallerman. 2016. On Pseudo-non-finite Clauses in Welsh, *Proceedings of the Joint 2016 Conference on Head-driven Phrase Structure Grammar and Lexical Functional Grammar*, 104–124. Stanford, CA: CSLI Publications.

Bonami, Olivier & Gilles Boyé. 2007. French Pronominal Clitics and the Design of Paradigm Function Morphology. In Geert Booij, Luca Ducceschi, Bernard Fradin, Angela Ralli, Emiliano Guevara & Sergio Scalise (eds.), *Proceedings of the Fifth Mediterranean Morphology Meeting* (MMM5), 291–322. Università degli Studi di Bologna.

Bonami, Olivier, Danièle Godard & Jean-Marie Marandin. 1999. Constituency and Word Order in French Subject Inversion. In Gosse Bouma, Erhard Hinrichs, Geert-Jan M. Kruijff & Richard T. Oehrle (eds.), *Constraints and Resources in Natural Language Syntax and Semantics*, 21–40. Stanford, CA: CSLI Publications.

Börjars, Kersti, Elisabet Engdahl & Maia Andréasson. 2003. Subject and Object in Swedish. In Miriam Butt & Tracy Holloway King (eds.), *Proceedings of the LFG '03 Conference*, 43–58. Stanford, CA: CSLI Publications.

Börjars, Kersti & Nigel Vincent. 2005. Position versus Function in Scandinavian Presentational Constructions. In Miriam Butt & Tracy Holloway King (eds.), *Proceedings of the LFG '05 Conference*, 54–72. Stanford, CA: CSLI Publications.

Borsley, Robert D. & Kersti Börjars (eds.). 2011. *Non-transformational Syntax: Formal and Explicit Models of Grammar*. New York: Wiley-Blackwell.

Bouma, Gosse, Rob Malouf & Ivan A. Sag. 2001. Satisfying Constraints on Extraction and Adjunction. *Natural Language & Linguistic Theory* 19:1–65.

Bresnan, Joan & Ron Kaplan (eds.). 1982. *The Mental Representation of Grammatical Relations*. Cambridge, MA: MIT Press.

Broadwell, George Aaron. 2006. *A Choktaw Reference Grammar*. Lincoln, NE: University of Nebraska Press.

Bruce, Kim & Donka Farkas. 2007. Context Structure for Dialogues. Ms., Pomona College & UC Santa Cruz.

Caponigro, Ivano & Jon Sprouse. 2007. Rhetorical Questions as Questions. In Estella
Puig-Waldmüller (ed.), *Proceedings of Sinn und Bedeutung 11*, 121–133. Barcelona: Universat Pompeu Fabra.

Carlson, Greg. N. 1977. *Reference to Kinds in English*. Ph.D. thesis, University of Massachusetts Amherst.

Chomsky, Noam. 1981. *Lectures on Government and Binging: The Pisa Lectures* (Studies in Generative Grammar 9). Berlin & New York: Mouton de Gruyter.

Chung, Sandra & William Ladusaw. 2003. *Restriction and Saturation*. Cambridge, MA: MIT Press.

Clark, Herbert. 1996. *Using Language*. Cambridge: Cambridge University Press.

Cooper, Robin. 2012. Type Theory and Semantics in Flux. In Ruth Kempson, Tim Fernando & Nicholas Asher (eds.), *Handbook of the Philosophy of Science*, vol. 14: *Philosophy of Linguistics*, 271–323. Amsterdam: Elsevier.

Cooper, Robin. 2013. Update Conditions and Intensionality in a Type-theoretic Approach to Dialogue Semantics. In Raquel Fernández & Amy Isard (eds.), *Proceedings of the 17th Workshop on the Semantics and Pragmatics of Dialogue* (SEMDIAL 2013 DialDam), 15–24. Amsterdam: University of Amsterdam.

Cooper, Robin. 2019. Type Theory and Language: From Perception to Linguistic Communication. Ms., University of Gothenburg. [Book draft]

Cooper, Robin, Simon Dobnik, Staffan Larsson & Shalom Lappin. 2015. Probabilistic Type Theory and Natural Language Semantics. *Linguistic Issues in Language Technology* 10:43.
https://www.clasp.gu.se/digitalAssets/1608/1608274_cdll_lilt15.pdf

Cooper, Robin & Jonathan Ginzburg. 2015. Type Theory with Records for Natural Language Semantics. In Shalom Lappin & Chris Fox (eds.), *Handbook of Contemporary Semantic Theory*, 2nd edn., 375–407. Oxford: Blackwell.

Coquand, Thierry, Randy Pollack & Makoto Takeyama. 2003. A Logical Framework with Dependent Types. *Fundamenta Informaticae* 20:1–21.

Corazza, Eros. 2002. Temporal Indexicals and Temporal Tems. *Synthese* 130(3):441–460.

Corazza, Eros. 2004. On the Alleged Ambiguity of 'now' and 'here'. *Synthese* 138:289–313.

Corblin, Francis & Tijana Asic. 2016. Une nouvelle approche de l'opposition *ici/là* et *ovde/tu*. *Travaux de linguistique* 72:29–48.

Creissels, Denis, Sokhna Bao Diop, Alain-Christian Bassène, Mame Thierno Cissé, Alexander Cobbinah, El Hadji Dieye, Dame Ndao, Sylvie Nouguier-Voisin, Nicolas Quint, Marie Renaudier, Adjaratou Sall & Guillaume Segerer. 2015. L'impersonnalité dans les langues de la région sénégambienne. *Africana Linguistica* 21:29–86.

Creissels, Denis & Séckou Biaye. 2016. *Le balant ganja: phonologie, morphosyntaxe, liste lexicale, textes*. Dakar: IFAN.

Creissels, Denis & Pierre Sambou. 2013. *Le mandinka: phonologie, grammaire, textes*. Paris: Karthala.

Croft, William. 2012. *Verbs: Aspect and Causal Structure*. Oxford: Oxford University Press.

Dalrymple, Mary & Irena Nikolaeva. 2011. *Objects and Information Structure*. Cambridge: Cambridge University Press.

Dargnat, Mathilde. Forthcoming. Les particules discursives. In Anne Abeillé & Danièle Godard (eds.), *Grande Grammaire du français*. Arles: Actes Sud.

Dargnat, Mathilde, Katarina Bartkova & Denis Jouvet. 2015. Discourse Particles in French: Prosodic Parameters Extraction and Analysis. In Adrian-Horia Dediu, Carlos Martín-Vide & Klára Vicsi (eds.), *Statistical Language and Speech Processing: Third International Conference, SLSP 2015, Budapest, Hungary, November 24–26, 2015, Proceedings* (Lecture Notes in Computer Science), 40–49. Cham: Springer.

Dekker, Paul, Maria Aloni & Alastair Butler. 2007. The Semantics and Pragmatics of Questions. In Paul Dekker, Maria Aloni & Alastair Butler (eds.), *Questions in Dynamic Semantics*, 1–40. Oxford: Elsevier.

Demberg, Vera. 2012. Incremental Derivations in CCG. *Proceedings of the 11th International Workshop on Tree Adjoining Grammars and Related Formalisms* (TAG+11), 198–206. Paris.

Demberg, Vera, Frank Keller & Alexander Koller. 2013. Incremental, Predictive Parsing with Psycholinguistically Motivated Tree-adjoining Grammar. *Computational Linguistics* 39(4):1025–1066.

Diaz, Thomas, Jean-Pierre Koenig & Karin Michelson. 2019. Oneida Pre-pronominal Prefixes in Information-based Morphology. *Morphology* 29(4):431–473.

Diderichsen, Paul. 1946. *Elementær Dansk Grammatik* [Elementary Danish grammar]. København: Gyldendal.

Ducrot, Oswald. 1972. *Dire et ne pas Dire*. Paris: Hermann.

Ducrot, Oswald. 1984. *Le Dire et le Dit*. Paris: Éditions de Minuit.

Engdahl, Elisabet. 2006. Semantic and Syntactic Patterns in Swedish Passives. In Benjamin Lyngfelt & Torgrim Solstad (eds.), *Demoting the Agent: Passive, Middle and Other Voice Phenomena*, 21–45. Amsterdam: John Benjamins.

Engdahl, Elisabet, Maia Andréasson & Kersti Börjars. 2004. Word Order in the Swedish Midfield: An OT Approach. In Fred Karlsson (ed.), *Papers from the 20th Scandinavian Conference of Linguistics*, 1–13. Helsinki: University of Helsinki, Department of General Linguistics.

Erteschik-Shir, Nomi. 2007. *Information Structure: The Syntax–Discourse Interface*. Oxford: Oxford University Press.

Erteschik-Shir, Nomi. 2019. Stage Topics and their Architecture. In Valéria Molnár, Verner Egerland & Susanne Winkler (eds.), *Architecture of Topic*, 223–248. Berlin: de Gruyter Mouton.

Fălăuş, Anamaria. 2014. Presumptive Mood, Factivity and Epistemic Indefinites in Romanian. *Borealis: An International Journal of Hispanic Linguistics* 3(2):105–124.

Farkas, Donka. 1985. *Intensional Descriptions and the Romance Subjunctive Mood*. New York: Garland.

Farkas, Donka. 1992. On the Semantics of Subjunctive Complements. In Paul Hirschbühler & Konrad Koerner (eds.), *Romance Languages and Modern Linguistic Theory: Papers from the 20th Linguistic Symposium on Romance Languages (LSRL XX)*, 69–104. Amsterdam & Philadelphia, PA: John Benjamins.

Farkas, Donka. 2003. Assertion, Belief and Mood Choice. Presented at the Workshop on Conditional and Unconditional Modality, Vienna. (Available at http://people.ucsc.edu/~farkas/papers/mood.pdf, 1 March 2018)

Farkas, Donka. 2018. Non-canonical Questions: The Case of *oare* Interrogatives. Presented at the University of Bucharest, 28–29 September 2018.

Farkas Donka & Kim Bruce. 2010. On Reacting to Assertions and Polar Questions. *Journal of Semantics* 27:81–118.

Fassi Fehri, Abdelkader. 1993. *Issues in the Structure of Arabic Clauses and Words*. Dordrecht: Kluwer.

Fernández, Raquel. 2006. *Non-sentential Utterances in Dialogue: Classification, Resolution and Use*. Ph.D. thesis, King's College London.

Fernández, Raquel & Jonathan Ginzburg. 2002. Non-sentential Utterances: A Corpus Study. *Traitement automatique des langues. Dialogue* 43(2):13–42.

Fitelson, Branden. 2001. *Studies in Bayesian Confirmation Theory*. Ph.D. thesis, University of Wisconsin–Madison.

Frâncu, Constantin. 2010. *Conjunctivul românesc şi raporturile lui cu alte moduri.* Iaşi: Casa Editorialǎ Demiurg.

Frey, Werner. 2006. Contrast and Movement to the German Prefield. In Valéria Molnár & Susanne Winkler (eds.), *The Architecture of Focus*, 235–264. Berlin: Mouton de Gruyter.

Gardent, Claire & Michael Kohlhase. 1997. Computing Parallelism in Discourse. *Proceedings of the Fifteenth International Joint Conference on Artificial Intelligence* (IJCAI–97), vol. 2, 1016–1021. Nagoya.

Gaucher, Damien. 2013. L'accord du participe passé en français parlé en tant que variable sociolinguistique. In Fabrice Marsac & Jean-Christophe Pellat (eds.), *Le participe passé entre accords et désaccords*, 115–129. Strasbourg: Presses Universitaires de Strasbourg.

Gazdar, Gerald. 1981. Speech Act Assignment. In Aravind Joshi, Bonnie Weber & Ivan A. Sag (eds.), *Elements of Discourse Understanding*, 64–83. Cambridge: Cambridge University Press.

Gazdar, Gerald, Ewan Klein, Geoffrey K. Pullum & Ivan A. Sag. 1985. *Generalized Phrase Structure Grammar.* Cambridge, MA: Harvard University Press.

Geurts, Bart. 1999. *Presuppositions and Pronouns* (Current Research in the Semantics/Pragmatics Interface 3). Oxford: Elsevier.

Giannakidou, Anastasia. 2009. The Dependency of the Subjunctive Revisited: Temporal Semantics and Polarity. *Lingua* 119:1883–1908.

Giannakidou, Anastasia. 2016. Evaluative Subjunctive and Nonveridicality. In Joanna Błaszczak, Anastasia Giannakidou, Dorota Klimek-Jankowska & Krzysztof Migdalski (eds.), *Mood, Aspect, Modality Revisited: New Answers to Old Questions*, 177–217. Chicago, IL: University of Chicago Press.

Ginzburg, Jonathan. 1994. An Update Semantics for Dialogue. In Harry Bunt (ed.), *Proceedings of the 1st International Workshop on Computational Semantics*. Tilburg: ITK, Tilburg University.

Ginzburg, Jonathan. 2012. *The Interactive Stance: Meaning for Conversation.* Oxford: Oxford University Press.

Ginzburg, Jonathan, Raquel Fernández & David Schlangen. 2014. Disfluencies as Intra-utterance Dialogue Moves. *Semantics and Pragmatics* 7(9):64.
http://dx.doi.org/10.3765/sp.7.9

Ginzburg, Jonathan & Dimitra Kolliakou. 2009. Answers without Questions: The Emergence of Fragments in Child Language. *Journal of Linguistics* 45:641–673.

Ginzburg, Jonathan & Massimo Poesio. 2016. Grammar is a System that Characterizes Talk in Interaction. *Frontiers in Psychology* 7:1938.

Ginzburg, Jonathan & Ivan A. Sag. 2000. *Interrogative Investigations: The Form, Meaning and Use of English Interrogatives.* Stanford, CA: CSLI Publications.

Giorgi, Alessandra & Fabio Pianesi. 1997. *Tense and Aspect: From Semantics to Morphosyntax*. Oxford: Oxford University Press.

Giurgea, Ion. 2018. The Romanian Interrogative Particle *oare* in a Comparative and Historical Perspective. In Gabriela Pană Dindelegan, Adina Dragomirescu, Irina Nicula & Alexandru Nicolae (eds.), *Comparative and Diachronic Perspectives on Romance Syntax*, 401–432. Newcastle: Cambridge Scholars Publishing.

Godard, Danièle. 2012. Indicative and Subjunctive Mood in Complement Clauses: From Formal Semantics to Grammar Writing. In Christopher Piñón (ed.), *Empirical Issues in Syntax and Semantics*, vol. 9, 129–148. Paris: Centre National de la Recherche Scientifique.

Grice, Paul. 1975. Logic and conversation. In Donald Davidson & Gilbert Harman (eds.), *The Logic of Grammar*, 64–75. Encino, CA: Dickenson.

Grice, Paul. 1978. Further notes on logic and conversation. In Peter Cole (ed.), *Pragmatics* (Syntax and Semantics 9), 113–127. New York: Academic Press.

Groenendijk, Jeroen & Martin Stokhof. 1984. *Studies in the Semantics of Questions and the Pragmatics of Answers*. Amsterdam: Akademish Proefschrift.

Grohmann, Kleanthes. 2000. Null Modals in Germanic (and Romance): Infinitival Exclamatives. *The Belgian Journal of Linguistics* 14:43–61.

Gundel, Jeanette K. & Thorstein Fretheim. 2004. Topic and Focus. In Laurence R. Horn & Gregory Ward (eds.), *The Handbook of Pragmatics* (Blackwell Handbooks in Linguistics 16), 175–196. Malden, MA: Blackwell.

Gundel, Jeanette K., Nancy Hedberg & Ron Zacharski. 1993. Cognitive Status and the Form of Referring Expressions in Discourse. *Language* 69(2):274–307.

Güngördü, Zelal. 1997. *Incremental Constraint-based Parsing: An Efficient Approach for Head-final Languages*. Ph.D. thesis, University of Edinburgh.

Gutzman, Daniel. 2015. *Use-conditional Meaning: Studies in Multidimensional Semantics*. Oxford: Oxford University Press.

Haddican, Bill & Anders Holmberg. 2019. Object Symmetry Effects in Germanic: Evidence for the Role of Case. *Natural Language & Linguistic Theory* 37:91–122.

Hamblin, C. L. 1971. Mathematical Models of Dialogue. *Theoria* 37(2):130–155.

Hamblin, C. L. 1973. Questions in Montague English. *Foundations of Language* 10:41–53.

Haugereid, Petter & Mathieu Morey. 2012. A Left-branching Grammar Design for Incremental Parsing. In Stefan Müller (ed.), *Proceedings of the 19th International Conference on Head-driven Phrase Structure Grammar, Chungnam National University Daejeon*, 181–194. Stanford, CA: CSLI Publications.

Heim, Irene & Angelika Kratzer. 1998. *Semantics in Generative Grammar*. Oxford: Wiley-Blackwell.

Hoekstra, Teun. 1984. *Transitivity: Grammatical Relations in Government-Binding Theory*. Dordrecht: Foris.

Hough, Julian. 2015. *Modelling Incremental Self-repair Processing in Dialogue*. Ph.D. thesis, Queen Mary University of London.

Hough, Julian, Casey Kennington, David Schlangen & Jonathan Ginzburg. 2015. Incremental Semantics for Dialogue Processing: Requirements, and a Comparison of Two Approaches. In Matthew Purver, Mehrnoosh Sadrzadeh & Matthew Stone (eds.), *Proceedings of the 11ᵗʰ International Conference on Computational Semantics* (IWCS 2015), 206–216. London.

Huddleston, Rodney. 2002. Clause Type and Illocutionary Force. In Rodney Huddleston & Geoffrey K. Pullum et al., *The Cambridge Grammar of the English Language*, 851–945. Cambridge: Cambridge University Press.

Jayez, Jacques. 2010. Projective Meaning and Attachment. In Maria Aloni, Harald Bastiaanse, Tikitu de Jager & Katrin Schultz (eds.), *Logic, Language and Meaning: Revised Selected Papers of the 17th Amsterdam Colloquium, Amsterdam 2009* (Lecture Notes in Artificial Intelligence 6042), 325–334. Berlin: Springer.

Jayez, Jacques. 2015. Orthogonality and Presuppositions: A Bayesian Perspective. In Henk Zeevat & Hans-Christian Schmidtz (eds.), *Bayesian Natural Language Semantics and Pragmatics* (Language, Cognition and Mind 2), 145–178. Cham: Springer.

Jespersen, Otto. 1924. *The Philosophy of Grammar*. London: Allen & Unwin.

Jurafsky, Daniel & James H. Martin. 2009. *Speech and Language* Processing, 2nd edn. Englewood Cliffs, NJ: Prentice Hall,

Kamp, Hans & Uwe Reyle. 1993. *From Discourse to Logic*. Dordrecht: Kluwer.

Kaplan, David. 1989a. Demonstratives. In Joseph Almog, John Perry & Howard Wettstein (eds.), *Themes from Kaplan*, 481–563. New York: Oxford University Press.

Kaplan, David. 1989b. Afterthoughts. In Joseph Almog, John Perry & Howard Wettstein (eds.), *Themes from Kaplan*, 565–614. New York: Oxford University Press.

Karagjosova, Elena. 2003. Modal Particles and the Common Ground: Meaning and Function of German *ja, doch, eben/halt* and *auch*. In Peter Kühnlein, Hannes Rieser & Henk Zeevat (eds.), *Perspectives on Dialogue in the New Millenium* (Pragmatics & Beyond New Series 114), 335–349. Amsterdam: John Benjamins.

Karttunen, Lauri. 1971. Some Observations on Factivity. *Papers in Linguistics* 4(1):55–69.

Karttunen, Lauri. 1977. Syntax and Semantics of Questions. *Linguistics and Philosophy* 30:669-690.

Karttunen, Lauri. 2016. Presupposition: What Went Wrong. In Mary Moroney, Carol-Rose Little, Jacob Collard & Dan Burgdorf (eds.), *Proceedings of the 26th Semantics and Linguistic Theory Conference, Held at the University of Texas at Austin May 12–15, 2016* (SALT 26), 705–731.

Kathol, Andreas. 2004. *Linear Syntax*. Oxford: Oxford University Press.

Kayne, Richard S. 1975. *French Syntax: The Transformational Cycle*. Cambridge, MA: MIT Press.

Keenan, Edward L. 1976. Towards a Universal Definition of Subject. In Charles Li (ed.), *Subject and Topic*, 303–333. New York: Academic Press.

Keenan, Edward L. & Denis Paperno (eds.). 2012. *Handbook and Quantifiers in Natural Language*, vol. I. Dordrecht: Springer.

Keenan, Edward L. & Jonathan Stavi. 1986. A Semantic Characterization of Natural Language Determiners. *Linguistics and Philosophy* 9:253–326.

Kempson, Ruth, Ronnie Cann, Eleni Gregoromichelaki & Stergios Chatzikyriakidis. 2016. Language as Mechanisms for Interaction. *Theoretical Linguistics* 42(3–4):203–276.

Kempson, Ruth, Wilfried Meyer-Viol & Dov Gabbay. 2001. *Dynamic Syntax: The Flow of Language Understanding*. Oxford: Blackwell.

Koenig, Jean-Pierre & Karin Michelson. 2012. The (Non)universality of Syntactic Selection and Functional Application. In Christopher Piñón (ed.), *Empirical Studies in Syntax and Semantics*, vol. 9, 185–205. Paris: Centre National de la Recherche Scientifique.

Koenig, Jean-Pierre & Karin Michelson. 2014. Deconstructing Syntax. In Stefan Müller (ed.), *Proceedings of the 21st International Conference on Head-driven Phrase Structure Grammar*, 114–134. Stanford, CA: CSLI Publications.

Koenig, Jean-Pierre & Karin Michelson. 2015a. Invariance in Argument Realization: The Case of Iroquoian. *Language* 91:1–47.

Koenig, Jean-Pierre & Karin Michelson. 2015b. Morphological Complexity à la Oneida. In Matthew Baerman & Greville G. Corbett (eds.), *Understanding and Measuring Morphological Complexity*, 69–92. Oxford: Oxford University Press.

Koenig, Jean-Pierre & Karin Michelson. 2019. Extended Agreement in Oneida (Iroquoian). In András Bárány, Oliver Bond & Irina Nikolaeva (eds.), *Prominent Internal Possessors*, 131–162. Oxford: Oxford University Press.

Koev, Todor. 2017. At-issueness does not Predict Projection. Ms., University of Konstanz. (Available at https://todorkoev.weebly.com/uploads/5/2/5/1/52510397/atissuen ess_does_not_predict_projection.pdf, 14 September 2019)

Kranstedt, Alfred, Andy Lücking, Thies Pfeiffer, Hannes Rieser & Ipke Wachsmuth. 2006. Deixis: How to Determine Demonstrated Objects Using a Pointing Cone. In Sylvie Gibet, Nicolas Courty & Jean-François Kamp (eds.), *Proceedings of the 6th International Conference on Gesture in Human-Computer Interaction and Simulation*, 300–311. Berlin & Heidelberg: Springer.

Krer, Mohamed. 2013. *Negation in Standard and Libyan Arabic: An HPSG Approach*. Ph.D. dissertation, University of Essex.

Krifka, Manfred. 1999. At Least Some Determiners aren't Determiners. In Ken Turner (ed.), *The Semantics/Pragmatics Interface from Different Points of View*, 257–291. Oxford: Elsevier.

Laanemets, Anu. 2012. *Passiv i moderne dansk, norsk og svensk. Et korpus-baseret studie af tale- og skriftsprog* [Passive in modern Danish, Norwegian and Swedish: A corpus based study of spoken and written language]. Ph.D. thesis, University of Tartu.

Lambrecht, Knut. 1994. *Information Structure and Sentence Form*. Cambridge: Cambridge University Press.

Landman, Fred. 1996. Plurality. In Shalom Lappin (ed.), *Handbook of Contemporary Semantic Theory*, 425–457. Oxford: Blackwell.

Langendoen, D. Terence & Harris B. Savin. 1971. The Projection Problem for Presuppositions. In Charles J. Fillmore & D. Terence Langendoen (eds.), *Studies in Linguistic Semantics*, 4–60. New York: Holt, Rinehart and Winston.

Lambrecht, Knud. 1990. What, me Worry? 'Mad Magazine Sentences' Revisited. *Proceedings of the Sixteenth Annual Meeting of the Berkeley Linguistics Society* (BLS 6), 215–228. Berkeley, CA: Berkeley Linguistics Society.

Larsson, Staffan. 2002. *Issue based Dialogue Management*. Ph.D. thesis, Gothenburg University.

Lau, Jey Han, Alexander Clark & Shalom Lappin. 2017. Grammaticality, Acceptability, and Probability: A Probabilistic View of Linguistic Knowledge. *Cognitive Science* 41(5):1202–1241.

Lee, Felicia. 2008. On the Absence of Quantificational Determiners in San Lucas Quaviní Zapotec. In Lisa Matthewson (ed.), *Quantification: A Cross-linguistic Perspective*, 353–381. Bingley: Emerald.

Leeman, Danielle. 2004. Les aventures de Max et Eve, j'ai aimé. À propos d'un C.O.D. "Canada Dry". In Christian Leclére, Éric Laporte, Mireille Piot & Max Silberztein (eds.), *Lexique, Syntaxe et Lexique-Grammaire / Syntax, Lexis & Lexicon-Grammar: Papers in Honour of Maurice Gross* (Lingvisticae Investigationes Supplementa 24), 405–412. Amsterdam: John Benjamins.

Levelt, Willem J. 1983. Monitoring and Self-repair in Speech. *Cognition* 14(4):41–104.

Lødrup, Helge. 1999. Linking and Optimality in the Norwegian Presentational Focus Construction. *Nordic Journal of Linguistics* 22:205–230.

Lounsbury, Floyd. 1953. *Oneida Verb Morphology* (Yale University Publications in Anthropology 48). New Haven, CT: Yale University Press.

Lücking, Andy & Jonathan Ginzburg. 2019. Not Few but All Quantifiers can Be Negated: Towards a Referentially Transparent Semantics of Quantified Noun Phrases. *Proceedings of the 2019 Amsterdam Colloquium*. Amsterdam.

Lücking, Andy, Thies Pfeiffer & Hannes Rieser. 2015. Pointing and Reference Reconsidered. *Journal of Pragmatics* 77:56–79.

Lüpke, Friederike (ed.). Forthcoming. *The Oxford Guide to the Atlantic Languages of West Africa*. Oxford: Oxford University Press.

Maling, Joan. 1988. Variations on a Theme: Existential Sentences in Swedish and Icelandic. In Benjamin Shaer (ed.), *Comparative Germanic Syntax*: Special issue of *McGill Working Papers in Linguistics* 6(1):168–191.

Marandin, Jean-Marie. 2008. The Exclamative Clause Type in French. In Stefan Müller (ed.), *Proceedings of the 15th International Conference on Head-driven Phrase Structure Grammar*, 436–456. Stanford, CA: CSLI Publications.

Martins, Ana Maria. 2016. The Portuguese Answering System: Affirmation, Negation and Denial. In Ana Maria Martins & Ernestina Carrilho (eds.), *Manual de linguística portuguesa* (Manuals of Romance Linguistics 16). Berlin & Boston, MA: Mouton de Gruyter.

Matthewson, Lisa (ed.). 2008. *Quantification: A Cross-linguistic Perspective*. Bingley: Emerald.

Matthewson, Lisa. 2014. The Measurement of Semantic Complexity: How to Get by if your Language Lacks Generalized Quantifiers. In Fredrick J. Newmeyer & Laurel B. Preston (eds.), *Formal Complexity*, 241–263. Oxford: Oxford University Press.

Michelson, Karin. 1991. Semantic Features of Agent and Patient Core Case Marking in Oneida. In Robert Van Valin (ed.), *Buffalo Papers in Linguistics*, vol. 91-II, 114–146. Buffalo, NY: Linguistics Department, University at Buffalo.

Michelson, Karin. 2015. Gender in Oneida. In Marli Hellinger & Heiko Motschenbacher (eds.), *Gender across Languages*, 277–301. Amsterdam: John Benjamins.

Michelson, Karin, Norma Kennedy & Mercy Doxtator. 2016. *Glimpses of Oneida Life*. Toronto: University of Toronto Press.

Mikkelsen, Line. 2002. Reanalyzing the Definiteness Effect: Evidence from Danish. *Working Papers in Scandinavian Syntax* 69:1–75.

Miller, Philip H. 1992. *Clitics and Constituents in Phrase Structure Grammar*. New York: Garland.

Miller, Philip H. & Ivan A. Sag. 1997. French Clitic Movement without Clitics or Movement. *Natural Language & Linguistic Theory* 15:573–639.

Milsark, Gary L. 1974. *Existential Sentences in English*. Ph.D. dissertation, MIT.

Milward, David. 1994. Dynamic Dependency Grammar. *Linguistics and Philosophy* 17:561–405.

Milward, David & Robin Cooper. 1994. Incremental Interpretation: Applications, Theory, and Relationship to Dynamic Semantics. *COLING '94: Proceedings of the 15th Conference on Computational Linguistics*, vol. 2, 748–754. Stroudsburg, PA: Association for Computational Linguistics (ACL).

Monachesi, Paola. 2005. *The Verbal Complex in Romance: A Case Study in Grammatical Interfaces*. Oxford: Oxford University Press.

Montague, Richard. 1974. The Proper Treatment of Quantification in Ordinary English. In Richmond. H. Thomason (ed.), *Formal Philosophy: Selected Papers of Richard Montague*, 247–270. New Haven, CT: Yale University Press.

Morrill, Glyn. 2000. Incremental Processing and Acceptability. *Computational Linguistics* 26(3):319–338.

Mount, Allyson. 2008. The Impurity of 'Pure' Indexicals. *Philosophical Studies: An International Journal for Philosophy in the Analytic Tradition*, 138(2):193–209.

Müller, Stefan. 2013. *Head-driven Phrase Structure Grammar: Eine Einführung.* Tübingen: Stauffenburg.

Munro, Pamelo. 2017. Chickasaw Quantifiers. In Paperno & Keenan (eds.), 113-201.

Murray, Sarah E. 2014. Varieties of Update. *Semantics and Pragmatics* 7(2):53. doi:http://dx.doi.org/10.3765/sp.7.2.

Nunberg, Geoffrey. 1993. Indexicality and Deixis. *Linguistics and Philosophy* 16:1–43.

Onea, Edgar. 2016. *Potential Questions at the Semantics–Pragmatics Interface* (Current Research in the Semantics/Pragmatics Interface 33). Leiden & Boston, MA: Brill.

Paperno, Denis & Edward L. Keenan (eds.). 2017. *Handbook and Quantifiers in Natural Language*, vol. II. Dordrecht: Springer.

Partee, Barbara 1986. Ambiguous Pseudoclefts with Unambiguous *Be*. In Stephen Berman, Jae-Woong Choe & Joyce McDonough (eds.), *Proceedings of the North Eastern Linguistic Society* (NELS 16), 354–366. Amherst, MA: GLSA.

Partee, Barbara. 2014. A Brief History of the Syntax–Semantics Interface in Western Formal Linguistics. *Semantics–Syntax Interface* 1(1):1–21.

Pavlidou, Theodossia. 1991. Cooperation and the Choice of Linguistic Means: Some Evidence from the Use of the Subjunctive in Modern Greek. *Journal of Pragmatics* 15:11–42.

Peters, Stanley. 2016. Speaker Commitments: Presupposition. In Mary Moroney, Carol-Rose Little, Jacob Collard & Dan Burgdorf (eds.), *Proceedings of the 26th Semantics and Linguistic Theory Conference, Held at the University of Texas at Austin May 12–15, 2016* (SALT 26), 1083–1098.

Peters, Stanley & Dag Westerståhl. 2006. *Quantifiers in Language and Logic.* Oxford: Clarendon Press.

Peterson, Tyler. 2013. Rethinking Mirativity: The Expression and Implication of Surprise. Ms., Arizona State University.

Perry, John. 1997. Indexicals and Demonstratives. In Bob Hale & Crispin Wright (eds.), *Companion to the Philosophy of Language*, 586–612. Oxford: Blackwells.

Perry, John. 2001. *Reference and Reflexivity.* Stanford, CA: CSLI Publications.

Platzack, Christer. 1983. Existential sentences in English, Swedish, German and Icelandic. In Fred Karlsson (ed.), *Papers from the Seventh Scandinavian Conference of Linguistics*, 80–100. Helsinki: University of Helsinki, Department of General Linguistics.

Platzack, Christer. 2005. The Object of Verbs like *help* and an Apparent Violation of UTAH. In Hans Broekhuis, Norbert Corver, Riny Huybregts, Ursula Kleinhenz & Jan Koster (eds.), *Organizing Grammar: Linguistic Studies in Honor of Henk van Riemsdijk*, 483–494. Berlin: Mouton de Gruyter.

Platzack, Christer. 2009. Towards a Minimal Argument Structure. In Petra Bernardini, Verner Egerland & Jonas Granfeldt (eds.), *Mélanges plurilingues offerts à Suzanne Schlyter à l'occasion de son 65ème anniversaire*, 353–371. Lund: Lund University, Språk- och litteraturcentrum.

Platzack, Christer. 2010. *Den fantastiska grammatiken. En minimalistisk beskrivning av svenskan* [The fantastic grammar: A minimalist description of Swedish]. Stockholm: Norstedts.

Poesio, Massimo & Hannes Rieser. 2010. (Prolegomena to a Theory of) Completions,
Continuations, and Coordination in Dialogue. *Dialogue and Discourse* 1:1–89.

Pollard, Carl & Ivan A. Sag. 1987. *Information-based Syntax and Semantics*. Stanford, CA: CSLI Publications.

Pollard, Carl & Ivan A. Sag. 1994. *Head-driven Phrase Structure Grammar*. Chicago, IL & Stanford, CA: University of Chicago Press & CSLI.

Portner, Paul. 2016. On the Relation Between Verbal Mood and Sentence Mood. Ms., Georgetown University.

Potts, Christopher. 2005. *The Logic of Conventional Implicatures*. Oxford: Oxford University Press.

Pozdniakov, Konstantin & Guillaume Segerer. Forthcoming. Classification of Atlantic
languages. In Friederike Lüpke (ed.), *The Oxford Guide to the Atlantic Languages of West Africa*. Oxford: Oxford University Press.

Predelli, Stefano. 1998. Utterance, Interpretation, and the Logic of Indexicals. *Mind and Language* 13(3):400–414.

Prince, Ellen. 1981. Toward a Taxonomy of Given–New Information. In Peter Cole (ed.), *Radical Pragmatics*, 223–255. New York: Academic Press.

Prince, Ellen. 1992. The ZPG Letter: Subjects, Definiteness, and Information Status. In William C. Mann & Sandra A. Thompson (eds.), *Discourse Description: Diverse Linguistic Analyses of a Fund-raising Text*, 295–326. Amsterdam: John Benjamins.

Pullum, Geoffrey K. & Barbara C. Scholz. 2001. On the Distinction between Model-theoretic and Generative-enumerative Syntactic Frameworks. In Philippe de Groote, Glyn Morrill & Christian Retoré (eds.), *Logical Aspects of Computational Linguistics: 4th International Conference* (Lecture Notes in Artificial Intelligence 2099), 17–43. Berlin: Springer.

Purver, Matthew. 2006. Clarie: Handling Clarification Requests in a Dialogue System. *Research on Language & Computation* 4(2):259–288.

Purver, Matthew, Arash Eshghi & Julian Hough. 2011. Incremental Semantic Construction in a Dialogue System. In Johan Bos & Stephen Pulman (eds.), *Proceedings of the Proceedings of the Ninth International Conference on Computational Semantics* (IWCS 2011), 365–369. Oxford.

Purver, Matthew, Jonathan Ginzburg & Patrick Healey. 2001. On the Means for Clarification in Dialogue. *Proceedings of the Second SIGdial Workshop on Discourse and Dialogue (SIGdial01)*, 116–125.

Quer, Josep. 2009. Mood Management: An Updated Toolkit. *Lingua* 119:1909–1913.

Quine, Willard van. 1976. *The Ways of Paradox and Other Essays*, 2nd edn. Cambridge, MA: Harvard University Press.

Ranta, Aarne. 1994. *Type Theoretical Grammar*. Oxford: Oxford University Press.

Recanati. François. 2001. Are 'here' and 'now' indexicals? *Texte* 127(8):115–127.

Reinhart, Tanya. 1981. Pragmatics and Linguistics: An Analysis of Sentence Topics. *Philosophica* 27(1):53–94.

Richter, Frank & Manfred Sailer. 2004. Basic Concepts of Lexical Resource Semantics.
Collegium Logicum, vol. 5: *ESSLLI 2003 Course Material*. Vienna: Kurt Gödel Society Wien.

Riegel, Martin, Jean-Christophe Pellat & René Rioul. 1994. *Grammaire méthodique du français*. Paris: PUF.

Roberts, Craige. 2012. Information Structure in Discourse: Towards an Integrated Formal Theory of Pragmatics. *Semantics and Pragmatics* 5(6):69.
doi:http://dx.doi.org/10.3765/sp.5.6. (A reissue of 1998 version at http://ling.osu.edu/~croberts/infostr.pdf, 14 September 2018)

Rohde, Hannah. 2006. Rhetorical Questions as Redundant Interrogatives. *San Diego Linguistic Papers* 2:134–168.

Rooth, Mats. 1992. A Theory of Focus Interpretation. *Natural Language Semantics* 1:75–116.

Rouchota, Villy. 1994. *Na*-interrogatives in Modern Greek: Their Interpretation and Relevance. In Irene Philippaki-Warburton, Katerina Nicolaidis & Maria Sifianou (eds.), *Themes in Greek Linguistics* (Current Issues in Linguistic Theory 117), 177–184. Amsterdam & Philadelphia, PA: John Benjamins.

Sadock, Jerry. 1971. Queclaratives. In Douglas Adams, Mary Ann Campbell, Victor Cohen, Julie Lovins, Edward Maxwell, Carolyn Nygren & John Reighard (eds.), *Papers from the 7th Regional Meeting of the Chicago Linguistics Society* (CSL 7), 223–232. Chicago, IL: Chicago Linguistics Society.

Sag, Ivan A. 1997. English Relative Clause Constructions. *Journal of Linguistics* 33:431–484.

Sag, Ivan A., Gerald Gazdar, Thomas Wasow & Steven Weisler. 1985. Coordination and How to Distinguish Categories. *Natural Language & Linguistic Theory* 3:117–171.

Sag, Ivan A. & Thomas Wasow. 2015. Flexible Processing and the Design of Grammar. *Journal of Psycholinguistic Research* 44(1):47–63.

Sag, Ivan A., Thomas Wasow & Emily M. Bender. 2003. *Syntactic Theory: A Formal Introduction,* 2nd edn. Stanford, CA: CSLI Publications.

Salvi, Giampaolo. 1991. L'accordo. In Lorenzo Renzi, Giampaolo Salvi & Anna Cardinaletti (eds.), *Grande Grammatica Italiana di Consultazione,* vol. II: *I sintagmi verbale, aggettivale, avverbiale,* 227–244. Bologna: Il Mulino.

Sato, Yo. 2011. Local Ambiguity, Search Strategies and Parsing in Dynamic Syntax. In Ruth Kempson, Eleni Gregoromichelaki & Christine Howes (eds.), *The Dynamics of Lexical Interfaces,* 205–233. Stanford, CA: CSLI Publications.

Schlangen, David. 2004. Causes and Strategies for Requesting Clarification in Dialogue. *Proceedings of the 5th Workshop of the SIGdial Workshop on Discourse and Dialogue* (SIGdial04), 136–143.

Schlangen, David & Gabriel Skantze. 2011. A General, Abstract Model of Incremental Dialogue Processing. *Dialogue & Discourse* 2(1):83–111.

Schlesewsky, Matthias & Ina Bornkessel. 2004. On Incremental Interpretation: Degrees of Meaning Accessed during Sentence Comprehension. *Lingua* 114(9–10), 1213–1234.

Sells, Peter. 2001. *Structure, Alignment and Optimality in Swedish.* Stanford, CA: CSLI Publications.

Shieber, Stuart M. 1986. *An Introduction to Unification-based Approaches to Grammar.* Stanford, CA: CSLI Publications.

Simons, Mandy. 2007. Observations on Embedding Verbs, Evidentiality, and Presupposition. *Lingua* 117:1034–1056.

Simons, Mandy, David Beaver, Craige Roberts & Judith Tonhauser. 2017. The Best Question: Explaining the Projection Behavior of Factives. *Discourse Processes* 54(3):187–206.

Simons, Mandy, Judith Tonhauser, David Beaver & Craige Roberts. 2011. What Projects and Why. In Nan Li & David Lutz (eds.), *Papers Presented at the 20th Conference on Semantics and Linguistic Theory (SALT) Hosted by the Departments of Linguistics at the University of British Columbia and Simon Fraser University, in Vancouver, British Columbia on April 29 – May 1, 2010* (SALT 20), 309–327.

Smith, Quentin. 1989. The Multiple Uses of Indexicals. *Synthese* 78:167–191.

Stalnaker, Robert. 1974. Pragmatic Presuppositions. In Milton Karl Munitz & Peter K. Unger (eds.), *Semantics and Philosophy,* 197–214. New York: New York University Press.

Stalnaker, Robert C. 1978. Assertion. In Peter Cole (ed.), *Pragmatics* (Syntax and Semantics 9), 315–332. New York: Academic Press.

Stassen, Leon. 1985. *Comparison and Universal Grammar.* Oxford: Basil Blackwell.

Steedman, Mark. 1996. *Surface Structure and Interpretation* (Linguistic Inquiry Monographs). Cambridge, MA: MIT Press.

Stroh, Hans. 2002. *L'accord du participe passé en occitan rouergat et en français.* Rodez: Grelh Roergàs.

Świątkowska, Marcela. 2006. L'interjection: entre deixis et anaphore. *Langages* 161(1):47–56.

Teleman, Ulf, Staffan Hellberg & Erik Andersson. 1999. *Svenska Akademiens grammatik* [Swedish Academy grammar], 4 vols. Stockholm: Norstedts.

Ţenchea, Maria. 2001. *Le subjonctif dans les phrases indépendantes. Syntaxe et pragmatique.* Timişoara: Hestia.

Tian, Ye, Takehiko Maruyama & Jonathan Ginzburg. 2016. Self Addressed Questions and Filled Pauses: A Cross-linguistic Investigation. *Journal of Psycholinguistic Research* 46(4):905–922.

Tomić, Olga Mišeska (ed.). 2004. *Balkan Syntax and Semantics.* Amsterdam & Philadelphia, PA: John Benjamins.

Tomić, Olga Mišeska. 2006. *Balkan Sprachbund Morpho-syntactic Features* (Studies in Natural Language and Linguistic Theory 67). Dordrecht: Springer.

Tonhauser, Judith, David Beaver, Craige Roberts & Mandy Simons. 2013. Toward a Taxonomy of Projective Content. *Language* 89:66–109.

Turri, John. 2013. The Test of Truth: An Experimental Investigation of the Norm of Assertion. *Cognition* 129:279–291.

Vallduví, Enric. 2016. Information Structure. In Maria Aloni & Paul Dekker (eds.), *The Cambridge Handbook of Formal Semantics*, 728–754. Cambridge: Cambridge University Press.

Vallduví, Enric & Elisabet Engdahl. 1996. The Linguistic Realization of Information Packaging. *Linguistics* 34(3):459–519.

van der Sandt, Rob A. 1992. Presupposition Projection as Anaphora Resolution. *Journal of Semantics* 9:333–377.

Van Eynde, Frank 2009. On the Copula: From a Fregean to a Montagovian Treatment. In Stefan Müller (ed.), *Proceedings of the 16th International Conference on Head-driven Phrase Structure Grammar*, 359–375. Stanford, CA: CSLI Publications.

Vasilescu, Andra. 2013. Sentence types. In Gabriela Pană Dindelegan (ed.), *The Grammar of Romanian*. 537–550. Oxford: Oxford University Press.

Vasilescu, Andra & Ileana Vântu. 2008. Tipuri de enunţuri în funcţie de scopul comunicării. In Valeria Guţu-Romalo (ed.), *Gramatica limbii române*, vol. 2, 25–46. Bucharest: Editura Academiei.

Viberg, Åke. 2008. Swedish Verbs of Perception from a Typological and Contrastive Perspective. In María de los Ángeles Gómez González, J. Lachlan Mackenzie & Elsa M. González Álvarez (eds.), *Languages and Cultures in Contrast and Comparison*, 123–172. Amsterdam: John Benjamins.

Villalta, Elisabeth. 2007. *Context Dependence in the Interpretation of Questions and Subjunctives*. Ph.D. dissertation, University of Tübingen.

Villalta, Elisabeth. 2008. Mood and Gradability: An Investigation of the Subjunctive Mood in Spanish. *Linguistics and Philosophy* 31(4):467–522.

Vydrin, Valentin. 2009. On the Problem of the Proto-Mande Homeland. *Вопросы языкового родства – Journal of Language Relationship* 1:107–142.

Wharton, Tim. 2003. Interjections, Language, and the 'showing/saying' Continuum. *Pragmatics and Cognition* 11:39–91.

Williams, Edwin 1983. Semantic vs. Syntactic Categories. *Linguistics & Philosophy* 6:423–446.

Wiltschko, Martina. 2016. The Essence of a Category: Lessons from the Subjunctive. In Joanna Błaszczak, Anastasia Giannakidou, Dorota Klimek-Jankowska & Krzysztof Migdalski (eds.), *Mood, Aspect, Modality Revisited: New Answers to Old Questions*, 218–254. Chicago, IL: University of Chicago Press.

Zaenen, Annie, Elisabet Engdahl & Joan Maling. 2017. Subject Properties in Presentational Sentences in Icelandic and Swedish. In Victoria Rosén & Koenrad De Smedt (eds.), *The Very Model of a Modern Linguist: In Honor of Helge Dyvik* (Bergen Language and Linguistic Studies 8), 260–281. Bergen.

Zafiu, Rodica. 2008. Modalizarea. In Valeria Guţu-Romalo (ed.), *Gramatica limbii române*, vol. 2, 702–726. Bucharest: Editura Academiei.

Zafiu, Rodica. 2011. Observaţii asupra semanticii conjunctivului românesc. In Rodica Zafiu, Camelia Uşurelu & Helga Bogdan-Oprea (eds.), *Limba română. Ipostaze ale variaţiei lingvistice*, 163–171. Bucharest: Editura Universităţii din Bucureşti.

Zafiu, Rodica. 2013. Modality and Evidentiality. In Gabriela Pană Dindelegan (ed.), *The Grammar of Romanian*, 575–584. Oxford: Oxford University Press.